WHAT IT REALLY TAKES TO START AND RUN A HORSE BUSINESS

AND HOW TO DO IT RIGHT THE FIRST TIME

By

Sheri Grunska

Original Text Copyright 2014 © Sheri L. Grunska

Revised 2019

All Rights Reserved

Front Cover Photo
by
Lauren Ashley Grunska

DEDICATION

First, I want to dedicate this book to my husband David for supporting me for many months while I wrote this book and being so patient during the very long process. The house did not get cleaned nor did I do much cooking especially during those months and he took all of it in stride. Also to my girls Kaeli and Lauren, I want to thank you for taking care of yourself much of the time that I was working on this book. I am so proud of you both and I am blessed to have you in my life.

SPECIAL THANK YOU

I want to give a special thank you to my wonderful father Bill Cannon and David's wonderful parents Bob and Sharon Grunska. Without your support our dream of having our own business would never have become a reality.

ACKNOWLEDGMENTS

So many wonderful people have come into my life during this journey from having a dream to making it a reality. I would like to thank the following people who have helped us in the very beginning all the way through to the birth of this book.

I would like to thank the following people: Lori Kohls, you were there from the start and you spent countless hours, days and weeks working on fencing and the run-ins with David. Thank you also for working so hard with me on the business plan. Without your computer skills I am sure I would not have had such a professional looking plan. Deb Koerth, thank you for giving of your time to help David clean 27 stalls during the week even in the coldest of weather. You made his job easier. Tom

McDermott, you were there with us from the very beginning. Thank you for getting us through some of the tougher times. Thank you for proof reading and editing parts of the book for me and for teaching me over the years the legalities of this business. Meryl Morton, thank you for taking the time to go over my chapter about writing a business plan. I truly value your expertise in this area and I am glad we have become friends through this whole process. Cheryl Jacklin, those early years were tough at times and I will always remember when you told me "The show must go on!" right before we were going to be on television and when it looked like things couldn't get any worse at our barn. You taught me more then you will ever know and for that I will forever be grateful. Karen Debney, thank you for teaching me about composting horse manure like they do in England. I wish you the very best with your new venture in the horse business.

Over the years so many people have come through our barn doors and each one of them have taught me so much about life, relationships and running a business. I want to thank all the wonderful people that have made Vinland Stables their barn home over the years.

Why I wrote this book

Over the last few years I have had many people ask how we started our business and things we would do differently now. This book is the story of my family's journey of starting a horse boarding business from absolutely nothing. All we had in the beginning was farmland and an old dairy barn. This book is about Vinland Stables in Neenah Wisconsin. We have been open now since 2006 and have the honor of caring for forty beautiful horses. It is a book about building our barn and all the mistakes we made when it came to building and running the business during the first few years and how through the hardest of times, we never gave up on it.

This book is very unique in the fact that it is two books in one. It is divided into two parts. The first half of the book is my family's journey of building our barn and all that it took to get the loan and get the barn up. The reason I wrote the first part of the book is to help others that want to build a barn and show them all that goes with the building process both good and bad. The rest of the book is about actually running a barn on a day to day basis with clients and horses. It is a complete "How to" book with our story included.

You will not find another book that talks about what it really takes to start up and run a horse business from nothing and takes you behind the scenes into the day to day life of running a horse boarding facility.

I am hoping that if you take the time to read this book, it will inspire you and help you in the areas that you are having problems with in your business. Are you are struggling with the day to day operations of your horse business? Are you are constantly running into issues with your clients and not sure how to fix the problems? If you are then this book will teach how to be the leader you need to be to run your business successfully. I hope to educate and answer the questions that no one else wants to talk about when it comes to building and running a horse boarding business.

When most people think of owning and running a horse business they usually only think of the physical labor that will go with it. After you read my book you will realize very quickly that there is an emotional and common sense side to running a horse business and it is equally and many times more important. Sometimes the emotional side of running a business can help and sometimes it can make things worse. I will give you honest straight forward examples of what we have done right and what we have done wrong through the years. I will give practical, common sense advice and make you think of things you have not thought of before. My goal is that by reading my book it will help you to run your horse business with confidence and efficiency and make your days working and running a horse farm a lot easier from the very start.

When I was growing up through my young adult years, I assumed that all the people I came in contact with that were horse trainers or owned horse farms came from generations of horse families where they just followed in their parents footsteps. I had this vision that most of them came from the mountains of Montana or something silly like that. I never dreamed that I would own a large horse boarding operation but I always loved the idea. Back then I figured you needed to be born into a horse family to be in the business.

Another thought that would creep into my mind many times over the years was the fallacy that I would never know as much as these horse professionals because they had been doing it for so long and they must know everything. That idea alone is what stops most people from achieving their dreams. Many years later, I decided I wasn't going to let the lie stop me from starting and running my own horse operation.

It has been a very eventful thirteen years in the horse boarding business with very highs and extreme lows and learning everyday how to better take care of our equine friends and their owners and always trying to evolve when need be. This book is for anyone that has ever had the dream of owning and running a horse business. Whether your farm is small or large, a boarding barn, breeding barn or training barn, I truly believe you will be able to relate to what is inside this book.

I still love the horse industry and it is a wonderful business but it can be an extremely hard business. If you are not scared to work harder than you ever have worked before (and a lot of times seven days a week!) and be open to change when something isn't working, then I encourage you to keep reading this book. I definitely look at our business differently than I did when we started. Still after all these years I love going out in the barn at 5am each morning (okay 5:30) and hearing the nickers. It is truly my favorite time of the day! We started our business from the ground up with nothing but empty farmland and a dream.

Wishing you many blessings in your horse business,
Sheri Grunska

Disclaimer

The purpose of this book is to acquaint the reader with how we started our horse boarding business. The information is drawn from the author's extensive experience owning and operating a horse business.

It is not all-inclusive, however, and is not intended to cover all circumstances or every situation which may arise. The author does not make any representations or warranties, either expressed or implied, regarding the technique's discussed and assume no liability therefore.

Table of Contents

~1~ 17
Like any other little girl 17
~2~ 22
My new life in Wisconsin 22
~3~ 27
The perfect barn design 27
~4~ 40
Finding a bank that does 40
agricultural loans 40
~5~ 43
Finding a builder we can afford 43
~6~ 45
Gathering information for our 45
business plan 45
~7~ 48
The business plan for a horse facility 48
   What is a business plan? 48
   Categories inside our business plan: 51
   Mission Statement 52
   Keys to Success 52
   The Company Summary 53
   Company Ownership 54
   Start-Up Summary 55
   Services 57
   Market Analysis Summary 59
   Market Segmentation 61
   Market Segment Strategy 63
   Service Business Analysis 65

Competition and Buying Patterns	66
Strategy and Implementation Summary	67
Competitive Edge	68
Sales Strategy	72
Sales Forecast	73
Marketing Strategy	74
Management Summary	75
Table-Start-up Funding:	78
Important Assumptions	80
Twelve Month Income Statement	83
Three Year Income Statement	89
Cash Flow Statement	89
~8~	92
The waiting game for a loan	92
~ 9 ~	97
Hurricane Katrina and	97
Building Supplies	97
~10~	102
Is this all we have so far?	102
~11~	108
A new year, new builder and a lawyer	108
~12~	113
Building problems on the horizon	113
~13~	121
Welcome to the business world	121
~14~	126
Our barn is under water!	126
~15~	129
Crunch time	129

~16~ 132
The indoor arena 132
~17~ 137
Unexpected expenses 137
~18~ 143
The builder and the rest of the story 143
~19~ 151
business insurance for a 151
horse farm 151
~20~ 154
Estimating how much everything will cost 154
~21~ 157
The final push before the 157
horses arrive 157
~22~ 160
We are finally open for business! 160
~23~ 162
Many firsts to come 162
~24~ 166
Changes in our first year 166
~25~ 172
The early years of running 172
our boarding stable 172
~26~ 175
The ever changing weather 175
~27~ 178
Our first winter season running 178
our horse facility 178
~28~ 185

Boarding contracts and liability waivers 185
    Vinland Stables Boarding Agreement: 189
    Emergency Information Form 202
    Liability Waiver 203
~29~ 204
Trainers at our barn 204
~30~ 208
Barn and arena rules 208
    Vinland Stables Barn Rules 212
    Vinland Stables Arena Rules 218
~31~ 221
The multi-discipline barn 221
~32~ 224
Extra charges for services done 224
    Vinland Stables extra charges for services 227
~33~ 231
Barn amenities–trying to 231
please everyone 231
~34~ 234
When things get broken who pays? 234
~35~ 237
Invoices and billing 237
    Setting your rates and when to raise them 238
~36~ 240
How much hay do we need? 240
~37~ 245
Grain and supplements 245
    Giving special supplements 249
~38~ 251

Not prepared for special requests 251
~39~ 255
Herd management 255
~40~ 261
The boarder and herd management 261
~41~ 266
Horses on pasture grass 266
~42~ 270
Challenges of outdoor board 270
~43~ 276
Veterinarians and Farriers 276
   Farriers 276
   Veterinarians 277
~44~ 280
Boundaries 280
~45~ 284
Handling the boarder's horse 284
~46~ 288
Asking a boarder to leave 288
~47~ 292
Saying good-bye to a horse 292
~48~ 295
It's a working farm 295
~49~ 299
Let them know you care 299
~50~ 302
encouragement goes a long way 302
~51~ 305
Things I've learned over the years 305

to make the job easier 305

~52~ 307

Clinics are always good 307

~53~ 312

Things we would do differently 312

    Grooming stall 313

    Automatic waterers 313

    Wash Stall 314

    Hay, Grain & Shavings Room 314

    Barn Design 315

    Storage for arena stuff 315

    Location of paddock automatic Waterers 315

    Insulating our barn 316

~54~ 318

Life lessons in running a business 318

    Going into Debt 319

    It's not personal, it's business 319

    The buck stops with the business owner 320

    Be patient and forgiving 321

    It is a service orientated business 321

    Don't act like you know it all 322

    Things never stay the same in business 323

    Owning a horse business is harder than I thought 324

~55~ 326

Business ownership is a love/hate relationship 326

    Sheri's Books and Website 328

~1~
LIKE ANY OTHER LITTLE GIRL

Before I go right into the building of our barn and how we run our boarding operation now, I thought I would share with you a little about my history and my early years with horses. I was not born into a family that was in the horse business. In fact I was born into a loving family that had zero experience with horses. We were city folks all the way.

My roots and beginnings of my affair with horses are all too familiar. Like so many other little girls before the age of ten, I fell in love with horses.

I was born in Burbank, California in 1962 and grew up living in apartments my whole young life. During my elementary years my whole world was about horses. I didn't have one of my own but I knew the homes that had horses in their backyard. I can remember riding my bike down the street from my apartment building to this house that had some beautiful white horses in the back of the property. I know it's hard to believe that there would be horses in Los Angeles now but back in the 1970's there were horses in many backyards. I loved to go and watch them and they were magical to me. They were white and I would sit on the fence for hours just hoping one of them would notice me and come over. I was only about eight or nine years old and I can remember asking the owner one day when he was outside riding if I could help with chores so I could ride one of his horses. He never told me his name but he was very nice and he gently told me no. I was disappointed but it never stopped me from looking for someone that would let me ride their horse.

My first job was working at a horse farm. I was in fourth grade and I would ride (back then we rode our bikes everywhere) to a small ranch in Van Nuys and it was called Studs Lane! What a name for a breeding farm but that is what it was called and they bred many horses. It was summer and again I asked the owner if I could clean stalls just to brush the horses. I thought I would start off slower and not ask to ride so quickly. They said yes and I had my first job cleaning stalls. It was my first experience with physical labor on a horse ranch and it was hard work and I remember it was very hot. I didn't last very long but I went there often to see the horses.

To this point I only had ridden a horse at the pony rides or with my dad at Griffith Park where you could rent a horse for an hour. In my mind, I was a great rider that would one day compete at the Olympics on the most beautiful horse in the arena. I think I had watched too many Bonanza shows and of course I wanted to be just like Elizabeth Taylor riding "The Pie" (that was the horse's name) at the Grand National in National Velvet. I knew I could ride just like her if I had a horse of my own. She made it look so easy.

Like so many other horse crazy little girls, I must have asked my dad for a horse at least once a week. He always said no in a gentle way because he knew I was going to be disappointed. Every few months I would ask him again and finally one day as I was entering the fifth grade my father came up to me and told me I could have a horse. What followed that decision changed my life forever.

We were not a horse family at all and really didn't know anyone that owned horses. Back then there was no internet to search for horses that were for sale so he started to ask around. Before I knew it we were driving to a city called Shadow Hills to look at a horse. I don't think I was ever so excited in my life. I didn't care what the horse looked like; I just knew it was going to be the perfect horse! To every little girl that is horse crazy, every horse is perfect.

Me and my first horse Rusty back in 1972

There he was. He was a strawberry roan and very stocky. His name was Rusty and it was love at first site. I hopped on and we rode down the street. It was a done deal. I am sure my father had no idea what he was getting into but he went along with it.

Our first experience with boarding a horse was an interesting one. If you lived in the San Fernando Valley back in the 1970's you would see dirt lots everywhere and horses living in small back yards. Horses were kept on very small acreage and because the valley was growing so fast, you wouldn't see any large horse farms (or ranches) in the valley like you see in Wisconsin. Because Southern California is so hot and dry you never would see horses out in rolling hills of grass where I lived. Only in the winter and early spring for a few short weeks would we get rain and if we were lucky the grass would grow long enough to let the horses graze for a couple of weeks in the backyard if you had a little more land than most.

About four miles from where I lived there was a little sub-division and a street that had horses on it. One of the homes boarded horses so that is where we would keep Rusty. It was close enough that I could ride my bike to see him and the city still had not cemented the entire place yet, so I could ride on the dirt sidewalks of the streets in this little sub-division.

Rusty was delivered with a saddle, bridle and pad so I was set. I just needed a few brushes and hoof pick and we were good to go. Things back then were so simple. Well I was about to learn the hard way that I wasn't that good of a rider. The little place I boarded Rusty at had lots of kids that rode and in the summer everyone rode bareback because it was so hot all summer long. If they could do it, so could I. I must have fallen off every day for the first few weeks. I still can't believe I never broke anything considering I landed on hard dirt which was the sidewalk at that time. I wasn't going to give up.

I must have owned Rusty only a couple of months and one Saturday my dad drove me to see my horse. On this particular day we drove into the stable and right away I knew something was wrong. We had only been there a short time but the place always had kids around and lots of activity and as we drove in, it was very quiet with only a couple of parents standing there. We got out of the car and walked to the back and right away people were coming around to tell us the owners had left and taken everything with them. They had taken horses and saddles and tack and were gone. I ran in the back and to my relief Rusty was still there! They didn't take him. All my tack was gone but I didn't care about that at the time. As I am writing this, I only now realize that my poor father was probably wondering what we were going to do and I am sure it was a stressful time for him.

I know the good Lord was watching over us because a nice family that lived around the corner had come by to see if they could help and they took Rusty and me into their home. Their daughter was my age and they must have thought it would be good for her to have someone to ride with. It was one of the best things that could have happened in my childhood. This family taught me a lot about horses and how to care for them. Over the next few years of middle school and high school, I did a lot of living at their home. I finally did outgrow Rusty and my parents surprised me with a very young quarter horse that wasn't broke yet when I was fifteen years old. I moved up to Hansen Dam Stables and spent my high school years there.

I boarded at a few different places over the years and with that came many different experiences in boarding facilities. Most are good memories of good places but I have had my share of places that didn't feed enough to the point where my horse lost a lot of weight. I've boarded at places where people would ride my horse without my permission, places where they were extremely mean to the horses and places that were not safe for a sixteen year old girl to be alone. I've been at a boarding facility that had flash flooding and no one let my parents know and I had to evacuate my horse (the only horse left on the property) during the flash flood! I now believe all these places have molded me into who I am today. And now that I own and run my own barn I definitely know what I want to do to make it the best and safest place for my boarders and their horses.

It was so different back in the 1970's. People did not have boarding contracts and I never saw a helmet except at shows when riders were jumping. It was a much simpler life but also a time when the boarder was not protected at all and neither was the barn owner.

I wanted to give you a little background into my life and where I came from so you will understand my story of building a horse business from the ground up. I now understand and have lived through many challenges as a barn owner and I truly understand the worries the boarder has. I have been on both sides of the fence and I am glad I have. If you have had the opportunity to board your horse then it will help shed some light on what both sides go through especially once you become the barn owner or manager. I think it has helped me be more understanding of the very real worries a boarder has about the care of their horse because I had those same exact worries and nightmares years ago and you never forget them.

~2~
MY NEW LIFE IN WISCONSIN

Fast forward many years and I met David. He was in the Air Force in California and we fell in love. Our relationship was a whirlwind and we met in September and were married in July. I had never been to Wisconsin but we were flying out after the wedding to spend two weeks in beautiful Neenah Wisconsin. I can still remember flying into Appleton airport and seeing cornfields all around the runways. I had never seen anything like that before and I had never seen so much open land. It was truly heaven to me. As we drove around northeast Wisconsin I couldn't believe how green everything was and all the horses that graced the large fields everywhere I looked.

After spending time in Wisconsin I knew in my heart that it was where I wanted to move and raise a family. We flew back home and decided that after David got out of the Air Force we would move back to his home town. He was scheduled to get out the next year in January and we would move in February.

I didn't own any horses when I met David but he knew that I loved them. We did a little riding during our first year of marriage but that was the extent of it. February came and we packed up the U-Haul in eighty degree weather. I said good bye to my family in the city and off we drove for the next four days. I didn't realize I was about to have the shock of my life. As we drove east the weather started to get colder and colder. I can still remember the day we drove into David's grandfather's farm. It was three degrees outside and more snow than I had ever seen before. Where was the beautiful country that I had seen just a short six months earlier? I was speechless. I had never been so cold in my life!

We were going to stay at his grandfather's farm until we could get our life figured out over the next couple of months and I needed to decide what I was going to do for work. I didn't do much until late spring. I was too cold to do anything. Finally the days warmed up and summer was right around the corner. David was going to be in flying school for work in

Georgia for a few months in the summer and I was going to get a job and stay on the farm.

Pretty quickly I met a friend who loved horses. She had a horse and worked at a horse farm. I told her I was looking for a job and she told me they were looking for some extra help and I should apply. It was a show barn and it was beautiful. It was a twenty-five minute drive from where I was living to the horse stable but I didn't mind. The country side was beautiful to look at and I couldn't get over how green everything was.

I can still remember driving up to this horse facility and in awe of how beautiful it was. I had never seen any farms like this in Southern California. I met the owners of the farm and I was extremely nervous. It had been a few years since I had worked at a horse farm and I was sure I had forgotten how to put a halter on! Right away I was into the thick of it, taking horses out of the barn and cleaning stalls and other things that needed tending. The basic care of the horse was all coming back to me. I loved it. With David gone to flying school the job kept me busy and tired. It was a great summer of meeting new people and being around many horses.

David came home after a couple of months and summer was ending. What do you mean summer was ending? It had just arrived. I was in shock about how fast summer came and went. By September the days were getting much cooler and I needed to get some fall clothes. I really had such a limited wardrobe for working outside. I came from California with basically shorts, dresses and a couple pair of jeans. You really needed clothing for all four seasons in Wisconsin. I was only used to two seasons in California. Hot and a little cool.

The days were cooler and I was dressing like I was in twenty degree weather. Fall was beautiful on the horse farm but I was cold every day. I was not sure what I was going to do when the snow arrived. How could I work in these cold temperatures? The barn was a heated barn which I had never seen before but I thought it must be a necessity for winters in Wisconsin. I just assumed at the time that the heated barn would be warm enough to take off my snow pants! I also didn't realize back then that most horse barns are not heated.

Winter came and the snow came with it. Off to the barn I would go every day to work and with that came many layers of clothes. It was a very long winter for me. I learned fast that a heated horse barn does not mean seventy degrees. The barn was kept a little above freezing and compared to outside that was warm to everyone else but me. I was in a constant state of frozen. No matter how much clothing I put on I could not get warm and no matter how many stalls I cleaned I would go home and have to crawl under my covers or take a hot bath to finally warm up.

I was starting to wonder how anyone would want to have horses in this state. Who would want to ride when the temperatures were so cold? As I got to know more people in the horse world I started to realize that even though people didn't like the cold weather they dealt with it because they loved horses. They kept on riding and doing everything you would do with horses through all types of winter weather. It was ME that was having the problem adjusting to winter. Everyone else was doing fine. I had worked my first whole winter at a horse farm in Wisconsin and survived. Spring was a welcome site and the job seemed a little easier.

I worked at that horse farm for a year and as winter was coming in the second year I decided I couldn't do it anymore. It was just too hard for me working with horses and doing chores in the cold temperatures. I gave my notice and decided to find a different job.

After I was done working on the farm I moved on and I decided in my mind that I was done with horses. There was no way I could buy a horse of my own and want to ride it living in a place with such cold winters. At this point I decided I would just enjoy looking at them in someone else's field and be content with that.

A few years later David and I bought his grandfather's farm and with that came a wonderful old dairy barn. I loved that barn more than my house. We were able to buy six acres of land with the barn and house. To me six acres of land was incredible. I had never known anyone to own that much land in California. Land is too expensive out there and you would need to be a millionaire to afford land of any amount. It was amazing to me the difference in prices from one state to the next when it came to buying real estate.

We started our family and soon we were blessed with two little girls. I was very busy with them and for the next couple of years I spent all my time taking care of them. As my girls got to be about 3 and 5 years old, all of a sudden I had the itch real bad to get another horse. It had never left. I just had put it way down deep inside of me and every once in a while I would think about the idea of having another horse but then I would think about winter and usually the idea vanished pretty quickly. I was starting to get used to winters in Wisconsin and learning to enjoy them a little. They were not as bad to me as they were in the beginning.

As time went on David and I started to talk more and more about buying a couple of ponies for the girls. We had the barn and the land so it would not take much to keep a couple of ponies on the property. It was like a light was switched on inside of me. I was so excited again at the thought that we were going to have a couple of horses on our farm. I felt like I was ready to take care of them even during wintertime. We had an old dairy barn that we would work on and convert into a horse barn.

At this time the thought of starting a horse business had not entered our heads yet. That was the furthest thing from our mind. We worked on that old dairy barn for over a year, tearing the old cow stanchions out, filling the gutters with cement and we ended up building ten large stalls and tack room in that old barn. I loved it.

We found two wonderful ponies and home to our farm they came. We kept pretty busy with the girls and teaching them to ride. I am not a trainer but I figured I could teach them the basics of horse care and beginner riding. It was such a fun chapter in my life.

BUILD IT AND HE WILL COME

Well you know the old saying from the movie A Field of Dreams. "Build it and he will come." It is so true! We converted that old barn and all of a sudden we were boarding a couple of our friend's horses and we loved it. Doing chores for four horses was very easy and I never felt tied down because if we needed to go anywhere the two boarders would do chores for us and it worked out perfect.

David would go to work each day but soon he was yearning to stay at home and farm and the more he was at home on our farm taking care of the horses and chores the more we started to talk about the idea of him being home full-time. How were we going to make this happen? That was the million dollar question.

We slowly started to flirt with the idea of opening a horse boarding operation. We joked about it a little in the beginning but the more we talked about it the more the idea sounded intriguing. We had no idea where we would even start. We kept it to ourselves a lot during the first year that we talked about it. We had mentioned it a little to a couple of people we knew and they laughed lightly and said we were crazy. We continued to talk about it to each other and kept an open heart to where it might lead.

Starting a business of this magnitude was something that we prayed about and we took very slow. Over the next year we started looking at horse facilities in the area and what the need was just to see if there really was a need. There would be no reason to build a barn if we couldn't get boarders.

~3~
THE PERFECT BARN DESIGN

I have to say that one of my favorite things to do is tour other horse barns. I love everything about horse barns especially the different designs. I never get tired of walking into a barn for the first time and taking in the design, the wood and the wonderful smells. You know you love horses when you would rather go to the barn then go to the mall.

If David and I were serious about starting a horse boarding facility and we were going to build a barn, then we would need more acres of land for the horses. Our farm had the dairy barn and six acres but that would not be enough for a large stall barn and indoor riding arena plus dry lots and pasture. We decided before we went any further we would talk to David's parents and see if we could use the other acres of farm land attached to our property for our business. I had no idea how all this worked in the business world but we would take it one step at a time and see if this was at all possible.

We met with David's parents and they were very supportive of the whole idea. We didn't have any clear cut numbers for them or any answers to how this was all going to work but they were going to let us explore all the options and hopefully we could get some clear answers on how to start a business like this one. At this time I started looking online for books that talked about starting a boarding stable. I found a few books but none that really talked about the business from the very beginning stages and how to set it all up.

We would have to get a business loan from the bank and I had no idea what it would cost to build a barn or how much money the bank would even think of loaning us. I didn't realize at the time that we would spend many hours talking to bankers about business loans. We were really going into this with no idea of what we should be doing first. There was no road map to follow.

HOW MANY HORSES SHOULD WE BOARD?

Through that year we looked at many barns of all shapes and sizes. One of the most difficult things to decide was how many horses would we need to board to be able to make a living at it. Would we go big or scale down and would we both still need to have a second job? We tried to talk to some barn owners in our area but to our dismay most did not give us much information. I again went through the books I had purchased about these types of questions but I could not find the answers I needed on starting a business from nothing when it comes to boarding horses. This type of business is so different than buying a food or clothing franchise where there have been proven numbers exposed year after year. Now looking back, I believe starting a Taco Bell business would have been much easier!

There was one large boarding facility in our area that we were able to walk through and I liked the design so we started with them as our model and we would modify it from there. I spent countless hours designing the layout of the barn and then the next big thing was the size of the indoor arena. I was amazed at all the different indoor arenas and footing.

Remember I am from Southern California and out there no one has an indoor arena because it is too hot. I quickly realized here in Wisconsin you have to have one if you want to ride and have boarders during the winter months. Finally after a year we had decided on the design of our barn with the arena attached. It was still a huge guess on how this was going to work and we just kept going forward without any answers at this point.

Since 2005 when we built our barn, many people have asked us what the size of our stable and arena are. I thought I would give you the dimensions and a few visuals so that you have an idea of the size of everything in the barn itself.

Our barn at Vinland Stables is:

The building -25,000 square feet in size

-Our indoor arena is 80 x 200 feet

- 27-12x12 stalls

-Heated lounge with bathroom and shower

-Wash stall with hot and cold water

-2 - 12 x 24 insulated tack rooms

Our barn is 25,000 square feet.

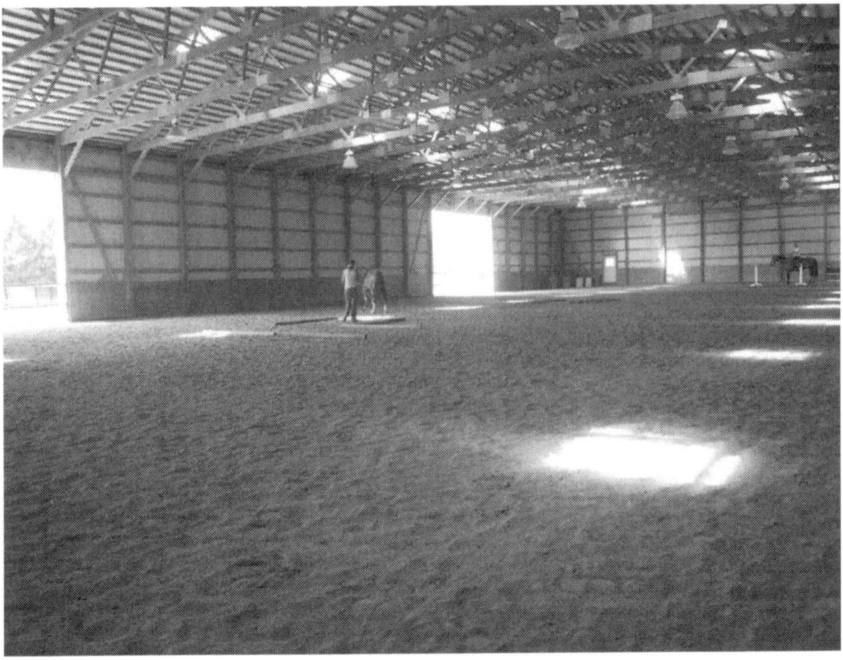

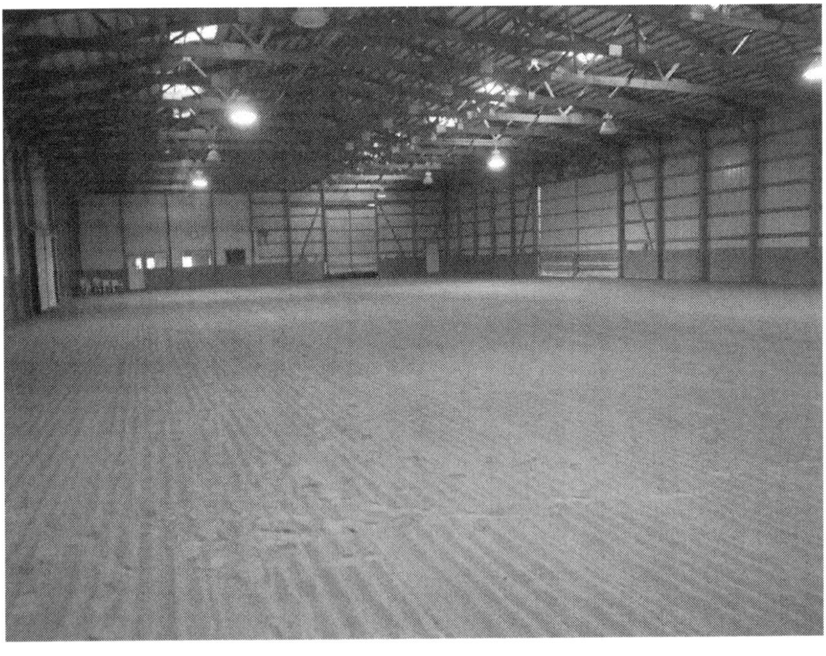

Our indoor arena - summer and winter

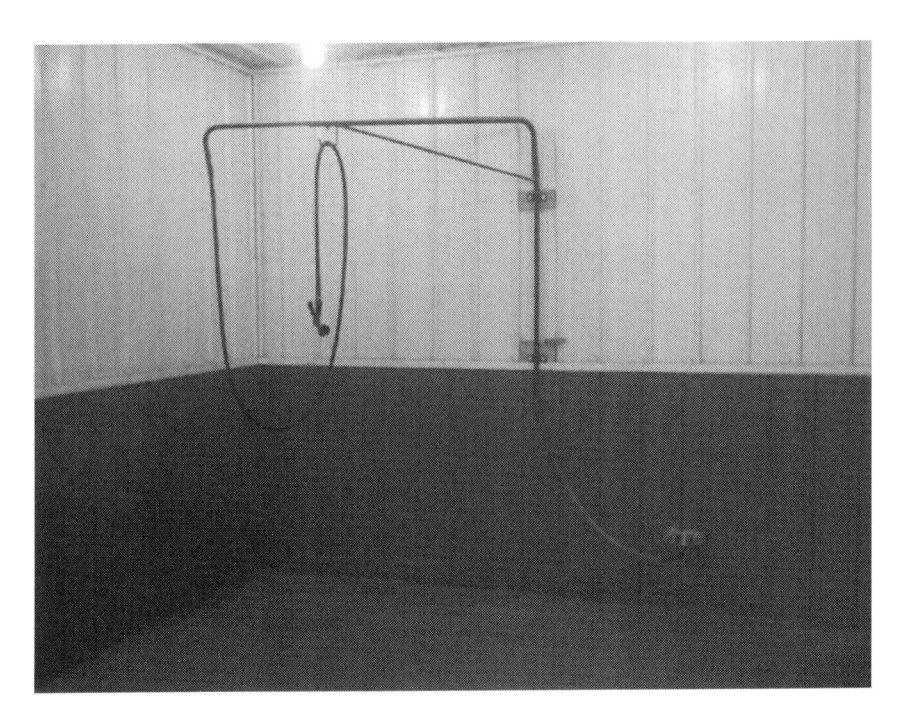

Our wash stall with hot and cold water

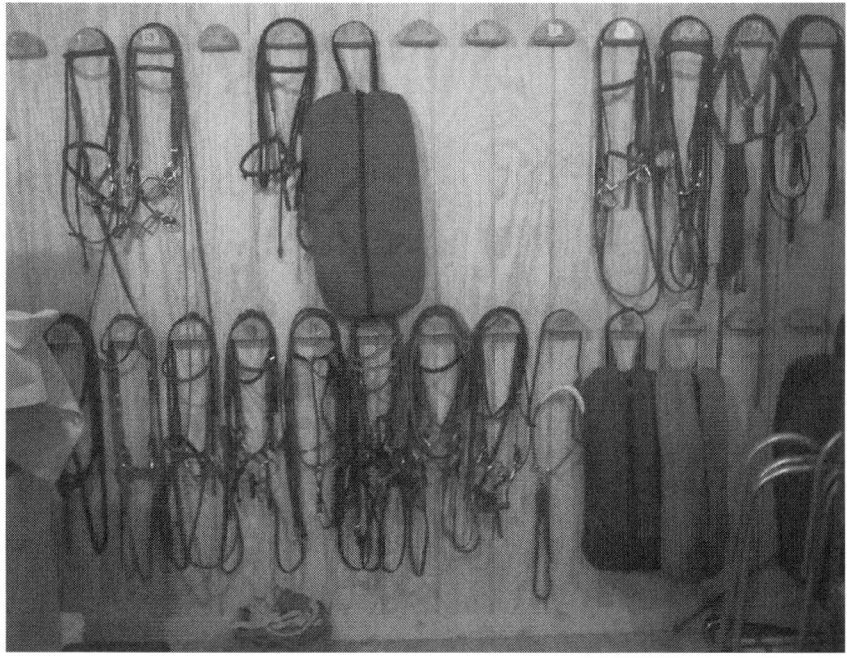

We have 2 - 12 x 24 insulated tack rooms

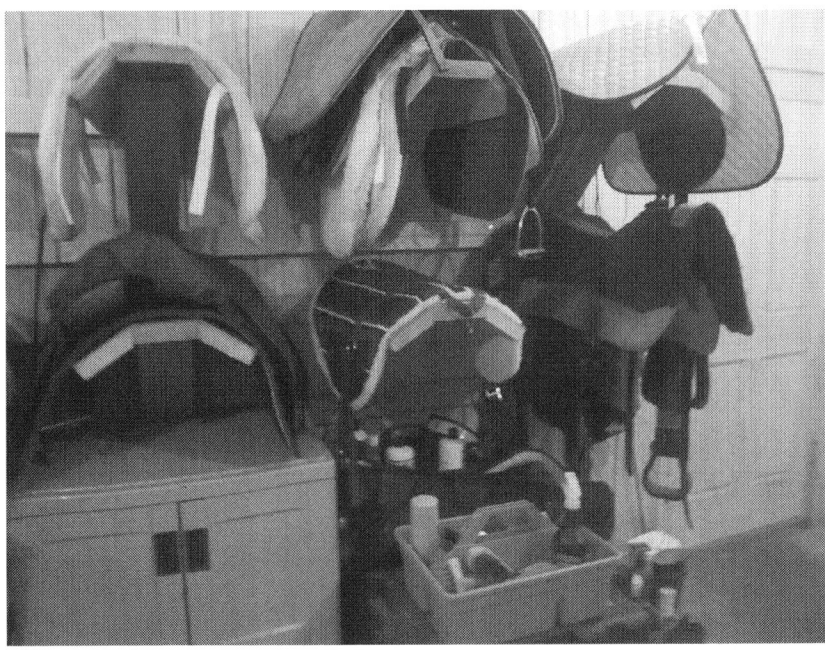

With 27 horses and we still have plenty of room

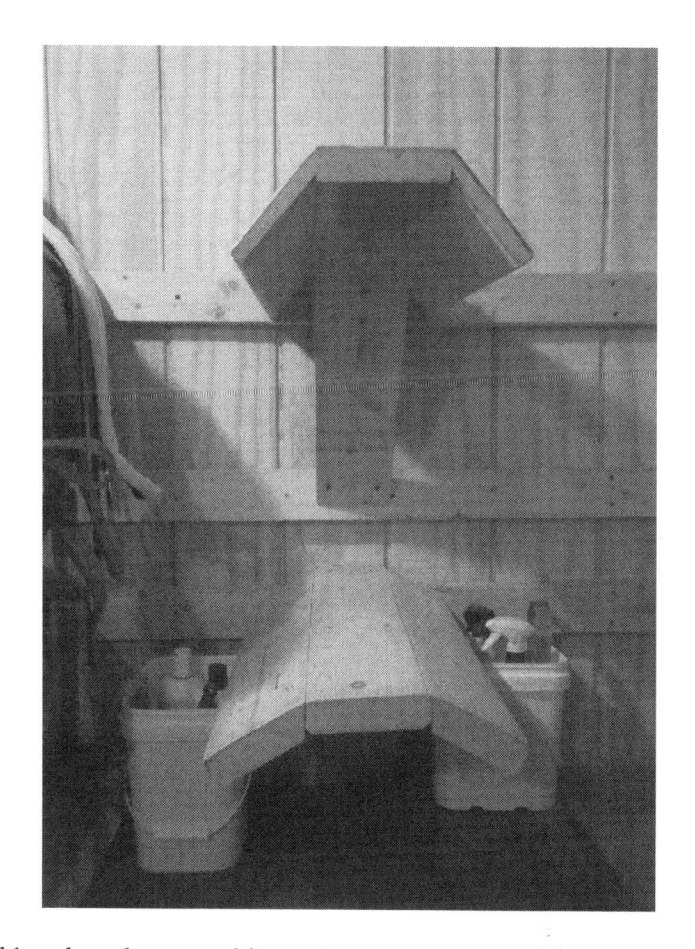

David hand made our saddle racks to save money. These racks handle the wear and tear of heavy saddle and it was definitely the right way to hang the saddles. Our saddle racks have lasted very well over the years.

Our hay and shavings room is 30 x 90 feet

We also have a 12 x 12 grooming stall which can be used for farrier and veterinarian calls. As you can see we decided to build a large barn!

We had our barn design on paper, now what do we do with it? Who is going to build it? How much was it going to cost and would we make enough to pay the mortgage? How much would we need to charge the boarders to cover all the expenses and would people pay it? And most important, how were we going to get a bank to give a loan to us on a business that had no proven record? It was a lot to think about and I could not find any formula or answers in any books I had read about starting a horse business. That is why I wrote this book.

Moving Forward With Our New Dream

The more that we talked about building a barn and starting a business of our own, the more excited we became for what could be. How was this all going to take place?

When I look back at those couple of years of preparing to start this horse business, boy did I have a lot more energy than I do now! It would have been so much easier to start our business before having kids so that we could devote 110% to the business but who does that?

Most of you will change careers a couple of times during your life. We were no exception. We still had not really told anyone of our venture except our parents so the only ones we had to talk to was each other. This was a good thing and a bad thing. Good because we talked a lot to each other but bad because we did not know what we were doing at all. We were just winging it with what we thought we should do next. We really should have been talking to people who already were operating boarding facilities successfully but we didn't do that. Looking back that was a big mistake but I will get more into that later in the book.

Before we could go to the bank to apply for a business loan we needed to see how much it would cost to build a barn of this size. I called and set up appointments with three well known builders in Wisconsin and we met with them and showed them our plans. After much talk of how we wanted our building to look, each of them came back in about a week with an estimate to build the building. Talk about sticker shock! I could not believe how much it was going to cost to build a barn and I am talking about just the shell. The inside was still empty!

David and I both worked but we were just your average middle income family. I worked for a school district as a teacher's assistant and David was an airplane mechanic. While we were meeting with builders to get estimates on putting up our barn, I also had been placing ads in the Buyer's Guide paper each week to see if people were looking for boarding. Remember this was long before Facebook. I ran an ad letting people know that a new barn was going to open in the Fox Valley in the near future just to see what the response was. The funny thing was there was no barn or even the approval for a barn. I needed to see if there was even a need before we went forward. It was exciting to see the great response I was getting from the ads. We went forward with what seemed like the logical thing to do next. Go to the bank.

Trying to Get a Loan

David and I really had not even started to think about the expense of building stalls in this barn or anything else we would need. We were so focused on the actually building that we had not checked into pricing for everything that needed to be done inside the barn once it was built.

I called our credit union that we did our banking with and asked them if they did business loans. They were a smaller banking institution and they told me they did not for what we wanted to build so I started looking for a bank that would be interested in our business. We made an appointment with another local bank and talked to the loan manager. We told him the approximate cost of the building and off the top of our heads gave him a price to complete the inside! Talk about a shot in the dark.

He was very nice and said he would get back to us in a few days. A few days passed and I called him and left a voicemail. No response. Then I called again and left another voicemail. Still no return phone call. I called him several times over the next couple of weeks and he never returned my phone calls at all! I was too timid to go into that bank and ask to talk to him in person and we just decided he was not interested. We never heard from him again! It was the craziest thing ever or he must have thought we weren't worth his time. Now years later, I would handle the situation so much different and I would go to the bank in person. Back then, I was so insecure about what we were trying to do that it was easier to move on.

We made an appointment with another bank and met with the loan manager. This man was very nice and after we talked for a long time he asked us if we had a business plan with us. What? What was a business plan? He had to explain what a business plan was to us and then he told us his bank did not do agriculture loans and that was the type of loan we needed. He suggested to us to find a bank that did agricultural loans and talk to their loan officer and go from there. I sure wish I had taken a business class in college! We were learning a lot about starting a business very fast. Now to find a bank that does agricultural loans. Off to the next bank.

~4~
FINDING A BANK THAT DOES AGRICULTURAL LOANS

Finding a bank that does agricultural loans is harder than you might think. I started calling around to banks in the valley to see if they dealt with agriculture loans. After many calls I did find a bank that had a department that only did agricultural loans. As I was writing this book it occurred to me that I live in the Dairy State and you would think most banks would do agricultural loans but they don't.

I got hold of the loan manager at yet another bank and set up an appointment to meet with him. We had to wait a week for our meeting so during that week I started doing some research on how to prepare a business plan. I was looking at books and reading articles on the internet and I was already getting overwhelmed.

I decided I would wait until our meeting with the bank. David and I went to our meeting and told our dream to yet again another banker. This time the loan manager understood what we wanted to do for a business. The only problem was he had only dealt with dairy farms and crops and farm machinery. He never had any huge horse barn projects come by him. What made this difficult for all of us was the fact that there was no proven income record for boarding facilities in the area that would be close to the size of what we wanted to do.

He was willing to go a little farther with us and so he explained to us what he wanted to see in a business plan and when we had that complete to call him and he would be willing to look at it. I was so excited that someone was actually taking us seriously!

We left and my head was spinning. Where do we start? I would have to find out the cost of everything we needed to buy to get this business up and running and have it typed out with graphs and charts. I would need prices on everything from stalls to every bucket and broom and how much hay we would use in a year's time. And of course our projected income! He even wanted to know what type of people I would be expecting to board their horse here at our barn. We needed to have information on what age of riders we would expect at our barn and even riding disciplines etc. That was a lot to wrap my head around. It would be nine months before we would see that loan manager again.

Learning to Write Up a Business Plan

During the next couple of months I was extremely busy getting prices on everything a horse farm would need. We live in a small town in Wisconsin and when you build anything you need to get it approved by the town board first. We had not done this yet because we did not want the word to get out on what we were thinking of doing. We knew it was time to apply with the township because there would be no reason to go forward if the board would not approve us to build our barn. I made an appointment for the next meeting with the board (which was usually held once a month) and gathered all the information the board wanted to know ahead of time.

Our township wanted to see the drawing plans for our barn. They wanted to know the size of the barn and how many horses we would board. Where would cars and horse trailers park? They wanted to know what we would do with our horse manure and water run-off. Again I found myself gathering and putting together information for a business that I really didn't have all the details for at the time. David and I wanted this so bad and didn't know what it would take to get it approved but we were going to try our hardest.

There were a lot of permits that were going to be needed in order to build and I needed to check into the application process for each of those and how much they would cost. We drove to the town hall meeting room and I was unbelievably nervous. I knew some of the local residents would be there and many faces we knew and this was their chance to ask us questions about our plans for our business and how we were going to run it. They could either support us or let the board know they do not. David and I had lived at the farm for a few years now so many people that knew us could drive by our farm any time of year and see how clean David kept everything. That was a plus for us. We were very happy because no one disapproved of our horse boarding business and we did get a lot of support.

I was relieved when the board approved us to build our barn and start our business. It is funny because we still didn't have a business loan and I kept wondering if we were putting the cart before the horse. So many times throughout this entire process I didn't know what we should be doing first and in what order to make it all come out together in the end. Again we were winging it but we never gave up. If anything, I was even more driven.

Now what to do about the barn and how much it was going to cost? I wasn't sure how much the bank would give us if we were approved so I decided to call the loan manager and after he ran some numbers over the next couple of weeks he was able to give us a ball park figure on a loan for everything from building the barn (the shell) to completing the inside and fencing and excavation.

They were rough numbers but it gave us a starting point. After I talked to him I realized very fast that the builders we were looking at for building the barn were out of our price range. Back to square one. We needed to find a builder that would build it for less than half of these other builders so that the rest of the loan money could go for finishing the inside and excavation, electric, fencing etc. I had no idea where to look. What kind of builder would build it for less than half the price of these other builders?

~5~
FINDING A BUILDER WE CAN AFFORD

Over the years I have found two kinds of business people in the equine industry. The people that want you to think they know more than anyone else and in reality they don't AND the ones that are very honest and will let you know if they don't have the answer but they are willing to help you find the answer. It is pretty easy to read who's who in the industry and when we were starting out I kept many things to myself because I was often overwhelmed with the whole process. If you don't realize it yet, you soon will and you will quickly find out that there are many very opinionated people in the horse world. You have to choose the people you go to for advice wisely. I have met many wonderful people in our horse community but I did not know them while we were trying to build. I felt like the new kid on the block trying to break into the business. I was not originally from the area and my Los Angeles horse roots did me no good in Wisconsin. I had been gone too long.

I started asking around about builders and trying to find someone that builds pole buildings. We thought we would have better luck finding someone if it was a person who wasn't so well known like the big name pole building companies in the area. We needed to find someone who was hungry to make a name for themselves. I called a guy who was a builder and talked to him and he came over to look at our plans. After he was at our home for a while he said he could do it and at a price we could afford!

Looking back, I think the only words I heard in that meeting were, "I can do it for the price you want." I was so excited that I never asked details about anything. We were way too trusting and not business smart at all. He also said he would take care of the sub-contractors for water, electric, cement and building the lounge and tack rooms. He quoted us a round figure that same night! I found this a little unusual because the previous three companies that had given us prices for building our barn took about a week each to get back to us with prices and bids for the job. If you are laughing right now I don't blame you. Talk about naïve and dumb!! That was us.

As I have been writing this book my mind has been flooded with many of the feelings I had all those years ago and all that took place to get this barn up and finally open for business. Jumping in blindly David and I found our man to build our barn. We asked very few questions. We really didn't know what questions to ask him. We just told him what we wanted. The only two things we wanted to know at the time were could he build it and could we see a contract? He assured us he would be able to build it with no problem. We had no idea what a builders contract should look like and what it should entail but he said he would be getting one to us. He was very personable and had a way of making you feel comfortable. We hired him and told him we would be in touch when we got the loan confirmed. You also need to remember this was long before the banking crisis and banks were giving out loans much easier than they do now. And this is how so many businesses got themselves into trouble years ago.

~6~
GATHERING INFORMATION FOR OUR BUSINESS PLAN

I started to work on our business plan which was extremely difficult to do since I had no idea what I was doing. As I was writing this book I went through and looked at some of the things we had in our business plan from years ago.

Mission Statement

Keys to success

Company Summary

Company Ownership

Start-up Summary

Services

Market Analysis Summary

Market Segmentation

Target Market Segment strategy

Service Business Analysis

Competition and Buying Patterns

That was just the start of it. I didn't even know what some of these words meant but I needed to learn fast and act like I knew exactly what I was talking about. We were at the beginning stages of writing our business plan.

David and I have been very blessed to have wonderful and very giving people come into our lives during this whole process. When it seemed like everything was working against us and would not be easy at all someone would step up to help us out.

We had a friend who kept her horse at our barn (our old dairy barn I had mentioned earlier) and when I told her about the business plan she was wonderful and said she would help me put it together. She knew how to do graphs and charts on the computer! That was fantastic because I knew absolutely nothing about putting together graphs and charts.

Over the next few months I started gathering prices of everything. Finding stalls I liked took a while but once I found them then I asked for a quote for 27 kits! Then we had to find stall mats for 27 stalls and 27 buckets, hooks for halters, salt block holders and blanket bars! And that was just the beginning. I am sure you get the picture now. It was 27 of everything. Our barn has two large tack rooms and we needed 2 saddle racks for each horse. Wow 54 saddle racks! We needed lights for the arena and aisle ways and grooming bays and wash stall and I can't even count how many light bulbs! Things were adding up fast. You don't think of all those things until you have to find out a price for all of them.

Now I see the importance of a business plan

I was slowly seeing how very important a business plan was. Next we had to get estimates on cement for the aisle ways that are twelve feet wide by two hundred feet long and also the back room where the hay and shavings were going to be stored. We also needed cement in the tack rooms and lounge. Then I needed to get prices on the arena sand. That was another story. I had looked at many arenas and everyone has a different idea of footing. Out of everything we did the arena footing took the longest to decide!

We needed to figure out our fencing. How many pastures and dry lots would we have and how many T-posts and wood posts and gates and bags and bags of insulators would it take to hang the electric braid we wanted to use? How many feet (or miles it seemed) of rolls of electric braid would we need?

I was gathering information about every part of the building in between work and taking care of two little girls. Many months later we were ready to start putting our business plan together.

~7~
THE BUSINESS PLAN FOR A HORSE FACILITY

When we learned years ago that we would need a business plan for any banker to even consider us for a loan it was overwhelming. I didn't go to college for business and neither did David. He knew how to run a farm and we both knew how to take care of horses. I am going to be very honest and tell you that our business experience was zero. The loan manager was willing to see us when we had our business plan together. He told us we could call him anytime if we had questions while we were putting it together. So I often did.

I had purchased several books on how to start and run a horse business but not one them went into detail about how to put together a business plan or what you would need in it. I read many articles online about business plans but I could not find one that pertained to the horse industry. Basically between my questions to the banker and what I read, I learned very fast what a business plan needed to have in it.

I decided when I wrote this book I wanted to devote an entire chapter to the core of what is in a business plan and what you need in it for the horse industry. My goal in this book is to help others out there that have the same dream as we had find the answers they are looking for.

WHAT IS A BUSINESS PLAN?

A business plan is your statement of your business goals. You are sharing your business ideas and why they are attainable and your exact and very detailed plan for reaching them. You are basically selling yourself and your dream.

This is a very simple description of a business plan but your business plan will be very detailed and in some cases very long. Our business plan was seventeen pages long. I know that there are many plans out there that are much longer depending on the size of the business and shorter if the business is smaller. Either way always remember the more detailed the better.

When David and I were starting to work on our business plan and gathering information I still did not grasp the whole reason why the bank needed so much detail. After we started to put it all together it was truly and eye opener and really made us realize all that it was going to take to get our business off the ground. It was one of the best things we ever did as far as teaching us about business.

When I decided to write a chapter solely devoted to an equine business plan, I knew that my original plan was already ten years old and some of it might be outdated. I decided to make an appointment with a woman who deals solely with agriculture loans and have her look at my old business plan and talk to her about what she would want on a plan in today's market. It is always fun to look at something that you did from years earlier. Sometimes it can really date you and in my case it made me laugh a little.

It was a nice surprise to find out my business plan from years ago was not too far off the mark. It was simplistic by today's standards and she told me where she would want more details and what she would change. I would like to pass this information to you. My goal in this chapter is to help you with your business plan.

When you start writing up your business plan remember you are sharing about yourself not just about numbers. The banker wants to know what kind of person you are. They will want to know about your history and what your experience is and how long you have been involved with horses.

Market Analysis Summary

When we started to put the plan together we were asked to put a Market Analysis Summary together. I had no idea how to do this or where to look. How do I find out about the market and if there is a need? We started with the Wisconsin Horse Council and learned what the statistics were for our state and the approximate number of horses back in 2004. I have to admit while we were going through the statistics for the state of Wisconsin I was learning many fascinating facts about horses in our state and the equine business industry.

We also took out ads in four newspapers (now you would use the internet instead of newspapers) to see what kind of response we would get for boarding. We talked to a countless number of people that responded and then we needed to decide what kind of barn we were going to have as far as riding disciplines. That was something I had not even thought of before. I had always boarded my horses out in California and the facility's I boarded at had many different breeds and different styles of riding. I just assumed that was the type of barn I wanted also.

With great response from our ads we truly believed there was a need for a multi-discipline type barn in the area. One of the most important parts to your business plan and is key to a successful start-up boarding stable will be to know what kinds of disciplines are prominent in your area. If you want to open a reining barn only and there are absolutely no reining horses in your area, you might have a much harder time filling all the stalls. On the other hand you might fill up extremely fast with people who have been waiting for a reining facility to finally open up in your area but you will need to find out for sure and the bank will want to know also. The more information you gather ahead of time about the riding needs in your area the better off you will be and the better your business plan will be. It is crucial to know what the market is in your area for the type of barn you want to have.

I am going to give you a detailed account of my business plan from many years ago. I am also going to tell you what each section means and what I would do differently now if writing up this plan again. There is a basic formula for what a business plan should look like and what the bank wants to see included. Though the formula might stay the same for most business plans, the type of business you want to start will make a big difference on what the details are like inside the plan. This is where I want to show you what ours looked like for the horse industry then and what it should look like now.

Remember, when putting together your plan communicate with your loan manager because each lending institution might want things done a little differently. They are there to help you and if you are in doubt about a section of the plan then call them and ask. They would rather have it done correctly the first time.

I wish many years ago I would have known of a book that had business plans in them for the equine industry. It would have saved me countless hours. My goal in this chapter is to educate and answer the questions you might have if you are looking to start a business.

CATEGORIES INSIDE OUR BUSINESS PLAN:

Mission Statement

Company Summary

Start-Up Summary /Expenses

Services

Market Analysis Summary

Market Segmentation

Market Segment Strategy

Service Business Analysis

Competition and Buying Patterns

Strategy and Implementation Summary

Competitive Edge

Sales Forecast

Marketing Strategy

Management Summary

Start-Up Funding

Break Even Analysis

Important Assumptions

Twelve Month Income Statement

Cash Flow Statement

Our business plan started with our mission statement and continued from there. It is a great way to introduce the banker to your business idea and values.

MISSION STATEMENT

Your mission statement tells the banker and everyone else that reads your business plan what your place is going to be about and what your mission is to make it the best place for people to bring their horses. It also tells a little about what your goals are for your farm. I have many times over the years read many mission statements from businesses and I always find them very interesting and some of them are so well written they make me want to do business with that establishment. Really think out what your mission statement is going to say. Set your business apart from the others right from the start with a great mission statement.

Here is an example of our mission statement from years ago.

Vinland Stables is a clean, attractive and safe horse boarding facility that strives for excellence in horse care and gives opportunity for horse owners to build a more intimate relationship with their horse, by promoting quality horse care, a healthy environment and natural horsemanship. By providing a comfortable environment, people of all horse backgrounds will find this a warm and friendly place to create long lasting relationships with other people and the horses they love.

Years later my mission statement would be longer and more detailed. Show the value of the company and what your core values are as the barn owner. Be as specific as possible. This gives you an idea of what a mission statement might look like. I would suggest going to different business establishments in your area and reading their mission statements. You will be surprised at how different and unique many of them are and the more of them you read, the easier it will be to write up one of your own.

KEYS TO SUCCESS

In this next section of your plan you will want to list the things that are going to make your business successful. Our business plan only had four points. Now that I have run a business for many years it would be easy to add many more.

Here is my example of our keys to success we put in our plan.

1. *Provide quality horse care.*

2. *Maintain a 100% lease rate*

3. *Maintain reputable and honest relationships with our boarders and the community.*

4. *Provide a return on investment that would allow Vinland Stables to offer more amenities such as two more outdoor arenas, round pen, groomed riding trails and the latest in care and technology.*

Please remember this is from years ago and now if I were to write this section over again I would have more detail for each point. I would give examples of how we would provide quality horse care and I would mention how I would advertise so that I always had a waiting list to keep a hundred percent lease rate. Remember the more detail the better.

THE COMPANY SUMMARY

The company summary is the section that you are going to tell your story. Tell about yourself and the area you live in. Write down the experience you have and what you will be contributing to on the farm. **If there is a need in your area then share it**. Explain how your facility can be an asset to the area. The bank will want to see your experience in the horse industry and if you have business knowledge that is a plus.

I am going to give you an example of what was in our Company Summary. After sharing my company summary with my friend that does agricultural loans, she told me she likes people to expand and tell their story. I finally see how important it is after all these years.

Our company summary was:

Vinland Stables is a professional horse boarding facility located in the Fox Valley. With massive growth in the Fox Valley and the equine industry, there is a great need for quality boarding stables. Vinland Stables is centrally located between Oshkosh and Neenah and is very easy to get to. Vinland Stables will provide housing facilities, quality care and the opportunity for the horse owner's to spend quantity and quality time with their horse. Vinland Stables will provide a family and community atmosphere.

If I was to write a company summary now for my business I would have much more detail about my experience running a large boarding facility and even touch on how we would run the business on a day to day basis.

COMPANY OWNERSHIP

This section is about the ownership of the business. It doesn't have to be long and in some cases like ours, we didn't have the details yet of the legal description of ownership. We were still just in the beginning stages of trying to see if we could get a loan so none of this was set up yet. Ours was very simple in our plan.

Here is what our Company Ownership read in our plan:

The final legal business entity format of Vinland Stables is yet to be determined. Lender/investor preferences, along with legal/financial counsel, will make this final determination prior to, and a condition of funding.

We just kept it honest. If you are already in a position where your company ownership is set up then put down exactly how it is set up. If things need to be changed in the future, your banker and lawyer will advise you on what needs to be done.

The next section on my business plan was the Start-up Summary. Gathering all the information for what it would take to start up our business was a true eye opener. Until you start to put it all together you don't realize what it really takes to get a horse facility off the ground from absolutely nothing. Doing this section for our business plan was one of the most educational parts of the whole process. I am going to give you a list of what our start-up summary consisted of. Yours will be different depending on what you have to start with and what you need to run your business.

START-UP SUMMARY

Cash for interest payment on construction loan
Legal expenses
Advertising, flyers, handouts etc.
Business insurance and Liability insurance
Computer for business
27 heated buckets
27 non heated buckets
27 corner feeders
27 salt block holders
27 blanket bars
10 blanket bars for drying blankets in back room
3 Wheelbarrows
4 picks
2 scoop shovels
2 100 ft. hose
2 floor brooms (heavy duty)
2 brooms
27 bucket holders
10 4 ft. gates
2 electric fence chargers
2 lightning constrictors
27 salt blocks
4 large salt block pans
4 large salt blocks
174 - 4 x 6 rubber stall mats
1 wash stall spray boom
3 100 gallon water tanks
3 165 foot hook up wire
Wood and screws for turnouts
24 handles for electric fence gates
1 entry mat for entrance
27 stall feeding chart liners
60 bridle hooks
54 wood saddle racks
1 50 ft. round pen
1 horse works program (for computer)
5 automatic waters
Tack room insulation
48 sheets-tack room liners

Grain storage bin
3 trash cans for lounge and tack rooms
Wood post (fencing)
T-Posts
Wood post Insulators
Bags screws
Ring insulators
Arena wood liner for walls
Stall hooks
7 pairs of cross ties
6 handles for arena doors/gates
Wood for stalls (back walls)
Wood for stalls
27 stall kits
Equine legal signs
2 ground rod kits
13 rolls of electro braid
Hay for one year
Grain for one month
Miscellaneous
Total Start-Up Expenses $0000

When you start to put everything down on paper it becomes clear very fast. It was amazing to us how much all this added up to. Even the smallest of items can add up. You will want to be as detailed as possible because anything you forget to include will throw your numbers off and you don't want to start off your business running out of money because you didn't figure in everything. We made that mistake in quite a few areas that we never gave any thought to. Our list was missing many items of things we needed for the barn. We did not realize in many cases all the things we would use on a daily basis until we were actually up and running with horses and people. Remember most new businesses do not have extra money just lying around. Better to be too detailed than not enough! It also shows the banker that you took the time to do your homework.

Our start-up expenses did not include the builders cost of building the barn, cement, electric and water and plumbing. That was all figured into the total later on.

When you are doing your business plan if you know how much the barn is going to be to build then you will want to add that on separate from your start up summary list and then total everything out. If you want to make sure you do it correctly for what your banker is looking for, then I would call and talk to your banker and ask him how he would like to see it done for your business plan. This was the way our banker wanted to see it laid out on our business plan.

The next part of our business plan was Services. This is a great area to really talk about what your facility is going to offer. Remember this is a service oriented business and we wanted to sell ourselves and set us apart from the other barns in the area so we needed to show we had great amenities and service. Service, Service, Service!!

SERVICES

Here is what our plan had in the services section. Yours will be different depending on what type of horse barn you have and what services you want to provide. This will give you a starting point and an idea of how to put it together in the business plan.

Vinland Stables is designed to provide safe and quality horse boarding services for equine owners of all riding disciplines. We will provide safe housing for horses inside with clean stalls and pasture board outside with shelter. Horses will be led outside every day to pasture individually and brought in every evening. The following is a list of initial services available at Vinland Stables.

Full Board (inside with stall and daily turnout) including twice a day personalized feeding program and visual inspection of each horse during feeding time.

Outside Board (horses live outside with shelter year round). In case of extreme weather in winter, horses will be brought into the barn overnight. They will have a personalized feeding program and visual inspection of each horse during feeding time.

80 x 200 ft. lighted indoor arena (groomed six days a week)

70 x 120 ft. outdoor riding arena

100 x 250 ft. outdoor riding arena

Large pastures with shelter

Private turnout

Foaling stalls

Trailer parking

Heated viewing room and lounge

Bathroom with shower

Rubber mats in all stalls

Wash stall (Hot and cold water)

Grooming, Farrier and Vet stall for separate care of horse

Owners live on site to provide emergency care to any horse at any time.

Vinland Stables will contract with local horse services to include, Veterinarian, Farrier, Trainer and others to be decided. Vinland Stables will host special events and clinics for boarders and the community. These may include educational clinics, 4-H Horse and Pony project and FFA. Additional services will be added to Vinland Stables as sources and demand is identified.

Now that you have read what we had in our business plan for services it gives you an idea of where to start and it also was a great tool for me really to think about what our barn was going to offer. If you are going to contract with local equine services then be as specific as possible. If you know already who you will contract with then include that in your plan. The more detail you give about your business the better.

MARKET ANALYSIS SUMMARY

Working on our business plan and the market analysis was an eye opener. It made me think of things that I would have never otherwise thought of.

We had to do an analysis of the different boarding facilities in the Fox Valley and close surrounding areas. How were we going to do that? I felt uncomfortable going to other facilities and telling them we wanted to open a new boarding barn in the area and ask what they offered at their barn. I am positive they would not have given me much information. I was able to go to one barn and ask the owner a few questions but I really didn't get much detailed information. I decided to have a friend of mine start calling different barns and ask what their rates were and what they offered. I know it sounds a little deceiving but I didn't know how else to get the answers I needed. Also this was long before Caller ID.

Remember what I had said earlier. There really was no clear numbers on the economic outcome of the facilities in area. It would have been so much easier to find out the economic records of any fast food restaurant in the area. When you compare the horse farm to the clothing store or fast food chain you can now see why it would be hard. Family farms are much harder to keep track of economically then the small business that sells food or clothes in the mall.

When I started gathering information for the Market Analysis Summary section I went to the Wisconsin Horse Council and checked on their records for the current number of horses in the state. We also contacted Veterinarians in the surrounding areas to get a number of how many horses they service in a month's time in the valley and surrounding areas.

We took out ads in four newspapers in the Fox Valley (now you would also use the internet) to see what kind of response we would receive.

In our market analysis section I talked in great detail about the responses I received for people wanting to move their horse because they were living in unsatisfactory conditions or the lack of pasture for their horse. I had a list of what people were looking for in a boarding facility and we were ready to have it for our clients.

Here is a sample of what I had written in our market analysis summary:

Please remember this was written years ago so it is going to be outdated with statistics but it will give you an idea of what our banker was looking for.

According to the Wisconsin Horse Council there are nearly 120,000 horses in Wisconsin. This is a number that is being updated right now in 2004. We know the numbers are larger now but I do not have the new totals. The number of potential boarders in the Fox Valley and a fifty mile radius around the Fox Valley is in the thousands alone. In contacting many equine veterinarians in the valley it is safe to say they are serving thousands of horses alone. This number does not include the many people who choose to give vaccinations to their horses themselves and many who do not vaccinate at all.

We also took out ads in four newspapers in the Fox Valley and surrounding areas to see what kind of response we would receive. With countless calls many people are ready to move now because of unsatisfactory conditions or lack of pastures for their horses. They would also like an indoor arena, personal care and the list goes on and on. Through this survey we have people who would like to be first on our registrations list. The most important thing everyone agreed on is there is a definite need for a new modern boarding facility in the area. The people I talked to were even ready to drive a longer distance to have the perfect place for their horse to live.

When writing your summary be more specific on what clients are going to be looking for. I only mentioned a couple of areas when we put ours together and I would highly recommend being more detailed. For example if you can give a percentage of how many people are looking for hunter jumper facilities or trail riding barns in your area then put that in your business plan. Tell the banker why an indoor arena is a very important asset in your area if you live in a state where the winters can be very cold.

This summary gives you an example of what to put in your market analysis. We also had one more section in the market analysis that was targeting people and the type of riders they are. When sharing about the types of riders that are in your area you will want to talk about the financial high end and low end for clients in your area. If your barn is going to be on the higher end of cost for the boarder, then you will want to convince your banker that there are plenty of people who are willing to pay more to make sure they have a quality facility for their horse.

For example, in some parts of the state of Wisconsin there are people that do reining as their choice of discipline and show their horse at reining shows. They are willing to pay more money to have a facility that meets their needs for their choice of discipline. In the Fox Valley where our barn is located there are very few reining prospects. Most of them have to travel a couple hours away to find a reining facility. It doesn't mean a reining facility won't be successful. In fact, it might be the perfect business opportunity. If you are able to hit a market that is not in your area, that could be great for business but find out first. Do a market analysis to find out how many people in your area are looking for a reining facility. Find out what the capacity is of other barns in the area and how full they are. Make sure there is a need!

MARKET SEGMENTATION

This is the area where you would divide a broad target market into smaller sets of consumers that have common needs. For the horse industry and boarding, the large market will be horse owners and the smaller subsets are the different types of horse owners looking for housing for their horse.

This is what our market segmentation looked like when we did our plan. Again, this is going to be a little different for everyone depending on what type of horse business they are going into.

Horse People come from all walks of life and all ages. The American horse love affair runs throughout our history and has never faded. We often hear of the little girl who sits by the fence for hours and watches as the horse of her dreams grazes peacefully in the pasture. That little girl grows up and the passion has never gone away. We always think of the little boy who plays cowboy and dreams of riding off into the sunset on his big horse. As that little boy grows up his passion is still as strong as when he was a little boy. Many of these children begin taking riding lessons and then eventually get their own horse and start showing at the 4-H horse shows and many of them move on to the class "A" shows. We would like Vinland Stables to be a place where children can ride their horses and be involved. We know the passion does not stop when the child grows up. Many adults begin careers in the horse industry and many adults own horses their entire life. Here are some of the target areas for the boarding industry.

1. Children-these children have horses and ponies and their parents want them to have a safe place for the horse and also a safe facility for their child. Vinland Stables is located in a wonderful location between two cities and just off a major highway so it will be very close and easy for the busy parent to get their child to the barn.

2. Teenagers and college age people-These young adults are wanting more from their horse experience and many of them are showing on a more competitive level. In Wisconsin they will need an indoor arena during the winter months to keep themselves and horse in top physical condition.

3. Single Men and Women-This group of adults are looking for a place to interact with other horse people and ride and participate in many social events together.

4. The Serious Adult Competitor-This is a person who needs to train year round and Vinland Stables would give them an opportunity to do serious training with the use of a very large indoor arena.

5. The Trainer-This is the person who trains horses and riders for a living and needs to be able to do this year round in a modern and safe atmosphere. Vinland Stables would meet this person's needs.

Now depending on what kind of equine business you are going to be starting, your plan will take on the details of your particular area of business. If you are going to breed and sell horses then you will want to really go into detail about the type of clients you will be looking for. The same is true for the trainer that is starting a business. You are going to need to be specific on what kind of training you do and with that what type of clients you are hoping to attract for business. Remember, the banker might not know much about the horse industry and everything that goes with it. If you take the time to put down as much detail as possible and explain in a language that he will understand, it will make your business plan that much better. He is not going to give you a large sum of money if he doesn't understand what you are going to do with it. Educate him as much as possible so he feels secure about how your type of business works.

MARKET SEGMENT STRATEGY

This is a sub set of the market segmentation and it just breaks down the classes of clients a little more. You are showing the banker that you have given this area much thought and you have a strategy. Your strategy may change and evolve as you go but you need a starting point. Our starting point was extremely simple at first.

In our Business Plan we had three target strategy areas for our barn.

1. Existing "pleasure" horse owners desiring to board and enjoy their horses in a safe, clean and modern barn with little or no specific care responsibilities on their part.

2. Existing "Show" horse owners who desire to have a safe, modern barn with all the amenities available to make getting ready for a show an easier task.

3. Non-horse owners who have long desired to become a horse owner but have not done so before and now would have a place to keep their horse that is extremely close to both Oshkosh and Neenah and surrounding areas. This would make it worthwhile as they wouldn't have far to drive to see their horse.

As you have just read my target areas that were written into my business plan, you have to remember that I was not at all a business person when we wrote this. It is extremely simple and now if I were to write it all over again my target areas would be much more detailed. Keep that in mind when you are writing your plan. I would talk about what is available near to your barn that will benefit your clients. Are there tack stores close by to pick up any horse related supplies or get last minute horse show items? How far is the equine veterinarian clinic from your facility? How far is your facility from public riding trails or horse show arenas? These are details that will make your plan stand out. Your business plan will be much better if you really know your market and what's available for your future clients.

We put in a closing statement in our business plan for the market strategy. It was as simple way of emphasizing one more time that we had thought about our strategy for getting customers and keeping them.

Here is what our business plan said:

The marketing strategy behind Vinland Stables is simple and very sound. A marketing survey was taken and it was greatly conveyed that there is a growing need for a new modern boarding facility with high quality care. Above that was the demand for a facility with more pasture for horses to be outside with other horses without overcrowding. Horse owners are now realizing that it is far healthier for their horses to be outside in a natural setting and spending less time in their stall. With the growing populations and cities, land is becoming harder to come by. The older boarding facilities that just have a barn now have no place to expand because of all the new homes and business being built in the Fox Valley. That is a plus for Vinland Stables because of the large amount of pasture we can offer that other boarding facilities cannot. We will be targeting all horse owners not just certain age groups or income levels. When it comes to horse owners they do not hold back when it comes to the care of their horse.

Marketing has already begun a year in advance with newspaper advertisements and giving future customers the opportunity to call us and ask questions and prepare them for our grand opening. The response has been great. Getting them excited about the future building of a new much needed boarding facility will prepare them for moving their horse to Vinland Stables. Once the building starts going up another ad will be placed in the newspaper letting people know they can come out and take a walk through. Word of mouth will also play a big part. Horse people talk! Flyers will also be sent to all call-ins, 4H groups and other horse groups throughout the Fox Valley to let them know we have started building and to come out and see. Vinland Stables will also be creating a website for people to look at and contact us through. We want to make this accessible to all so that anyone can contact us at any time.

Some of the ways you advertise will be different from years ago. Now one of the best ways to advertise is social media and Facebook. I use Facebook to advertise all the time now but back then we didn't have it. It is a fantastic tool! It is even a better tool when linked up to your website.

SERVICE BUSINESS ANALYSIS

As you can see our business plan was getting very long and detailed but there was a lot more to go. The next part of our business plan was the Service Business Analysis. This analysis is a report of a business that thrives on services. Our horse boarding facility is solely a service business. Without the service there is no business. In this section you want to be very descriptive about what your barn is going to offer and how it affects everyone else that works in the horse industry. It definitely has a pyramid effect. This is what ours looked like on our business plan. This will give you an idea of what the banker is looking for.

The Service Business Analysis from our business plan:

In the Fox Valley there is a great need for quality horse boarding facilities. The boarding facilities that are in the Fox Valley with similar amenities as Vinland Stables have waiting list. Some of them have a year wait. When we did an analysis of the area and what the other boarding facilities were offering, the one thing that set us apart was the amount of pasture we have to offer for the horses to get outside as much as possible. Many boarding barns in our area are older and do not have pastures at all. Many years ago the school of thought for many people was "Ride your horse for an hour and they will be fine for the other twenty-three hours in their stall." We know that is not the healthiest way for a horse to live. We think our service of hand walking out the horses each morning and bringing them in each evening will get the horses outside and also give us a chance to look them over twice a day and make sure they do not have any cuts or lameness issues. We will offer a safe and very healthy living environment for each horse that is kept at Vinland Stables.

An economic study done by the American Horse Council Foundation validates what the industry has known for some time; the horse industry is highly diverse, national, serious and *economically significant. Through this study we know that are 6.9 million horses in the United States. We know that 7.1 million Americans are involved in the industry as owners, service providers, employees, and volunteers. 1.9 million people own horses. The industry alone provides 338,500 full-time jobs. The horse industry has a 112.1 billion dollar impact in the United States. There are nearly 120,000 horses in Wisconsin with twenty-five percent being used for sporting events, breeding, racing and work. Each year almost $150 million is spent on horse feed, health care, tack and many other services.*

Now after reading what we had in our plan many years ago you can get the idea of what a service business analysis is about. I am sure the numbers for the statistics have changed and grown since we wrote our plan but when it is all said and done, it is about service. Your barn that you build will affect many other jobs out there. The people that you buy your shavings, grain and supplements from and the farmer that brings your hay are just a few to start.

COMPETITION AND BUYING PATTERNS

In our plan this section was very short. Looking back all those years we really didn't have a good grasp on competition and buying patterns in the boarding industry. It is something that I am very familiar with now for our area but back then we were trying to figure this all out.

What you really want to do in this area is have knowledge of what is out there in your field. You need to be very familiar with your competition and what is going to separate you from the rest of the competition.

This is what ours looked like when we did our plan:

Competition and Buying Patterns

People that love horses are a tight knit group of people. They form a network within each barn and keep each other aware of what is going on in their own barn and the surrounding areas. If something good is happening at your barn, it is guaranteed other people from different barns will find out very fast. The same is true when something bad happens. Word travels fast in the horse world. In that respect, building trust and a good reputation is the key element for a successful boarding facility. The competition in the area does advertise, but by building a trustworthy reputation, Vinland Stables is confident that customer loyalty will come from developing a trust between the customer and the owner of business.

STRATEGY AND IMPLEMENTATION SUMMARY

A business plan's strategy and implementation summary emphasizes what makes your business compelling and how you will attract and maintain your customers with a solid business relationship.

Our strategy and implementation summary was the area where we wanted to tell our banker what the one thing was we have at our barn that will separate us from the rest and is solid and true. This is what we wrote in our business plan to give you an idea.

Emphasize service

We will differentiate ourselves with SERVICE! We will establish our business offering a clear and viable alternative for our target market.

Build a relationship

Build long-tern relationships with our boarders. Make them feel completely secure at where their horse will be living.

Focus on target markets

Our target market will be all people that own horses. It is very simple and very sound.

This area of our business plan was extremely simple but very clear. If you are going into a target area (for example-training or breeding) then your target market is going to be different.

When we were writing our business plan this was all new concepts for me to think about. I would explain why it is important to have a good relationship with your boarders and how I would do that. I also would have a more direct target market because I know that our barn is not really conducive for certain riding disciplines and I would explain what disciplines I would be aiming for. Our arena is great for most disciplines except reining horses and speed horses. With the exception of those two disciplines, it leaves a huge number of possible clients out there looking for boarding. When you are writing your plan include some of those details.

COMPETITIVE EDGE

In our business plan the bank wanted to know what our experience was with horses and what our competitive edge was. We were mentally getting ready for the Shark Tank at this point. We were really going to have to sell ourselves!

Before you know what your competitive edge is, you must know what your competitors have to offer. It is very important to know what other facilities in your area are offering and what you have that they don't. Do you have something unique?

When we put our competitive edge section together in our plan it really was not descriptive enough. I will give you a sample of what our competitive edge looked like and then I will tell you what I would do differently now if I was writing a business plan today.

Our competitive edge on our plan:

The major competitive edge that Vinland Stables will emphasize is the high quality of its customer service, high quality care of the customers' horses and very close communication with the owners about daily care and well-being of their horses. Other areas that will set Vinland Stables apart are the large amount of pasture for horses, a very attractive and very clean barn, and top quality amenities at a very competitive price.

One of the greatest assets Vinland Stables has is our location. Our location is unbeatable. We are just five to ten minutes from both Neenah and Oshkosh cities yet when you come to our stable you will feel like you are out in the country. This is a definite plus for the average person who works till 5pm Monday thru Friday and would still like to come out and see their horse after work and have time to ride.

We have extensive equine experience and knowledge in care and horse management. With combined twenty-five years of experience the owners feel very comfortable with all breeds of horses. The owners, David and Sheri Grunska have taken horse management classes and will continue to educate themselves each year with different learning venues so they can learn the latest in all around horse care and welfare. Sheri also has had experience working at different horse barns including one barn for a year and a half in Wisconsin. This facility showed horses and bred horses for business. David and Sheri are currently boarding horses and have for the last year. With the combined experience and always being updated with the latest information in horse care, we are confident that Vinland Stables will be set apart as far as horse boarding facilities with the latest in equine horse care and with a well thought out building structure that is safe and designed with the horse in mind.

If I was to write this now, I would still have the same content I wrote in the original text but I would elaborate on details. If you have a very large indoor arena which helps during peak hours of riding then that would be a plus and give you a big competitive edge in the market place. If you have a cross country course in your plans then that would give you a great competitive edge against other barns that don't have a jump course. Those are the kind of things I would include in this section.

When doing an analysis of your competitive edge, the information you find out will be very useful for marketing, pricing, barn management and it will give you strategic plans for getting clients.

You are going to want to ask (and do a lot of detective work) when trying to establish what your competitive edge is. Here are some questions you will want to ask and find answers to regarding the horse industry.

Where are your competitors located in conjunction with yours? Are there a lot of barns in a close proximity? When we were checking into the competition there were only two other large barns within a forty mile radius.

What are the competitor's strengths? It is very valuable to find out what the other barns offer and their strengths. What do they do that sets them apart? Do they cater to Hunter/Jumpers or Dressage? Are they strictly a Quarter Horse barn? How do they feed and what do they offer with hay. Do they offer grain and supplements? Do they hand walk out the horses or do they let them run out to the pasture? Do the horses go out every day and for how long? Can you bring your own trainer in or do you need to use the barn's trainer? These are just a few of the many questions you could ask.

There are so many differences between barns and trainers that if you do your homework it will be a big help in really seeing what your competition is.

How do the barns in the area compare to what you are building in terms of quality, appearance and how it is kept up? One of the most common things I hear from potential boarders that I am giving a tour to is that the barn they are currently at does not repair things when they become broken. If you have horses things are going to get broken in the barn or outside and what happens at many facilities is that things get broken and then they don't get fixed. I hear that constantly and to this day if you were to ask one of our present boarders (or even past boarders) if we fix everything that gets broken I can tell you with confidence they would tell you yes. We have earned that reputation and we plan on keeping it. That is a fantastic competitive edge!

What is their price structure compared to yours? This is great information to gather about your competitors. I still keep tabs on what other barns are charging. I want to be in the right price range for what we offer and I don't want to be too low nor do I want to bust the ceiling either. It is a delicate balance. Find out if they are offering grain with the hay as part of the price or if they charge extra for grain and supplements. Find out if they charge for blanketing and holding a horse for the farrier and all those other little things that can add minutes or hours to your very long day.

When we were trying to figure out what other barns charged I didn't feel comfortable calling barns myself so I had a friend of mine call barns looking for boarding and she would ask all those questions. Nowadays it is much easier to find out information because most of the boarding facilities in our area have websites. You can just click on them and find out what they have to offer. That wasn't the case years ago.

Are the boarding facilities in your area full? This is a very important question and you really need to take the time to find out if barns are full with a waiting list or if they have many empty stalls. Empty stalls make for less income and the banker will want to know that information. Many years later I still get asked that question from my banker when I see him. He always will ask me, "Are you full?" and "Do you have a waiting list?" Thank goodness I have always been able to say yes!

What are the company's supply sources for products? Where are you going to get your hay? Are you going to make your own on your own land or buy it from a supplier? The difference in price between the two choices will be the difference in thousands of dollars. If you have forty horses like we do at our farm it is extremely expensive. Find out what other barns do for hay? Where do they get it if they have to buy it? The bank is going to want to know who you have set up to be your supplier and do you have a backup if the first supplier can't meet your order for hay.

If you are going to supply grain as part of the board then where are you going to get your grain from? What is going to be the cost? The banker will want to know how other barns handle grain and supplements in your area and cost is a big part of it.

Don't forget about shavings. Shavings will be one of your biggest expenses and make sure you have at least two suppliers available. What are you going to do as far as bedding and how do other barns bed their stalls? Find out all these things so if your banker asks you about it you will truly know what you are talking about.

Your banker may want to know what you paid for hay or shavings and how does that compare to what others are paying. Remember, he wants to make sure you are smart with your money and running your business and if you are paying five dollars for one bale of hay and everyone else is buying hay for three dollars per bale he will probably question why you are paying so much more. Can your sales from your business cover the cost? These are all things to think about.

What is the company's marketing activities? Find out what other barns are doing to promote their business. Are they on Facebook or a website? Do they host clinics or have horse shows? Do they sponsor 4H or FFA? There are so many things you can do to market your barn and when you are writing your business plan think about the things you want to do at your barn and include it. Clinics are a wonderful way to market your barn and now with Facebook it is so easy to advertise. These are all really positive things to get your business out there and make your barn a familiar place in the community. When writing down your ideas on your business plan, share how it is going to give you a competitive edge.

Remember, you are selling yourself to the banker. If you are good at something then flaunt it! If you are a trainer and have had a waiting list for two years then write it down. Let the banker know you are an expert in your field and you are willing to work hard and you are good at your job working with horses and people. You're not bragging, you're just confident in what you do and you want the banker to believe in you.

Believe me when I tell you that years ago when we were putting this business plan together I had no idea what I was talking about. I had never given any of the things we are talking about a moment's thought. Now that we have run our own business for many years I finally understand why a business plan is so important and why the banker wants a detailed plan. It really makes you think long and hard about your business and everything that you need to do to get it up and going strong and keeping it that way.

SALES STRATEGY

I didn't have a sales strategy back then and I wasn't sure how detailed the banker wanted our sales strategy. When we wrote ours it looked like this:

The sales strategy behind Vinland Stables is simple but very sound. Excellent horse care and open communication between David and Sheri Grunska and the horse owners will keep Vinland Stables at one hundred percent capacity.

Like I said, it was very simple. It was too simple by today's standards. I have never been much of a sales person at all and I have always believed if you have a good product it will sell itself. That was what I went with when we wrote our sales strategy. I still feel the same about sales now but now I would tell you that in today's market you must make your sales strategy much more detailed.

When talking about the communication strategy like we had put down in our plan, I would elaborate and talk about how you are going to reach your customers. When we had built our barn many years ago I used the newspaper and flyers. That was pretty much it. Nowadays that would be outdated. I would still use flyers and post them but I would also use the internet. There are so many wonderful tools on the internet to use and it will get your name out there very fast. If you are going to use brochures or other printed material also write that down in your plan.

Once you get your clients then share your sales strategy on how you are going to keep them. That is what I was saying when we were talking about excellent care and communication in our plan.

SALES FORECAST

We needed a sales forecast for the first three years after we opened. How was I going to do that? All I can say is boy I wish I had taken a business class in college!

Working on the sales forecast for our business plan was interesting and very difficult.

I wish I could tell you we had a magical or even educated way of doing this and making the numbers work but we didn't. Simply, we just played with numbers a lot. We multiplied what we wanted to charge for each stall by twenty-seven (That is how many stalls are in our barn) then did the same with our outdoor boarded horses and the total monthly gross income was the answer. Now the problem was we didn't know exactly what our monthly bills were going to be and all we had was a rough estimate. We did this several times until we came up with a monthly number that seemed safe to start with. This number had to be projected three years out and that meant including the rise in hay, grain, gas, electric cost and everything else that you would use on a farm to keep the farm going. You also want to take into account a percentage of stalls that might be empty. Remember empty stalls mean less income. You need to be real when you are projecting your sales forecast. Talk about a guessing game!

What we had was a graph with a three year sales forecast. It was pretty simple but we just projected out three years what our estimated sales would be for board. When figuring out your numbers for your sales forecast it is important to include a percentage for turnover also. You will have turnover and that could mean a loss in revenue during that time. The bank wants a very real picture of your sales.

Yours might different if you offer other types of boarding or training packages but for us our income was coming from boarding alone along with David and I working second jobs. The bank definitely will want to see other sources of income when starting up. David and I had also included in this whole money scenario that I would still work full time for a couple more years but he would gradually cut back on hours at his second job to the point where he would be able to stay at home and work fulltime at the farm.

The one very important thing about an animal farm is that you never close not even for one day. They always need to be fed and watered even on Sunday and holidays. Many people don't think of those things when looking at starting a business with animals. We did because David had milked cows for years and understood that way of life. We had to sell ourselves to the bank that we would be able to handle this lifestyle seven days a week (Holidays included).

Our plan was to eventually have employees on weekends so we could have some time off. At least that is what we thought at the time of doing our plan for the bank. The bank liked the idea that we would be bringing outside money in also. I was planning on working a second job for only a couple more years after we opened and I didn't mind working weekends at home for a little while. In today's market the bank will most likely want a second income for a safety net. The banks are much more conservative now than they were years ago.

MARKETING STRATEGY

This is what ours read:

The one thing that is great in the horse community is the fact that if you do a good job taking care of other people's horses and the owners are happy, they will spread the word for you. That also can go the other way just as fast. The horse community is a close group of people and when they start talking word travels. We will have a website in place so people can find us at any time and contact us with any questions they might have about our facility.

Looking back at our business plan for our marketing strategy ours was pretty lame! Our marketing strategy said nothing about what we were going to do. Instead all I wrote was the fact that we were going to put up a website but did not have it done at the time. When writing down what your marketing strategy is, always talk about what you are going to do and make it all positive. Have a timeline and let the bank know you plan to achieve the future task by a certain date. Don't wait four years like we did to get a website up! Websites are so easy to create and they will help your business in a huge way. Having a website is one of the most important marketing tools you will ever have. I realized after reading my marketing strategy that it was not very positive and had poor detail.

When you put down what your marketing strategy is remember it is the process of finding and bringing in customers. Every business will have its own marketing strategy unique to its business. Your marketing strategy will hover around the horse industry and every part of the horse industry can filter into your business whether it is training, breeding or boarding. I have had many calls from potential boarders that have gotten my number from their farrier or veterinarian. Even our local tack store has brought me a lot of business. Include those details in this section. There are many ways to market your business and remember the horse industry is a large industry with many wonderful options of marketing your product. Most off all if your boarding barn or training skills are good, word of mouth is a fantastic tool.

MANAGEMENT SUMMARY

The bank wanted to know our experience in running a horse facility and how we were going to do the day to day job of running a large horse boarding operation. Well I have to be very honest here. I really had no experience in running a forty horse operation. I had worked at different horse farms through the years but never ran one solely. We were planning on running the farm ourselves and we had to sell ourselves to the banker on the fact that we had many years' experience with horses and hoped that was good enough. *Let me tell you there is a huge difference between owning a horse or two at your own place or even boarding a horse at a stable and completely running your own horse farm.*

Looking back we were never nervous about it. We knew we could do it. We just needed the chance. David and I both had different jobs on the farm and with our new barn we each would have different roles. To this day we still each have our own roles and jobs and it works great. I laugh because sometimes we try to step into each other's job and change things and it usually causes a little stress between us.

When we wrote out our management summary, this is a sample of what it looked like:

The initial management team depends on the founders themselves. David and Sheri Grunska own Vinland Stables and will run the barn themselves. This is something they have experience in. They are currently boarding horses and have for the last year. David will handle more of the physical work load and both will handle the horses. Sheri and David will both handle the financial books with a system that works for them.

Resume Overview:

David and Sheri have a combined twenty-five years' experience in every aspect of the equine industry.

David has many years' experience working in the dairy business and fully understands an industry dealing with animals and the day to day special needs that may arise. He also understands that this is more that an eight hour a day job and is very ready to make this his career. Having this business would not change too much the hours that David already puts in at his job (away from home) and here at our farm as it exists now with the horses we board and our own personal horses.

Sheri has the experience of working at a horse farm and dealing with very expensive show horses, brood mares and foals.

David is extremely versatile in range of "hands-on" technical and trade abilities.

Good computer skills

Extremely good creative abilities

Very Flexible

Extensive reputation for organizational skills and time management.

Very dependable and honest

Great contacts both in general business and equine activity

Great contacts with both local veterinarians and farriers.

In addition, David and Sheri Grunska will be backed by a very strong family team in complete support of this endeavor. David and Sheri are partners in every part of this business and balance each other out. When decisions need to be made they each have the support of each other and are both equally hopeful for the implementation of the business plan.

There is nothing more important than good team management between myself and David. I was truly blessed to have him as my partner in our business endeavors as well as life. On our plan as you see we had to list the role and jobs David and I would take on working at our farm and what we excel at. This was something I had not thought about before regarding myself but this part was much easier for David because he had many years working on dairy farms and with equipment. David is great at hands-on technical and trade abilities (basically he would be able to fix anything that a horse could break and they break a lot!).

I felt more comfortable talking with people and problem solving and the day to day care of the horses. We were really starting to define our jobs and sell ourselves on paper to the bank. The wonderful thing about a business plan is it really makes you think of every detail of the business that you probably would not have thought of before. It is a fantastic and very important tool for anyone to see if they really want to start and run a horse business.

Our business plan was moving along and it became pretty complicated. We realized we needed graphs and charts and I needed help in this area. You will want visuals in your business plan and graphs and charts always look nice and give an easy visual of what you are trying to convey with numbers.

Our business plan included **Start-up Funding** and **Break Even Analysis**. Those were sections that I had no idea how to answer. I am going to admit that we had to take an educated guess. If you are applying for a loan for an existing horse facility, this area of your plan will be much easier because the barn will already be set up. I will show how we displayed our numbers then explain a little about it so it is easier to understand. This is what our start-up funding looked like when we first were applying for a loan

TABLE-START-UP FUNDING:

Start-up Funding

Start-up Expenses to Fund	$32,440
Start-up Assets to Fund	$367,560
Total Funding Required	$400,000
Assets	
Non-cash Assets from Start-up	$362,560
Cash Requirements from Start-up	$5,000
Additional Cash Raised	$0
Cash Balance on Starting Date	$5,000
Total Assets	$367,560
Liabilities and Capital	
Liabilities	
Current Borrowing	$0
Long-term Liabilities	$400,000
Accounts Payable (Outstanding Bills)	$0
Other Current Liabilities	$0
Total Liabilities	$400,000
Capital	
Planned Investment	
Owner	$0
Additional Investment Requirement	$0
Total Planned Investment	$0
Loss at Start-up (Start-Up Expenses)	$32,440
Total Capital	$32,440
Total Capital and Liabilities	$367,560
Total Funding	$400,000

Now that you have had a chance to look at our start-up funding, I will break it down for you and explain what it means.

Your business plan is not complete without planned start-up funding. You are going to need to explain where you are going to get the money for start-up expenses and start-up assets.

Start-up Expenses are the expenses you will need to start the business. They are at the beginning of the plan. For example, my start-up expenses were the cost of materials for inside the barn and advertising, fencing, brooms and insurance etc. It was not the barn itself at the time.

Start-up Assets is the cash when you start your long term building. For us it was the building itself. They are current and long term. Our stalls are a permanent part of our barn and they were included in the start-up asset category. When your barn is complete it will become your asset.

You will want to discuss this section with your banker when completing your start-up expenses and assets. Depending on whether you are building a new barn or trying to get a loan for an existing barn will make a difference on how your numbers are going to appear on your business plan. It is always best to ask your banker how he would like to see it done. Remember he would prefer you to ask and have it done correctly the first time then to put all the hard work into it and have it be wrong. They are there to help you with all of this.

Long Term Liabilities are notes or loans that are due longer than one year into the future. Our business loan was for twenty-three years so it was a long term liability.

The other part of this section in our business plan was the **Break-even analysis.**

It is an analysis to determine the point in when income received equals the cost associated with receiving the income. The break-even analysis will calculate what is known as a margin of safety. It is the amount that revenues exceed the break-even point. This is the amount that revenues can fall while still staying above the break-even point.

This was an area that David and I had no idea about or where our break-even point would fall. It was another guessing game because we didn't know at this point what our monthly mortgage was going to be along with all the other cost. We had to estimate the best we could under the circumstances and then be truthful with our banker and explain that we really didn't know what the break-even point was until we had an idea of what our loan amount was going to be for and what the interest rate was at the time. We are very lucky because we had a very understanding banker and we just laid it all out on the line. At this point we had nothing to hide and if we were trying to hide something, I am sure he would have seen right through us.

We only needed $5,000 cash requirement from the start-up. Remember this was years ago before the economy fell. Nowadays banks are going to want you to come up with more cash to put down in the beginning and more cash reserves for everyday business expenses. In today's market $5,000 dollars would be extremely low.

Our total funding for our loan to start was $400,000.00. Our situation was a huge risk even though we didn't realize it back then. We did not have any capital and we were borrowing everything but $5000.00 dollars which is peanuts compared to the amount we borrowed.

The one thing that made this whole loan possible was the land that we owned and I will go into detail with that later on.

Important Assumptions

Putting a business plan together is all about looking into the future and forecasting and confronting assumptions. Here are some questions when working on this section of your plan.

Is there a need in your area for your product or in our case a horse boarding facility? You can't just assume there is a need because you love horses and you think everyone else feels the same way. A lot of people love horses but not enough to want to own one. If they have a horse can they afford the board at your facility? These are things that you will need to find out and the banker will want to know what steps you used to find your answers. Is there a significant customer base? Is there enough people looking for boarding in your area?

We were lucky when we decided to build a horse barn. We live right in the middle of three close cities that are largely populated and our facility is only a little ways out in the country and very easy to get to. When people drive to our farm they feel like they are way out in the sticks but they are actually very close to everything including a major highway. If you live in an area that is a very long drive from any city, you might have a harder time filling your stalls. I know of a beautiful horse barn that is very new and they are at least forty five minutes from any large city and they have a hard time filling stalls due to their location. If they were closer to town I am sure they would be full all the time and have a waiting list. One of the problems they have is the fact that most of the people that live out in the county near them keep their horses on their own property because they have enough land. Those people don't need to board their horse.

Can your business turn a profit? This was a hard area for us because we still didn't know exactly what our mortgage payment was going to be at the time and we really didn't have a true idea of how much it would cost to keep the facility running for a year. The first year was a lot of guessing about everything.

Are you the right person to run a horse business? It will be a life transformation that you will not expect until you are far into it and then there will be no backing out. The banker wants to make sure you really know what you are getting yourself into. It's not something that you can buy and when winter arrives in full force you decide that you don't want to do it anymore. Unless your place is paid off you will still have a monthly mortgage payment that needs to be paid.

When we wrote up our section for important assumptions I really didn't have a full grasp of what the banker might be looking for. Ours is pretty short but I will give you an example of what ours said when we did our plan.

Important assumptions we are conveying are:

With the changes in the Fox Valley and the booming economic growth pattern, farm land is being sold for sub-divisions and with that goes precious land for grazing or making hay. Huge sub-divisions are being built out in the middle of what used to be farm fields. With more people moving out to the country, the country is disappearing and these people need to place to keep their horse which Vinland Stables will offer.

The horse business is a very rapidly growing economic business in the United States and is a business to be taken very seriously. It is no longer just considered a hobby sport but is a viable income to the nation's economy. We know Vinland Stables will greatly benefit the Fox Valley and will greatly boost the equine industry in this area. We have a positive assumption that our business will grow greatly in the next few years.

We feel that the 4H and FFA clubs in the Fox Valley would greatly benefit from our facility and we would greatly promote the horse and pony projects in the area. Having 4H and FFA horse clinics in the wintertime would give these kids a chance to work with their horses and learn at a time when otherwise they might not be able to take a clinic until late spring when snow season is over. This would help them get ahead start into the summer months.

When Vinland Stables is open it would also give local businesses more customers and more income when shopping for horse related items. This is a plus for the local merchants.

We can easily say that our competition does not have the quality of service or the size and modern facility to compete on a very professional and high quality level. Having large pastures will be one of our strongest assets because many boarding facilities do not have pasture or daily turnout at all.

Now that you have read what we put down in our business plan it is safe to say, if you are going to write your own, have more detail and answer the questions I brought up at the beginning of this section with as much information as you can give. Our assumptions were very vague and I am positive if a banker was to read this now they would not be impressed and would need a lot more information. Remember, it is going to be harder to get a loan today than it was years ago. I truly believe it can be done but the bank is going to be looking for a lot more then what was in our plan.

Take your time and do it right the first time. If you have a passion for 4H or other equine organizations then write it down and talk about it. The banker wants to know about you and what kind of person you are. He wants to know if this is your life because it will be once you open for horses and clients.

We were coming to the end of our business plan and now what was left to put down on paper were some numbers. The bank wants to know as much about the owners as possible but when it is all said and done, they really need numbers to go on. After all, you could be the nicest hardest working person they know but if your numbers don't match up and you lose your business then the bank loses and they don't want that and neither do you.

TWELVE MONTH INCOME STATEMENT

The projected income statement really just summarizes the operating activities of your horse business over a given period of time. Our banker wanted a twelve month period of time and that is pretty common. You would complete a twelve month table and if he needs something different you can change it accordingly.

I will give you an example of what our projected income statement looked like when we were putting it together back in 2004. We had to guess on a few things but I will go over it with you after you have read the table.

Revenue	June	July	Aug	Sept	Oct	Nov	Dec	Jan	Feb	Mar	Apr	May	Total
Outside Board	1125	1125	1125	1125	1125	1125	1125	1125	1125	1125	1125	1125	13500
Stall	2610	2610	2610	2610	2610	2610	2610	2610	2610	2610	2610	2610	31320
Window Stall	5400	5400	5400	5400	5400	5400	5400	5400	5400	5400	5400	5400	64800
X-% Occupancy	0.5	0.85	0.85	0.95	0.98	0.98	0.98	0.98	0.98	0.98	0.98	0.98	
TOTAL BD	9135	9135	9135	9135	9135	9135	9135	9135	9135	9135	9135	9135	109620
Other Income	590	709	823	942	1456	1588	1593	1793	1161	1161	1161	1161	14138
TOTAL INCOME	9725	9844	9958	10077	10591	10723	10728	10928	10296	10296	10296	10296	123758
EXPENSES													
Accounting	25	25	25	25	25	25	25	25	25	25	25	25	300
Advertising	200	200	100	100	20	20	20	20	20	20	20	20	760
Fuel	250	250	250	250	250	250	250	250	250	250	250	250	3000
Insurance	425	425	425	425	425	425	425	425	425	425	425	425	2700
Feed	510	650	750	850	1000	1000	1000	1000	1000	1000	1000	1000	10760
Bedding	156	187	218	250	290	306	306	306	306	306	306	306	3242
Office Supplies	20	20	20	20	20	20	20	20	20	20	20	20	240
Repairs	50	50	50	50	50	50	50	50	50	50	50	50	600
Supplies	50	50	50	50	50	50	50	50	50	50	50	50	600
Property Taxes	575	575	575	575	575	575	575	575	575	575	575	575	6900
Phone	50	50	50	50	50	50	50	50	50	50	50	50	600
Utilities	275	275	275	275	275	275	275	275	275	275	275	275	3300
Auto Expenses	60	60	60	60	60	60	60	60	60	60	60	60	720
Depreciate	954	954	954	954	954	954	954	954	954	954	954	954	11448
TOTAL EXPENSES	3600	3771	3802	4184	4044	4120	4120	4120	412	4120	4120	4120	48241
NET INCOME	6125	6073	6156	5893	6547	6603	6608	6808	6176	6176	6176	6176	75917

*Other income is derived primarily from optional services that the horse owners may want. It is not guaranteed income.

1) Put on/off blankets at $2.00 per day. Estimate 50% usage in the Fall/Winter/Spring months.
2) Holding horse for farrier and vet at $10.00 per time. Estimate 75% usage.
3) Training clinics
4) Walking horse for owner
5) Soda Machine.

Now that you have had a chance to look at my income statement you have to remember we were estimating to the best of our knowledge. *Most important our mortgage payment was not part of the twelve month statement.* Once we knew what our monthly mortgage would be then we would figure it into our equation and of course our net income would be much less. Some of the expenses that we put down were a close estimate because we had done the research and were able to get some hard numbers. Some of our numbers were way off due to the fact that we had to estimate and didn't have true numbers to start with. If you are buying an established horse business then the owners should have true numbers for you on what it cost to run the facility on a yearly basis. If you notice on our chart the numbers change from the beginning to the end of the year because we were estimated with a brand new (empty) barn and all horses came in over the course of a month or so. I will break down each section for you.

Revenue-is the money that you will be taking in each month from your business.

Outside Board-When we estimated what our revenue was for outside board we just figured out how many horses we would take in and add up all the income that we thought would be coming in and total it for each month. Our total for the year would be at the end of the twelve months.

Stall Board (without window)-In our new barn we would have 10 stalls without a window and the board was going to be ten dollars less per stall. We just did the same thing as the outside board. We added up total income for each month then totaled it out for the year.

Stall Board (with window)-In our new barn we would have 17 stalls with windows and we were asking ten dollars more per stall. Again we added up total income for each month and then totaled it for the year and that is how we came up with our revenue for the first year.

Occupancy %-This is just your goal of the percentage of stalls filled each month and all year. If you look at ours we started out with only .05% and then within a couple of months we were almost full. We have been very blessed to be one hundred percent full almost the entire time we have been in business but it would not be realistic to put that down and it is not guaranteed that you will be full all the time. The banker wants realistic numbers so you need to be very real and if you end up being a hundred percent full then celebrate!

Other Income-This was a very grey area for us. I knew there were many services we could offer to the boarders and charge a fee for those services but I really didn't know how many boarders would want to pay for them. Years later we really have never made a lot of extra money putting on blankets or holding horses for vets or farriers. Our estimates were way too high in this area and that was income that we really never saw and could never depend on. Remember that when you are doing your income statement you can add extra services and make a little extra money but look at it as extra income only. Think of it as a bonus but not always guaranteed. Unless it is something everyone has to pay for on a monthly basis don't depend on it as regular income. You can compare it to overtime pay. I have seen many people over the years work at a job that gives a lot of overtime. Soon they come to depend on the overtime because they have raised their living expenses according to the extra money they bring in. Then what happens next is that the overtime is cut out and all of a sudden they are panicking because they can't pay the large debt they have created. It can be a real mess. Think of that when you are budgeting for extra charges and fees for services offered.

Total Income-These were our totals for each month on revenue and then we totaled it for the year. In reality our numbers were much lower our first three years by about $10,000 to $12,000 dollars.

Expenses-This section was very hard to estimate because we really didn't know what everything was going to cost for a year for a forty horse operation. This part we muddled our way through a bit. It has been so interesting to look back at this section years later and now I can really see where we were close in numbers and where we were completely off the mark.

Accounting-This will be different for everyone. I did have a friend help me with our accounting for the first couple of years but now I do a lot of it myself. I do have an accountant that takes care of my quarterly reports and incomes taxes. Don't take chances when it comes to this stuff.

Advertising-The numbers we put in for advertising were estimated too high. In all reality you can advertise for almost next to nothing if you use the internet.

Fuel-Our estimate was pretty close in cost because David had a good idea of how much he would be using our equipment to run the farm. Years later our fuel bill is higher but the first couple of years were pretty accurate.

Insurance-Our business insurance estimate was too low. After we were open I realized we didn't have the complete coverage we should have for all the horses and when I took care of that our insurance went up another $1,200. You can talk to your insurance carrier but make sure he is familiar with the equine industry. If he is not, you might not be getting the correct coverage for your entire operation. That happened to us in the beginning.

Feed-In this section our numbers were low to start. When we first opened we included grain as part of the board along with hay. If you are going to include grain in your board rate then I would have your hay and grain separated into two sections. Do each one individually. It will give you a more accurate vision of all the costs for the year.

Bedding-Shavings are our second highest cost next to hay. This was something I did not realize. Until you have to start buying it in very large quantities you really don't realize how expensive bedding is. At least we didn't. We were too low in our estimate for bedding and it did take a large chunk out of our "extra income" each month.

Office Supplies-Taking care of the paperwork for a business can be very complicated or it can be relativity simple depending on what kind of business you have. What you order for supplies each month and if you have employees are a big part of the paperwork. We only have employees on a limited schedule so that decreases much of the paperwork. We had to guess on office supplies and for the most part we were pretty close to the cost in the beginning.

Repairs-This was a hard one to estimate. Now after many years I can say we estimated too low. It is amazing how much horses can break and destroy everything from fencing and wood to corner feeders and heated water buckets. I would have to say with a forty horse operation we spend a lot more money fixing things then we estimated. Some months are real good and some months are real bad. In the winter in Wisconsin, the extreme cold seems to be very hard on equipment and David is constantly fixing everything. If I was to do this part over I would estimate much higher. It will truly depend on how big your operation is.

Supplies-This was another one of those grey areas. Supplies could mean anything. We estimated too low in this area also. I never realized how many pitch forks, water hoses and insulators for the electric fence we would be replacing. We go through at least two new water hoses each year and we buy good ones that are supposed to last a lifetime! It starts to add up. I would now estimate higher on this one also.

Property Taxes-If you have an existing barn you will already know what your property taxes are going to be. If you are building a brand new barn you won't have any idea until the tax bill comes out. All we could do was go to public records and look up existing barns in the area and find out what they pay to get some idea. That was how we figured out our total.

Phone-This should be one of the easiest areas to estimate your monthly cost. You most likely have a phone and you are already paying your bill, so this one is a no-brainer.

Utilities-This was a shot in the dark. We had no idea how much our utility bill was going to be each month with a new barn. We have a heated lounge and a huge indoor arena to light up so all we could do is go by what the electrician told us. It turned out in the summer our bill is very low but in the winter our bill is extremely high due to all the heated water buckets. We were close but I would still estimate higher than we did back then.

Auto Expense-We have a farm truck that is used one hundred percent for the farm so we had to estimate how much to operate and maintain our work vehicle. This will differ with everyone depending on payments and how much it is used.

Depreciation-it is the decrease in value of an asset over a period of time. It can be real estate or in our case our new barn. This was something David and I didn't really understand and because I never took business classes I had to go to my banker and ask him how I was to estimate this in our expenses. We could only go off of what we thought it was going to cost to build the new barn and he understood that we didn't have hard numbers for this area. This is something that I would definitely talk to your loan officer about when you are working on your business plan.

After you get all your categories figured out and have your monthly cost then you can total out your monthly expenses and then total out the year. Subtract your expenses from your revenue for each month and that gives you a monthly total net income for each month. The last thing you do is total out the twelve months of net income and that gives you your net income for the year.

When you look at our numbers they might not seem high to you but what is not figured into the total is our monthly mortgage payment. That will make a huge difference in your net income.

This is the difference between an established business and a business that you are starting from absolutely nothing. If someone wanted to buy our business today I would be able to give them the exact totals for all the years we've been in business and what it truly cost to run our farm. The bank loves that. When you have nothing to show as history of the business it makes it much harder for the bank to decide if it is a safe business to invest their money in or not. They have a greater chance of losing everything on a business that is brand new than one that has been around for ten years and has a good track record.

I am not telling you this to scare you off, after all we did it and I am glad we did. I just want you to have a better understanding of everything that is involved in trying to get a boarding facility up and going. We didn't have anything like this when we were trying to start our business. We were going into it blind and I had bought many horse business books but not one of them broke it down into very simple terms so that I could understand it. My goal in this book is to break everything down into terms that you will be able to understand and relate it to running your horse business.

THREE YEAR INCOME STATEMENT

Doing a one year statement was hard enough but our banker also wanted a three year statement. This was extremely challenging and I had no idea what three years would look like.

Basically we had the first year done already so we just needed the second and third year. On the chart we didn't break it down by the month at all. We just used our totals from the first year and then estimated a growth percentage for year two and three.

It took us a while to figure out our numbers but once we decided what our growth percentage would be for the year, we just multiplied and went forward. I had to be very honest with our banker when he looked at our three year income statement and tell him that we had to estimate with some guessing involved. He understood and I think he liked the fact that we tried and were very honest with him. That is all anyone can do when you're starting from nothing and there is not a lot of other horse farms to compare income to in your area. I do believe it is better to try to get accurate numbers then to not put anything down. Remember it is all a learning curve and the more you put into it the more you will truly understand the core of running your business and all the financials that go with it. It is all so important!

CASH FLOW STATEMENT

Cash flow is essentially the movement of money into and out of your business. It is the cycle of cash in and cash out that determines your wealth and soundness of your business. Now when you show this in a cash flow statement it becomes much easier to see how much money is coming in and how much is going out.

When we were doing our cash flow statement for our business plan we really didn't have anything to go from so again we had to estimate. If you buy a business that is already established, you will be able to look at the numbers for cash flow from the owners records. Hopefully they kept good paperwork!

In our business plan we had a one year cash flow statement and a three year cash flow statement. We had no idea what to expect so again, we estimated.

This was the last part of our business plan and when we were done I have to say it taught me a huge amount about business. I felt like I had just taken a college course in business. We didn't have a loan yet but if anything, it opened my eyes to the cost of everything. Looking back, it was one of the best things we ever did before we started our business.

The last page of our plan was a picture of the barn we wanted to build. It was a good way to show the banker exactly what we wanted and give him the details of the design and everything that would go inside. I can't stress enough don't be afraid to give as much detail as you can about every part of the business. That is what he is looking for. He wants to see if you really know what you are talking about.

It's not just about the building, it is about where you will store your hay and grain and shavings. It is about where you will put your horse manure and how you will get rid of it. How much will it cost to get rid of your horse manure and how often? Where is your water coming from and what about water run-off? In a day of keeping a clean environment these are things that will be asked sometime during the loan application process and you want to make sure you covered everything. We know a person who built a horse boarding stable and about a year after they were open they were almost fined for not having proper clean-up and disposal of their horse manure and it was running off into a nearby stream. You don't want that to happen to you. You want to have this all taken care of ahead of time.

Your business plan is a vital and very important way to sell your dream to the bank. Don't go to the bank without knowing your stuff. Also when putting together your plan make sure it looks professional. Don't just give the loan manager a stack of papers. That doesn't cut it. Remember you are asking them to put their trust in you and give you a lot of money. When you have your plan complete put it in a nice looking binder with a title page, your name and date. Attention to those little details can go a long way and will really make you stand out as a professional.

Our business plan took about nine months to complete. It was a very long process but worth every hour we put into it. I learned so much about starting a business just in those nine months.

Well now it was done and it was time to take it to the bank. It would be a very long time before we heard from the bank. We just waited. I can't stress enough how long the entire process can take. If you think it will only take a couple of months to get the money, you will need to think again. Applying for a business loan is in no way like a home loan and it is treated in a much different manner. It will take a long time but if you are willing to do what is needed from the bank, it will be worth it.

~8~
THE WAITING GAME FOR A LOAN

Okay back to our story…A few weeks had gone by and the loan manager at the bank called and wanted to set up a meeting with David and myself. I remember feeling sick to my stomach because I had no idea what he was going to say about our business venture. We had waited for this day and now I was at a loss for words and we were going to have to really sell ourselves.

It really helped that our loan manager only did agricultural loans and understood the farming community and the way of life for people that live on and work farms. Since the horse boarding business was a new area for him we would have to explain a lot to him but the everyday work load, he already understood and respected. Now would he feel we would be able to handle this seven day a week job?

I was thrilled when he liked our business plan and I think he was pleased that we took it seriously and put forth a huge effort to make it detailed and complete to the best of our knowledge. I know the plan wasn't perfect but I think we got an "A" for effort.

The meeting went better than I could have dreamed of and he told us he was going to present our plan to the board at the bank and try to get approval for a loan. It all was based upon if we had enough collateral from the land we owned and our home on the property. It would have to equal out so that if our business failed they would be able to sell the business and all the land and hopefully not take a loss.

WHAT A HUGE CHANCE WE WERE TAKING

Years later, I now realize what a huge chance we were taking. Sometimes it sends shivers down my spine when I think about the risk we took. I never realized all the things that could go wrong back then and what we could lose. We were so naive. He told us it would be a couple of weeks before we would hear from him but in the meantime we needed to get a business name and talk to a lawyer about setting up an LLC or Corporation. We had already chosen our business name but we needed to make it legal. We chose an LLC per our lawyer. We just wanted everything in place legally in case they did give us the loan.

Over the next couple of weeks I kept going as if we were going to get the loan. We drew up our design on paper for our dry lots and pastures and how many horses would be in each herd. I also spent a lot of time figuring out all the details for the inside of the barn. Designing the tack rooms and lounge was so much fun for me. I had looked at many tack rooms and I knew I was on a budget but still when you love horses, the tack room becomes one of your favorite places to be. I love walking into tack rooms and smelling leather! If you love horses then you know exactly what I mean.

Finally three weeks later the loan manager called me. He had great news. The bank was willing to help us with the business loan but they would not guarantee it all on their name alone. They would only give us a loan if we had an SBA guaranteed loan. SBA stands for Small Business Administration. The government offers guaranteed loans to lending institutions for the person who has no other way to get a loan when wanting to start a business. Banks and other lending institutions offer SBA loan programs to assist small businesses. Through the SBA program they will protect and cover the loan to the bank if we (David and Sheri) fail in our business and we can't make the mortgage payments. It doesn't get us off the hook but it does protect the bank.

THE EXTRA PRICE TAG OF A **SBA** LOAN

The SBA approved loan came with a big price tag. It would cost us a few thousand dollars more to get the SBA loan and it also came with a higher interest rate. We didn't have to think about it (even though we should have!) We said yes and moved forward in getting the loan finalized. Another thing we learned at this time is when you are getting a business loan it is much different than a home loan. Business loans always have a higher interest rate. Years later I still don't understand why business loans need to be a higher interest rate. After all, if you buy a home for $400,000.00 and you lose your job and can't make the payments, then you will lose your home and the bank is stuck with trying to recoup the money on a home sale. If you go out of business and you can't make your business payments, then you lose your business and the bank has to recoup its money trying to sell the business. I understand it is much harder to sell a business than a home that is in foreclosure but higher interest rates make for a larger mortgage payment which in turn makes it harder to get a good financial foundation at the beginning of any business venture when most businesses start out in a lot of debt. That is when new business owners need the most help and higher interest rates do not help at all. Very few people make any money at the beginning of a new business. When we went through this process we were so excited that there was a good chance we were going to get the loan and it didn't matter what form it came in.

Because David and I were in our early forties the bank would only give us a loan up to around the age we would normally retire. The belief on this was that we would not be able to physically work as hard at seventy years old as we could at forty so therefore we could not get a thirty year loan. Our loan was for twenty-two years. Now at fifty-two years old I get it! I sure don't have the energy level I had when I was younger and I am so glad our loan was NOT for thirty years. With the shorter term on the loan it would now make for a higher monthly mortgage payment. These were things we had not planned on but our hearts were deep into it and we were not going to quit now.

The next couple of weeks were a whirlwind. We met with our lawyer to get everything drawn up and met with the bank several times to get everything finalized and I had to make sure I had every permit in order. The bank needed to see the contract from the builder including what specific jobs the sub-contractors would be working on.

SIGNING THE PAPERS

The title company would be involved once we signed the papers and the money would all be dispersed from them. The loan would be a construction loan for nine months. That meant we would have to get the building up and be open for business in nine months! During that time we would only pay the interest each month on the loan. After the nine months were over the loan would roll into a regular business loan. No pressure right? Wrong!! Everything had to be cleared from the bank and title company first. I felt like we were signing our life away but we were excited and I didn't see the vastness of our venture until many years later.

The day came. We went to the bank and signed so many papers it was unbelievable. David and I were both in a state of shock at what we had just done. We walked out of the bank becoming business owners with no business yet. The real work was just ahead.

After we got home I got on the phone and called the company that was going to do the excavation. A lot was going to be changed on our property. The area where the barn was going to be built needed to be raised three feet high. They were going to first have to take off the top soil and then fill in with crushed rock and then screenings over that. Our barn was going to be 250 feet long and 104 feet wide which made the excavation very expensive because they had to bring in a huge amount of material to raise the ground and make sure we wouldn't flood.

We also wanted a separate driveway so we could have some privacy for our family. A new road had to be made. We had to worry about our paddocks and make sure they were not going to flood due to the low area which meant the excavator would be working on that also. I never really knew all that went into building a large barn but I was going to learn. One of the sweetest memories about the whole excavation process was the fact that David's father worked for the company that was going to do the excavation and my wonderful father-in-law would be here working on our project during the early stages of ground moving. I can still remember him driving this huge machine and moving the earth. He always had a big smile and my girls thought it was the neatest thing watching grandpa drive this huge tractor.

After signing the papers with the company to start moving dirt I had my first experience with the title company. It would be my first of many trips to get money to pay whoever was working on the site. I would have to get money for the start of the job and then money at the end. There was a form that had to be filled out for each draw request and it was the title company's job to make sure the money was being spent properly. I felt like they knew what they were doing and I felt confident knowing they were checking everything as we moved ahead. It seemed like a perfect plan. As I am writing this I realize that the excavation of our property was probably the only part of the building process that went as planned.

The earth was moving and we were thrilled. It was nearing the end of summer and I worked for the school system so I had summers off. I had a couple more weeks until I had to go back to the classroom so I was so excited to see the excavation of our land. Who would of thought that a forty something woman would be excited to watch machines moving dirt. I sure was!

David was working full-time so I had to keep him posted a lot. Now if you live in Wisconsin or the neighboring states you will understand completely what I mean when I say the weather rules the day. It can be good weather or bad weather but it is always changing and we get a lot of rain. That would be a big factor in how fast we got our excavation done and all the dirt brought in. I remember back to that summer and it was a dryer than normal summer which was great for us but not good for the farmers in our area.

As we started all this I had to do some serious thinking about advertising now. I needed to get all 27 stalls filled in the new barn and six outdoor board spots by June 2006. How was I going to do all this and I had no barn to show them yet. I also was on the phone with the builder we had hired. We were going to meet with him within the next week to make our final plans so he could order everything. We just would not be able to have it delivered until the ground work was done which was coming fast. The excavation was just about finished and the transformation was fantastic. We would walk on the job site in the evening after the workers were gone and dream.

If you decide you are going to build like we did then be prepared because it will be a long process and waiting will be a big part of it. As I said earlier, applying for a loan for a business is much different than building a barn for personal use. The next several chapters are all about the nine months of building our barn and what it took to get it up and open for business. My goal as you read these chapters is to inform you of what can go wrong in the building process and what it takes to make it right. I hope to educate and inform you so that you know what to look for in contracts with your builder and how to protect yourself.

~ 9 ~
Hurricane Katrina and Building Supplies

We were extremely happy and the weather had cooperated for the most part during the excavation. Unfortunately in other parts of the country the weather had been devastating. Hurricane Katrina had flooded much of New Orleans in August of 2005 and now many builders were heading down there to rebuild the city and they were taking supplies from everywhere.

This terrible storm hit the same week we were meeting with our builder. We met with him a couple days after the storm and he told us that there was a sense of urgency to order the materials because there was going to be a shortage and prices were going to sky-rocket! Everything was moving at a fast speed and our heads were spinning. He had the plans for our building but I wanted him to have all the details so there would be no mistakes.

As I was telling him where I wanted the cement in the barn and plumbing for the kitchen sink and bathroom and where the cabinets should be hung he took very few notes. I also told him what I wanted for the two colors of steel for the building and how many service doors we wanted. We also wanted three huge double doors in our arena so in the summer we could open them all up. He told us this would be no problem and again I noticed he took very few notes.

We were also going to run electric and water from the well that is next to our house all the way to the barn. We would need to find out if the well was deep enough and if there would be enough water pressure for such a long distance. Because it is Wisconsin and the ground freezes, the ground would need to be dug up for the water and electric before the first of November. Otherwise there would be a surcharge by the company that does the digging and also the power company because of the frozen ground. It would add thousands of dollars to the cost.

The builder explained to us that all the building materials were on sale only through a certain date and we needed to order everything now.

After that date the prices would skyrocket due to what happened in New Orleans. He wanted me to go to the title company and get a very large check the next day. I called the title company and told them the situation and what our builder had told us. They told me they would need numbers and prices on materials. He asked me to go with him to the title company and he would explain the urgency. They cut him a check for the amount he was asking for. It was an incredible amount of money all at one time. I didn't know how these things normally worked but I assumed the title company knew what they were doing.

Five Hundred T-posts!

Off to the store the builder went to order everything for the shell of the barn. He said much of it had to be custom ordered so it would be a couple of weeks before materials were to be delivered. It was time to start putting in the T-posts and corner wood posts. This was something that David would do himself and every day after work if there was enough light he would go down the line of each pasture and one at a time he would pound them into the ground. I am still amazed at the hard work and all the T-posts he put in. We estimated about five hundred! He took vacation from work and spent a whole week of vacation putting T-posts in. Because of it being Wisconsin where the ground will freeze he was in a hurry to get them in before the ground became too hard. Then we would have to wait until spring and then pound the rest of the posts in. We were blessed to have a friend help David with the fencing throughout all four seasons and all types of weather. (Thank you Lori)

The entire family helped!

It was all a labor of love. As the pastures were being sectioned off, the girls and I started putting insulators on each post. My girls were five and seven years old at the time so they mostly hung out and pulled the sled or wagon depending on the season. We worked on fencing for an entire year!

It was mid-September 2005 and the builder called and told us the materials were going to be delivered. He told us he would not be there when they were delivered but he would be out the next day and get started. Huge semis delivering our barn in packages came and dropped everything off. We were so excited and I remember that particular day was beautiful outside. We had very little rain and everything was dry. We had the perfect weather to start building our barn. David came home from work and he looked at all the materials trying to find out if most of it was there. I kept looking at all the boxes wrapped up so nicely in perfect condition like they were Christmas presents.

The next day the weather was beautiful and I was anxiously awaiting the builder to come and start opening some of the items and to start digging where the huge support posts were going to be for the building. I waited and waited but he never showed. David called him that evening and asked why he didn't show up to start and he told us he got too busy at another job site and would be out the next day. The next day came and went and we never saw him.

~10~
IS THIS ALL WE HAVE SO FAR?

Every day David and I would go off to work in the morning and I would get home first and every day nothing seemed to get done. Right away I would call David at work with the news. At this point we really didn't know what was normal in building construction and what was not. After several more days the builder finally showed up. I breathed a sigh of relief. He and another guy got started marking off the area that was going to be our building. We were on our way.

The next day he came with a small digger. He was going to dig the holes that the large support posts were going into. They needed to go down seven feet into the ground to be sure they were below the frost line. Even though it now sounds silly, I didn't want to stand there and stare so I would go into our old dairy barn and watch from the window in one of the stalls. They started to dig the holes but it was evident even to me that after a couple of days they were running into all kinds of problems. The ground underneath the three feet of new dirt we had just added had huge rocks in it and the machinery he was using was too small and could not handle it. What should have taken just a couple of days, wound up taking a couple of months with many modifications.

The next two months were a complete blur. He would be here for a day or two with just one other guy and then the weather would turn bad and he would not be out for days. Even after the weather was nice he would tell us he was working on another job site and couldn't get out. Only about half the support posts were in the ground and now we were getting rain and the place was fast becoming a real mess.

During all this time the builder had not arranged a time to get the water line dug from the house well to the new barn. Wisconsin Public Service had a deadline for us to get this done before we had to pay a surcharge. Finally as we got days away from the November first deadline, the builder had someone come out and start to dig the seven foot deep trench from the house to the barn. The ground had already started to freeze and was very hard. We told him we would not pay the surcharge fee if we were charged. It was a slow process but the seven foot trench finally got done with frozen ground and snow/mud mix all around.

It would snow one day, rain the next, then snow again and the ground was getting harder. Everything on the site was a mess and large mounds of dirt were everywhere and they were starting to freeze. Finally the support posts were in the ground. We should have been happy but we were starting to feel sick inside about the whole building project. All we had after three months were support post and very little more. Throughout December we hardly saw the builder. He came out a few days to put a few more pieces of wood on the building to connect the beams but that was it.

This was our barn in January 2006

During this whole time the loan manager we were dealing with would check in every couple of weeks also to see how everything was going. There was a huge amount of money on the line and David and I were getting worried. We were way behind. It was now mid-December and nothing more was done.

HOW DID WE LET THIS HAPPEN?

I have had many people ask why we let our building project fall so far behind in the first three months of construction. I had to think hard about what was going on in our heads during this time. Our materials were delivered in mid-September and at that time we were filled with blind optimism and excitement. We were on top of the world and didn't think anything could go wrong. I am by nature an optimist so I just kept thinking positive that it was all going to come together. My husband by nature is a pessimist or realist but he was so excited about the new life we were starting that he put those feelings deep down inside for a while. I also felt like nothing could go wrong because the title company would be checking everything and making sure the money was not being spent foolishly. Our banker was checking in with us every couple of weeks so if he was good with everything to start then I must have believed it was okay at the time. Hind sight is always 20/20.

During this time between September and January 1st, I was starting to run ads in the Buyers Guide paper letting people know that a new boarding facility was opening June of 2006. I didn't have anything to show future clients except a drawing of our barn and layout of the inside. I would have to be a good salesperson to get people to sign on with us and want to keep their horse here when we open.

"IS THIS BARN GOING TO BE DONE BY JUNE?"

I was getting many calls but when people would come over to our farm the first thing they would ask was "Is this barn going to be done by June?" or "You will never get this barn done before June 2006." Many people left our home and I am sure just watched from afar to see what was going to happen next. I never would let on that we were having problems with the construction. I would reassure them the best way I knew how and say, "Yes of course it will be done." This was something that was very hard for me because I am a person that is very easy to read and I have a hard time hiding my feelings. I was so worried that they would see right through me and maybe they did. As of January 2006 we did not have one person signed up yet. I was not losing hope yet. I kept telling myself that people would soon start signing on to join our barn family.

My girls were very young the Christmas of 2005. David and I were trying to keep things light in the Grunska home during the holidays but it was very hard each time we drove into our driveway and saw only a bunch of large posts sticking out of the ground. David's parents who had been our biggest supporters also wondered what was going on but we did not say much to anyone other than our loan manager. I think we were too embarrassed and too much in shock about the whole thing.

By mid-December the ground was frozen solid. We were having a unique winter with very little snow but lots of rain/snow mix that was unfortunately falling inside our arena and stall area because there was no roof on the barn. There were frozen piles of dirt everywhere from the work that had been done. We were supposed to have cement poured for our lounge, aisle way between the stalls, the tack rooms and hay room. Given the weather and condition of the ground and with no roof and sides on the building there was no way we were going to get the cement poured anytime soon.

That wasn't all. The materials would be another disaster. The materials had been opened but never secured. One day when I was at work a huge storm had come through our area with incredible winds. I remember we had to detour to get home because there was an accident on the highway. I always got home before David and that day when I drove into my driveway I was shocked beyond belief. The storm we just had a couple of hours earlier had ripped through our place and the brand new steel siding for the building had been blown all over the place and crunched like aluminum foil! There were these long red and white sheets everywhere! The winds were still howling and I just sat there and cried.

Our siding for the barn sitting in frozen water

After a few minutes I managed to pull myself together and got my barn clothes on and started to retrieve the steel one sheet at a time. There were sheets of steel that were wrapped around each other like paper and had blown up against our outdoor arena. It was a good thing our outdoor arena was there otherwise I am sure there would have been steel a half mile down the road. I will never forget that afternoon. I called David and told him what had happened. As I waited for him to come home, I slowly started gathering the steel one sheet at a time in between a flood of tears. It was now raining again. No snow just rain.

David and I for the first time started talking about firing our builder. I can still remember going to church the next Sunday morning and crying the entire service because I was overwhelmed with stress and anxiety. This farm had been in David's family for generations and I was so worried we were going to lose it and everything we had. I am sure David was even more worried than me and even more upset since this was his family's farm. He was the strong one and kept it together. I prayed that whole service for an answer and help.

Christmas came and went and we had decided to let go of the builder we had and find a new builder. But what was the best way to do this and who were we going to get to finish the building before June? We were already months behind on the project and now it was the dead of winter.

~11~
A NEW YEAR, NEW BUILDER AND A LAWYER

It was the new year and back to work after the holidays. On my lunch break I called our loan manager at the bank and told him we were going to fire our builder. There was a moment of silence and with his calm voice he asked who we were going to get to finish the project. I had no idea who we were going to find to finish the project but I told him I would find someone as soon as possible.

The one thing I always liked about our banker was that fact that he was always very calm and didn't get worked up easy. He had to know for the last couple of months that there were some serious problems with the building project but he would always ask the right questions to get his answers without making us feel stupid and nervous. We already felt very stupid. He always put us at ease and made us feel like everything would be okay. He told us he felt there was enough time to get the barn done and open for business if we could find someone quickly to finish it. That was good enough for me. If he felt like there was time then there must be enough time. I trusted the fact that he knew what he was talking about and thought he must have gone through this before, even though I never asked him. After I got off the phone I felt like we could still do this. I felt like a weight was lifted off our shoulders for the time being. I told him I would contact him as soon as I found a builder to replace the one we were going to fire.

Well I had done my job. Now it was David's turn. He was going to have to call the builder or go see him in person to tell him we were letting him go. That evening David came home from work and we sat in the living room talking about the best way to do this. This was no small project. There were hundreds of thousands of dollars already gone and a lot on the line. I can remember David feeling sick to his stomach but he finally made the call. About ten minutes later he was off the phone. David had told the builder that he was done with the job. Wow, now what? We didn't have a builder and with him all the subcontractors were gone also. We were relieved and very nervous all at the same time. I had to get in high gear and get on the phone and try to find a builder and sub-contractors very fast. It was mid-January and time was ticking. We had until June to finish and be open!

LOOKING FOR A NEW BUILDER

The next morning came fast and David and I got up early to do chores and then off to work we went. My mind was flying and I needed to find a builder today or at least very quickly. I called our banker when I had a break at work and told him we had let our builder go and I would be calling him when I had a person to finish the barn. Years ago there wasn't Facebook and I wasn't on the computer as much as I am now. I still did things the "old fashioned way." On my lunch break I started calling friends and asking them to spread the word that we were looking for someone to finish the barn.

My work day was over and I headed back home. I walked in the door with the kids and again I was back on the phone. One of my friends that boarded her horses at our home knew there were problems and I went out to the barn and spilled my heart completely. I told her I needed to find someone to finish the barn and she called her husband and asked him if he might know someone that could do the job. I was completely shocked when he said he knew someone that might be interested. He gave me his name and number and told me to give him a call. He told me that he knew someone that had a house built by this guy and he did a great job and finished the job done on time! He didn't know if he had experience in building a pole barn but we could find out. I went back in the house and had some hope that maybe we would be able to find a builder soon.

AN UNEXPECTED VISITOR

From my kitchen window I can see everyone that drives in and out of our driveway. As I was looking out the window I saw a truck pulling into our driveway. It was the builder we had just fired the night before! He came up to the door, knocked and I answered it. He was angry and told me he would see us in court and he wanted all the money that was owed to him for all the work he had done! My heart was pounding! I am sure my face was pale. He drove off and I was in shock. I couldn't believe this was happening. He was threatening to sue us and wanted money he said he was owed. The work he did had been paid for in the first couple of installments. David got home and I told him what happened. We had decided that the next day I would call the lawyer that had set up our business with the LLC and talk to him.

I told David about the lead I had gotten for the guy who might be interested in finishing our barn. We needed to call him. Our minds were in a fog but David got on the phone again and called the guy. I think we were in fast forward motion and I am sure I was in survival mode as well as David. As I am writing this chapter I am flooded with all those emotions that I have suppressed for so many years. With God's grace I believe He kept us strong even when things got harder and they did.

Looking for a new builder on such short notice was a task in itself. What was even harder was finding someone who could get a project this big completed in five months and above all else could do it in our price range. It would be a huge undertaking. We only had so much money left. We still had no idea of the monetary damage that had been done and could we get the sub-contractors for the same bid as the previous ones? On top of all this, I was going to be calling our lawyer to tell him about the problems that were coming with the first builder and I had no idea what that was going to cost.

David got off the phone with the guy that possibly might be interested in finishing our barn. The guy said he would be interested in seeing what was done already and look into the project further. He was going to come over to our home the next evening.

The next day I got on the phone and called the lawyer that had set up our LLC for our business and told him what had happened in a short four months. I was embarrassed and felt so stupid but we could not turn back and we had to deal with this now. He set up an appointment for me to bring in the contract we had with the first builder and so I could tell him exactly what had taken place in the last four months. I would be meeting with him in the next week. I am sure he could hear the panic in my voice but he said let's just take this one step at a time. I got home from work, did chores and took care of the girls. David arrived and soon after that a vehicle drove into our drive. I watched from the window as a man drove into our driveway and parked in front of the construction site.

He got out of the car and started walking around. David went out to meet him.

They were out there for quite a while looking at the building structure and materials and of course the huge mess. Finally they both came up to the house. By first impressions this guy seemed very nice. He was very easy to talk to and seemed very understanding of our situation. We must have talked for over an hour telling him our horror story of the barn construction and he never made us feel like idiots.

He had never done a pole barn before but seemed confident that he could finish this barn. He asked if there were any barns in the area with a similar structure that he could look at to see a finished product. We told him of one that was very similar to ours and he wanted to take a ride over there the next day and look at it closely and take pictures if the owner would allow. We said good-bye and he would be calling us the next day after he looked at the other barn.

A NEW DAY

It was a new morning. I woke up with a great feeling that things were going to be okay. I waited for the man who might finish our barn to come over and talk with us. We had no idea what his thoughts were but he called and was on his way. Just like clockwork he drove over to our farm and with him he had pictures he had taken of the other barn that was similar to ours.

David and I and the new builder talked for quite a long time about what needed to be done to finish the project. He said he could do it and gave us a price for his part of overseeing the job. He would hire the sub-contractors to do all the work. He gave us a contract to sign and told us what his fee was and it would be final. We would not be charged anything extra for his services. David and I were unbelievably relieved. This guy made us feel like everything was going to be okay.

Now the new builder needed to find sub-contractors to do all the work from the foundation, building the barn and putting all the steel on. We needed people for the cement, electrical, tack rooms and lounge, mound system and bathroom and all the water to all paddocks and barn and more! This was all just the beginning. We only had so much money and it was based on the first builders bid and sub-contractors bids.

The next day our new builder got on the phone and started calling people he knew for the job of building the barn and everything else. The days following were absolutely crazy. We were on the phone constantly with him and he was at our farm quite a lot meeting with different sub-contractors for every part of the project. It was absolutely insane.

I called our banker and told him we found a new guy to finish the barn and we would keep him posted on when the building was going to start up again. While all this was going on, we were still putting up new fence for our paddocks and pastures in all kinds of weather. On top of that I was out price shopping for the best deals on everything a barn needs from wheelbarrows and muck buckets to mats for the stalls. The most important item we still needed to buy was the horse stalls.

I had looked at many different stalls with different materials for the stall grills. I wanted stalls that had grills on all three sides so the horses could see each other and they wouldn't feel isolated. I finally found a company in another state that had stalls that I liked the look of and the material was aluminum that they use in airplanes and was extremely strong and very nice looking. The best part was they would never rust! It was going to be expensive to order 27 stall kits but we did and they were going to be delivered in a couple of weeks. I was excited. We had no barn yet but we did have great looing horse stall kits coming. Twenty-seven of them!

Well a week had gone by fast and there had been a lot of people out at our place looking at the barn and talking to our new builder and giving bids. He had found a group of guys that would be able to get the barn shell up for a price we could afford. They would start work immediately. I wish I could say the rest of the sub-contractors were that easy but it didn't go that way. We were in for another financial blow.

~12~
Building problems on the horizon

It was now the end of January and we were starting to build again. On the first day a bunch of guys came to our job site and for what seemed like hours walked around and looked at materials and looked at the support posts coming out of the ground.

The foreman in charge called David and told him we have a problem. How could we have a problem already? He told us that the grade for the building was not set properly. The grade boards were not at the correct height for the finish on the outside of the barn and inside with the arena. After much discussion with many people they decided to leave the bottom grade boards and start fresh with new boards where the grade was supposed to be. This meant we would need more wood.

Starting over in January 2006

The new builder we hired came to us yet again and told us we had a second problem and it was a huge problem. In order to put up and secure the huge 80 ft. double trusses that went across the arena and the

24 ft. double trusses for the stall area, they needed to rest in a grooved out area in each of the large support posts. He went on to tell us that the support posts between the arena and the stall area were not at the correct height and they were already seven feet down in the frozen ground. What were the trusses going to rest on if the posts were at the wrong height? He explained that they would be able to get the 80 ft. trusses on but they were going to have to modify the support posts so they had a place to rest the 24 ft. trusses. It was getting complicated very fast. Our new builder was explaining all the modifications we were going to need to make and things became even more stressful from there. After discussing all the building modifications it was going to cost more than originally planned.

While things were starting to happen at the farm, I needed to start advertising to get boarders. I put a whole new ad in the Buyers Guide and waited for the phone to ring. I was feeling pretty positive and I thought if I could get people out here to look at our plans on paper and they saw the building actually going up and turning into a barn, they might be more likely to jump on board. The word was getting out and finally the phone began to ring.

Trying to get potential Boarders

Getting potential boarders when you don't have a barn to show is no easy task. I decided to go to the local copy place and get a very large print of our barn plans so I would have that to show people that might be interested. I found myself on the phone for long periods of time answering many different questions about our boarding facility.

I was asked things I had never even thought about before. I had been around horses most of my life but I was amazed at the questions I was asked and quite a few of them I didn't have the answer for at the time. I was responding to questions with answers that I hoped the person on the other end would be happy with. I wanted to be completely truthful with people but because we had not opened yet I was not fully able to predict how things would go on our farm. I knew how I wanted them to go but as we all know, what we want and how things really are can be very different.

Finally after a couple of weeks I had my first interested people come by our place. Because I was still working I would have to meet with them in the evening and it was dark so we really couldn't see the barn outside. Maybe that was a good thing I thought. They wouldn't be able to see the total mess out at the barn. It turns out after talking to many people I found out that people were driving by on a weekly basis to see if the barn was going to be completed. They saw the mess and they still came to talk to me. Either curiosity brought them to our farm or the hope for a truly better boarding facility in the area. I was just happy that they were coming for a look around.

With each new person that came by to hear about our boarding facility I would give the same tour and routine. If I was able I would show them around the construction and try to get them to visualize what the barn would look like when it was completed and then I would lay out the plans on my kitchen counter so they could look at it.

It was very interesting to me that I had a few people actually try to change things in our barn before it was even completed. I had someone tell me that we had too many large doors in our indoor and it would scare the horses and they asked if we would take out some of the doors since the barn was not built yet! It did not surprise me that this person did not come to board with us. I also had people tell me what paddock and pasture they wanted their horse in and would not take anything else. I was learning fast about the business world and the demands of some people.

It was a very fine line between trying to fill 27 stalls and trying to please everyone. At this point it was very hard to tell people that we would not be able to do some of the things they were asking for. I had not become a business person yet in my mind and I wanted to please everyone under any circumstances. I needed to fill all the stalls but I didn't want to compromise what we wanted our barn to be like. I was having a very difficult time saying no.

I thought they would be so happy just to have the pick of a brand new never used stall in a brand new never used barn. Their choice was completely up to them. This turned out to be an ever changing decision for some potential boarders. I was so naïve back then when it came to business and clients.

I can still remember being outside for a couple hours with one lady and trying to answer every question under the sun. Of course I didn't know all the answers and some of her questions I had never heard of before but I had to act like I knew what I was talking about. The whole time I was outside talking with her I was thinking about my very young girls in the house and what they were getting into. I was going to have to draw the line with people and learn how to do it without offending them. I remember walking back into the house after being outside for an incredibly long time and my youngest daughter had tried to make toast and it was burnt as black as can be! I decided I was not going to do that again.

THE CRAZY BUSY MONTHS AHEAD

The next four months would be a lot of meeting with many different types of people. Many of them were wonderful and very understanding of trying to get a new barn off the ground. We were so blessed to even have a few people that had signed on and offered to help with finishing off the tack rooms and stalls. Slowly we were starting to fill up our stalls. We would take a deposit to hold their stall until we would be open in June. I never let any of the people I had talked to know of the problems we were having during this construction time. I'm sure it would have been bad for business.

The builders were coming out to work on the barn daily weather permitting. Once they figured out how to fix the grade on the bottom of the barn, they started putting all the rest of the 2 x 6's on and attaching them to the support beams. Hopefully soon it would be time to put the trusses on. I had made an appointment to meet with our lawyer about being sued by the first builder. I know people have many different views of lawyers but I liked my lawyer and I felt like he was always very honest with David and me. We had told him what had happened with the first builder and what he said to me when he came to my home weeks earlier.

Our lawyer was another person in my business life that always was very calm and reassuring but very honest. We felt completely stupid telling him about all the things that had gone wrong in such a short time but he listened and he kept me calm when I just wanted to simply get very emotional and scream! It was only months earlier that we were setting up our LLC with him and driving home with the American dream in our reach. I am sure our lawyer had seen this many times in his career. After meeting with him he advised us to just sit and wait and see what the first builder was going to do. Maybe he would do nothing and it would be all over. We left and were back to the business at the farm or what we used to call it back in California, "back at the ranch." I sure do miss some of the western lingo I grew up with.

So much was happening all at once. We were still putting up fence all the time whenever we had free time. I was placing orders for much of the inside things we needed and running back and forth to the title company to get money. The wood was pretty much finished being attached to the support posts and our builder said it was time to put the trusses on. The 24 ft. double trusses were going to go on first. Also the trusses for our lounge would go up right away so work could begin on the lounge. It was going to be amazing to watch. As long as the weather cooperated and the wind was calm they might all be on in a few days or so.

The builder and the guys who worked under him had to figure out a way to put the 24 ft. trusses on because they said the posts that the trusses were supposed to fit into were not at the correct height. After they modified them, they started going up.

The front of the barn and lounge are coming together.

PROBLEMS WITH THE SUB-CONTRACTORS

Another new problem was developing. Our builder came to David and me and told us that he was not able to find sub-contractors that could finish all the other parts of the building for even near the same price our first builder had given us. We needed electricians, cement poured, the inside of the barn finished off which included the tack rooms, hay and bedding area, wash stall, lounge and bathroom. He wasn't sure how the first builder was able to do the work for the price he gave us but the people our new builder contacted would not do the job for that low of a price. We pretty much ran into the same problem with each sub-contractor we talked to. A big problem was on the horizon and it was coming fast.

We needed to find someone to pour the cement because the lounge area was to be the first area to be poured and it was ready. We could not move forward without the cement. I had four different companies give me bids for cement for our barn and we settled on one company. It was more than we were going to originally spend but we hired them. We did the same thing with several electricians and also settled on one company.

Looking back I am not sure why David and I started calling to find the sub-contractors ourselves. It was not our job to find sub-contractors. The builder we had hired should have been doing the work of finding people. Again, we were so naïve and maybe just so happy that the building was taking shape that we were willing to do whatever the builder asked. Stress can do so much to the mind and at that point we were willing to do anything to help the builder. Not an ideal situation at all but we did what we had to.

David had a friend that told him that he and his dad could finish the lounge and tack rooms after the cement was poured. He gave us a bid and we decided to stick with him plus we knew him and trusted he would do a great job.

The new bids were coming out at thousands of dollars more than we had in our budget. We decided to hire these guys and we would have to find a way to make up the money elsewhere. There was nothing we could do right now, we were stuck. The barn was moving forward and progress would stop without the cement and electric.

Asking for More Money

I called my loan manager and told him about the new problems we were having with all the sub-contractor bids and that it was going to cost us more money. He asked how much and I gave him the rough numbers and we would cut out some things in other places if need be. He asked how everything else was going at the barn and I said I thought well. I really didn't know for sure but it seemed at the time like it was going good. We hired the new sub-contractors and off to the title company I went again to get money for it seemed a small village of people. I was paying people left and right.

The date was set for the cement to be poured and a few days before, David and I took a walk through the lounge area where it was going to be poured. It was a good thing we did. I never noticed all this time that the water for the kitchen sink was on the wrong end of the room! The original builder had the design all wrong. Thank goodness the cement was not poured yet. We had to go in with machinery and move the piping to the front of the lounge where it was supposed to be. That was extra time and money to hire the guys to do that. They had to dig through frozen ground. They got it done but what a pain. This would not be the end of the mistakes. The cement truck came and poured the cement for the lounge.

David and I would sit down at night and try figure out what we were going to cut out from the barn due to the extra expenses we were already getting. The only thing we could think of to cut out was a large cement slab we were going to have in the back part of the property behind the barn for our manure. David thought it would be easier to have all the manure on a cement slab especially during the muddy months. It would make it easier to load in the manure spreader. We decided to axe the cement slab. He was disappointed.

I love the design of our barn but it is a simple design and we didn't have anything really fancy in it. It is a very practical horse barn so everything we had in it we were going to need. We could not find one more thing to cut out. I was thinking optimistic that it would all work out. We had no choice but to keep going and eventually ask our loan officer for more money.

~13~
Welcome to the Business World

Our construction loan was for nine months. We had only nine months to complete our barn. Now it was the end of February and we were cramming everything that should have taken nine months to build into four months. I was paying the interest each month on the money that had already been used which was hundreds of thousands of dollars and we were not bringing in any money at all except from our regular day time jobs. I was already starting to feel the pinch when I had received a letter from our first builder's lawyer that he was asking for a very large amount of money from us for the work he had done on our barn before we let him go. I am sure my face turned pale white as I read the letter. Before I knew it we had to hire our lawyer and this was going to cost us even more money. I couldn't believe this was happening. Welcome to the business world.

While all this was going on we were still trying to hire all the sub-contractors to complete the job. Our friend who we hired to do the lounge, bathroom and tack rooms had started on the lounge because the cement was poured.

More Mistakes With Our Building

The workers were starting to put the steel on the sides and all the insulation. As they were opening all the colored steel packages they were starting to realize that some of the steel was the wrong color for the inside walls of barn! They double checked everything and after it was all open, they were right. I wanted my walls on the inside to be white and a lot of the steel was bright red like the outside of the barn. We had all the receipts and our builder called the company and told them what had happened and they told us they could not take back any of the steel because it was custom cut to fit our barn. What were we going to do? I didn't want red walls on the inside because it would be too dark. I was sick about the whole thing.

Taking a walk around each evening after the workers left for the day.

The guys started putting the steel on the sides and we would see what we had left afterwards. They were also putting the insulation on the ceiling of the building and we were already running short of money so we decided not to put insulation on the walls and to return all the extra insulation so we could use the cash for other things we needed-like attorney fees. It was turning out to be a much more difficult job for our builder and the guys he had hired. It was becoming very complicated because of all the modifications they were doing along the way and taking everyone double the work hours to get things done.

EVERYONE WANTS MORE MONEY

The days were starting to get a little longer and with more sunlight the longer everyone could work. The biggest problem we were having were the windy days. Here in northeast Wisconsin it seems like it is windy every other day. Putting the long sheets of steel on the sides and roof was dangerous to say the least and if it was too windy then work would stop. Every day I was just hoping for calm weather.

The project was moving along and then the builder who was in charge came to David and me one evening and wanted to talk to us. We sat down at our dining room table and he told us that he was going to have to charge a little more money for his work of overseeing the project. It was taking him double the time to work on our project because of all the extra things he had to take care of or fix that normally would not be the case on a regular job. On top of that, the guys who were working on the building wanted more money also because it was turning out to be a much bigger job than anyone could have imagined.

At this point in the game David and I were so unbelievably happy and relieved that the building was going up at a good speed that we felt obligated to give him and the builders what they wanted. I know it was not what we had originally agreed upon but we were so thankful that the barn was being built that we thought we should pay them what they were asking. Looking back I am sure I was scared out of my mind that if we didn't give them what they wanted they would quit right on the spot and then we would be one step closer to losing the farm.

I was going to need to talk to the banker about paying out more money to the builders and get the okay from him. At the same time we were running into more problems with the materials. We were finding many things that were ordered way over the amount we needed and then other things that were never ordered at all. The company that the materials came from would not return the insulation but we were working on that. All of a sudden after figuring out the new numbers of what to pay everyone and order the rest of the materials, we became tens of thousands of dollars short! We did not have near enough to complete the project. Between the higher cost of all the sub-contractors, our lawyer fees and now the builders and the guy overseeing everything, we were almost out of money. There would not be enough to finish everything to open the barn. I am sure I was aging at an accelerated rate!

WHEN THINGS COULDN'T GET ANY WORSE...

Just when I thought things could not get any worse I was notified that a lien had been put on our property for the amount of money that the first builder wanted to be paid. I was running out of optimism. I got on the phone and first called our loan manager to tell him everything that was going on and then next I would be calling our lawyer. It is a funny thing about talking to your lawyer on the phone when you know you have to pay for those calls. You learn to talk fast and keep it short and to the point. This was something that was very hard for me to do because I was angry and definitely emotional. I kept thinking to myself we are good people. Why are all these things happening to us with this building project? I kept wondering if our dream of owning a horse boarding facility was slipping away. We decided to have a meeting about the whole project. We were going to meet at the lawyer's office with our lawyer, our banker, the builder, David and myself.

I know many of you reading this are wondering how we could ever let it get to this point. I cannot tell you the answer to that. It is so easy to say that you would never let this happen but the truth is, it happens to people every day. People like us that are so naïve and far too trusting of people. We were inside the eye of the storm and could not see out. It had overwhelmed and exhausted us and we were not business smart and we did not know what our legal rights were. We trusted the professionals that we were involved with and believed we were protected from all situations that could arise. That was not the case at all. We were not protected at all.

THE MEETING

A few days later everyone involved with the building project met at my lawyer's office. Here we were sitting at a large very nice looking table at his office with four other people discussing all the problems taking place at our farm. I never dreamed of having to do this. It was something I had only watched in movies and I looked around at all these men with different careers and watched how they all entwined together around this horse barn.

We each took a turn talking about what was done wrong, what was being done now, and what needed to be done in the future. How much more money it was going to cost and would the bank agree to help us? I have to say I was extremely relieved to feel like we had the support of everyone in the room. I think they all felt a sorry for us. Years later, David and I tell people we take full responsibility for what happened to us. It was our fault for not educating ourselves in the building process and business world. Most importantly we should have hired a lawyer to check through every contract before any building started on our property. It is a mistake that I am finding out more and more people make every day.

Our banker listened and did a lot of writing. Our builder explained in great detail why the project was going to cost tens of thousands of dollars more and had details on paper for the banker. As usual our banker was calm and never got upset. Everything was on the line at this point. If we didn't get the extra money from the bank, we would not be able to finish the barn and worst case scenario we could lose the farm. Most of the conversation was between us, the builder and the banker. Our lawyer listened and took notes.

After a very long time of discussion our banker knew we had reached the end and said he would go back to the bank and see what he could do to extend the loan amount. He wasn't going to make any promises but he understood the seriousness of the outcome if we didn't finish the barn and open for business. You would think with this news I would of been happy but I wasn't. I also knew with the bigger loan came a much bigger mortgage payment. How would this new mortgage affect our board rates we had already set and advertised? We couldn't raise the rates now and we already had quite a few people signed on and deposits given to hold their stalls. It was a mess!

After the discussion with the banker and builder were done. They left and David and I stayed to talk to our lawyer. We talked about the lien on the property and now all the problems that needed to be fixed on the barn. Our lawyer knew our financial situation and because he did this for a living knew this fight could go on for years. We simply did not have the money to pay a lawyer for how long it would take to fight this. He suggested a colleague that would be less expensive than him to work with us. There were no guarantees but we had to try to get the lien off of our property.

David and I went home that day very heavy hearted. It was a low point for both of us. Starting a business was not supposed to be like this. I was trying not to be bitter or angry but it was creeping in and I was fighting not to let it take over my life. I did a lot of praying.

~14~
Our barn is under water!

It wasn't very long until our phone rang with the news that the bank had extended the amount of our loan to cover the extra expenses. It was great news but also bad news. Our monthly mortgage payment would be much larger but we would deal with that when the project was complete. Full speed ahead we went and the next thing to get done was all the cement poured and we had another huge problem.

Have you ever had a bad dream where you are running and something bad is chasing you and you keep running as fast as you can to get away, but you can't get anywhere? That is exactly what building this barn was like!

The days were getting longer and warmer and the snow was melting at a rapid rate. There was a huge amount of water all over and it had filled into all the holes that were dug up in the fall and never filled back up. The water was in the building on both the stable side and arena side. Our new paddocks were also now a huge lake! The area in the building where the aisle way was going to be had large holes filled with water. There was no way we could get all the cement poured without first getting rid of all the water. We ended up using quite a few sump pumps all over the entire barn! We hooked them all over with hoses attached to pump the water outside the building. It took what seemed like endless hours to get rid of the water and we were praying more rain wasn't on the way.

Now that we had a roof hopefully no more water would come in the building. It was still in the forties and fifties and cool but David was out there for hours pumping water outside the building. He did that for days and it got old real fast for him. After he was able to get the aisle way dry he started working on our flooded indoor arena. We had water everywhere.

The cement for the aisle way and tack rooms is finally poured.

I thought our project was a mess but in the springtime everything looks even worse with the mud everywhere. I think the only ones that liked playing in it were my girls and dogs. Finally the time came that the barn was ready to have cement poured. It was a big project and it looked awesome when it was done. Now we could start on the tack rooms and the stalls. Once the cement cured in the aisle way, it was time to get the stalls built. We were going to have 27 stalls so a lot of work was ahead for David. He was going to do most of the work himself. We were blessed to have his brother and some wonderful friends come and help with the stalls whenever they could. It was going to take many long hours to build 27 horse stalls.

I was still giving lots of tours and now I could at least show them the barn and I think they felt confident that it would be done on time. The stalls were filling up fast and that was a huge relief. We finally got some good news. After many weeks of working with the company that had sold the first builder the insulation, they finally said they would take back the rest of the insulation and give us a refund. After most of the steel was on the outside of the building we didn't have enough of the correct color for the inside of the barn where the hay, grain and shavings would be stored. We were also short white steel for our indoor arena. I didn't want red in the arena because it would be too dark. Because we couldn't exchange it we decided to put the steel on backwards and the red side would show in the hay room (which I guess didn't matter because no one really goes back there) and the back of the steel which was an off color white would be facing the arena. It seemed to work. To this day I don't think anyone has ever noticed the difference in shades.

~15~
CRUNCH TIME

The next two months were probably the busiest I had ever known. It was crunch time. David was working unbelievably long hours between going to work and then coming home and working on stalls. When I picked out our stall kits I didn't realize they were not assembled when they arrived. The grills were all separate aluminum tubes that fit into each socket on top and bottom of the grill. There were thousands to fit into tiny holes on an aluminum molding and then it would be attached to wood. I love our stalls but if I had to do it all over, I would have never bought these stall kits. It took many long hours and days putting them all together.

Now that we have had these stalls for years there is one really good thing about them. When a horse kicks and dents one or someone ties their horse to the stall grill (which is not allowed) and the horse pulls back and bends the bar with it (which will happen eventually) we can replace the bar very easily. With a permanent stall grill you would not be able to replace the bar that was bent. When I come in the barn and find a stall grill bar that is bent and all the rest are completely straight it drives me nuts. It's like looking at a bunch of pictures hanging on the wall and one is crooked and you have to straighten it. The best part about these stalls is that we can replace any grill bar that needs to be changed and it is fairly easy.

The front of our stalls

PUTTING IN THE LIGHTS

The electrician was putting in all the lights and this was an area that there was much discussion about. I had been to many indoor arenas and the lighting is slightly different in each barn. I knew what kind of lighting I wanted in my arena but we disagreed on how many lights to put up. Our arena is 80 x 200 in size and I knew it needed a lot of lights but I wanted half of what the electrician wanted. It seemed crazy to me to have all the lights that they suggested. I felt like we were going to light up like the house in Chevy Chase's Christmas Vacation Movie. We settled on half the amount of lights and to this day I only use half of them at once! The only times I have ever put all of them on at once was during a television segment when our facility was on television or when we are having a clinic. It helps a lot also that we have sky lights on our roof and it keeps our arena pretty bright and saves on the electric bill.

Plenty of light in our arena with only half the lights turned on.

Between taking care of my girls and normal household chores, working full time and doing regular chores on top of all the new barn stuff going on, I was simply exhausted. I can still remember the evening when I went in to take a shower and I was so tired I forgot to take off my clothes and stood in the shower with them on! I think at that point I was more tired than I ever was giving birth to my girls.

The days were warmer and we were getting a lot of rain. The barn was staying dry but our paddocks were flooding and there was no place for the water to go. We thought with all the excavation we had done (and all the money we spent on it!) that we wouldn't have a water problem but we did. It looked terrible and now we had to get it fixed as soon as possible. We needed to get our automatic waters put in and electric and water line ran out to each of the paddocks but could do nothing with it all under water. It was a lake and the ducks loved it and we were sick about it. We had to talk to the company that did the excavation. Nothing was going to come easy for us.

~16~
THE INDOOR ARENA

It was time to start getting our indoor arena ready for sand. It was a big mess. Because of all the holes that were everywhere we needed to get it all smoothed out and then we had another problem. We were going to have screenings put down before the sand came but the base had tons of huge rocks in it. They were coming up after the winter and there were way too many rocks to even think of putting screenings and sand in. They were coming up through the newly excavated ground and it would be extremely unsafe footing for the horses. It was also a mess because of all the water we had to pump out of the holes. We decided we were going to have a rock picking party.

I found out quickly it wasn't easy to get people to come to pick rocks. Here in Wisconsin farmers do a lot of picking of rocks in the fields. You are always seeing skid loaders out in a field with someone picking rocks and throwing them in the bucket. I ended up putting an email out to my church and some youth came and helped. We picked rocks for many days. It seemed like they just kept popping out of the ground. This was something I was not expecting when we had our excavation done. Another lesson learned when getting an excavator. Make sure they understand that the footing is for horses! Finally it was time to get the screenings ordered, put down and rolled. We went with six inches of screenings and then had it rolled many times over for a great base. You can go with a little more screenings if you like but there is really no need to. Finally the best part was coming, the sand!

Our indoor arena was another area in the barn that seemed to always be up for debate with everyone I had come in contact with.

Our arena still looks great even after all these years. Skylights are a true benefit of any indoor arena.

I have been in many arenas all over Wisconsin and also California (even though I had never been in an indoor in Southern California-too hot!) and everyone has different footing. Some were way too deep and some were not. I never realized there were so many different types of sand until I started looking at them closely.

To this day, I still find myself looking at the footing of every arena I am at. There are so many beautiful arenas where the footing is like riding on air. With the large size of our arena it was going to be very expensive so I had to find something in the ballpark of what we could afford. We ended up using washed concrete sand that to this day I still really love. Unless the days are extremely cold (I'm talking below zero temperatures) or the air is extremely dry, the sand stays pretty dust free. We do have to water it now and then but not as much as you might think.

How much sand do we need?

Washed concrete sand is one of your more expensive sands but I was willing to pay the price to get great footing. This is where it gets confusing. How much sand do you get for an 80 x 200 ft. indoor arena? I called the place that I was going to buy the sand from and told them the size of our arena and that I only wanted at the most three inches of sand in the arena. They told me they could figure out the total truck loads according to the size of the arena. I assumed they knew what they were doing since they do this all the time. Again I assumed wrong!

The day came and the sand was going to be delivered. David was at work so I would be there at the barn when they came. One by one these twenty ton trucks came and dumped sand in our arena. They kept coming and coming and coming. It was crazy. I thought it would never end. When they were done I should have taken a picture. It was like being in the Sahara desert. There were mounds everywhere and you couldn't see over them.

I called David and told him that I think they brought too much sand. There was nothing we could do until he got home. He was shocked when he saw all the sand. Right away he got his skid loader out and started trying to level it out and after many long hours we both realized it was way too much sand. We had at the low point six inches of sand and at the high point probably ten to twelve inches of sand everywhere. Way too much for a horse to move in. We were fuming. We had paid thousands of dollars for sand we didn't even need and now we could not return it.

I spent the next day in the skid loader while David was at work taking bucket after bucket of sand out of the arena. Nothing like having extra time to do this on top of everything else I needed to do. When it was all done we had half the sand outside the arena in piles that would eventually need to be moved to another place. After all these years we still have sand left over in a pile outside the barn. Every year we have added some sand to the arena and we still are able to use the extra sand we purchased years ago. That was a lot of extra money we didn't have at the time.

The company that sold us the sand would not take any of it back and so we were stuck. Now I always tell people to do their homework and figure out themselves how much sand you will need. Don't leave it up to the company. You can always buy more but you can't return it.

THE RIGHT FOOTING FOR YOUR ARENA

When we were thinking about the footing for our arena, I had to really stop and think about what disciplines of riding I would have here at our barn. That would make the difference in our footing. I knew for our facility that we would most likely have dressage riders, jumpers and pleasure horses. We probably would not have too many speed horses or reining horses. I knew our arena would be too shallow for speed horses so this was something I would have to be up front with for potential boarders.

I came across many opinions on arena footing during this time and I listened to everyone's thought on the subject. This will be ultimately your choice for your arena. You won't be able to please everyone so I believe the best way to design your arena and footing is to do what you like best. I personally don't like a very deep footing but I have friends that love a deep footing for their horses. My daughters have shown in arenas that were so deep that I would be worried about the horse's legs when they were riding. You could physically see the strain the horse had while working through the deep sand. We chose to stay with a maximum of three inches of sand across the arena and I have been very happy with the footing ever since. We always have to add a little every year but since we have extra, it has worked out fine.

I love the washed concrete sand but it is more expensive. I think it is worth it in the long run and your arena will have less dust. You can always go to a quarry and get samples of all their sand in buckets and then compare what they are like when they are dry and then after you wet them down. Our garage was full of ice-cream buckets of many different types of sand when I was looking.

Our outdoor arenas have different sand. It is not a washed concrete sand and it does have some dust but is handles the rain nicely. You will want to feel the sand after it is wet because some sands become mushy and absorb the water and don't drain very well. If you live in a state like

Wisconsin it will make a difference on how soon you can ride after a heavy rain.

~17~
UNEXPECTED EXPENSES

As I am writing this book and trying to get the correct order of everything that took place during the building of our barn, I realize now how much of a blur May and June of 2006 really were. There was so much happening with all parts of the barn construction and they were happening all at the same time.

When we had first designed our barn we did not have drain tile or gutters planned into the design. I guess we were thinking with the overhang of the barn roof it would keep the water away from the barn. Our first builder never said anything about drain tile or gutters and we never gave it a thought. We were quickly learning that with such a huge roof and slope there was an enormous amount of water coming off the roof all at the same time and it was flooding everything. With the heavy rains we have here in Wisconsin there was no place for the water to go at such a fast rate.

Our barn with an extremely large roof

All of a sudden we were talking to our new builder and getting estimates for gutters, spouts and of course the most expensive part, putting in the drain tile. If you are unfamiliar with drain tile and what it does (which I was) I will explain. Basically they dig a trench below ground and put circular flexible piping in the ground starting from where the gutter is going to let the water down through the gutter spout and straight into the ground. Once the water is flowing underground it keeps going until the tubing ends somewhere on the property. We have our tile ending behind our barn at a natural low point of land where the water keeps flowing above ground all the way until it gets to a stream on our property. Drain tiling is common practice with farmers but again coming from Southern California I had never heard of it. I was learning something new every day about farm life.

This was something we had not budgeted for and digging up our ground and putting the tile in was going to be expensive but we knew we needed it because of all the flooding we were having. We were going to have to come up with the money somewhere. This was not an expense we had mentioned to our banker. Also because of all the flooding in our paddocks we were going to need tile in our lowest paddock where all the water drains to and then it would hopefully drain the water out of the paddocks much faster. Since we needed water lines and electrical dug out to the paddocks we were going to have it all done at once. The hard part was watching our excavation being torn up a second time. It was really becoming a big mess outside the barn again.

Flooding was a big problem in early spring. This was before drain tiles.

We had talked to the company that did our excavation and they said they were willing to do the rest of the work including fixing the flooding problem but it was going to cost even more money. We could not afford the price they gave us. I ended up talking to my farrier and he gave me the name of a guy who he knew that was very good and reasonable. We called him up and he came over and gave a look and a better price. We hired him.

HOW MANY DIFFERENT COMPANIES DOES IT TAKE TO BUILD A HORSE BARN?

I often asked myself during this time the great question. How many different companies and people does it take to build a horse barn? I think we had set a record! I find it interesting and very frustrating that you can have two builders look at the same project and they both have completely different ideas and views of what you would need and what is important to complete the project. I would think because of all the rain we get in Wisconsin that drain tiles would always be a strong consideration. It was never mentioned until we talked to our new builder and the rains started coming. That is when we knew we had a big problem.

We were so close to the end of the project and more and more unexpected expenses were popping up every day. We were spending money everywhere and because everyone wanted more money, we had to borrow money against a second mortgage for those unexpected expenses that were popping up. I know you are thinking how stupid and looking back you would be right. We didn't know what else to do and we were supposed to be open in the next month. The pressure was enormous and without dry paddocks we would not be able to put horses out.

After reading this book up to this point, I hope you can see the extreme importance of really knowing all the details of a building project before it starts. You will have many unexpected expenses and it can really make the start of your new business a nightmare if you are not careful.

THE MONEY TREE

Much to my surprise our barn was almost full with people who had signed on to bring their horse in June. We only had a couple of empty stalls left. I was on the phone constantly and people were stopping by all the time. The stalls were coming together and looked beautiful and so clean. It seemed like once or twice a week boxes of supplies were delivered to our barn. We were hanging buckets and feeders and blanket bars. Everything was done 27 times over.

There was a new problem. We were not going to be open in June like we had planned. We would need to tell our future boarders that they would need to stay one more month at the place they were at. This was extremely hard for me to do but to my amazement everyone was very understanding. We still had too much to do and we were going to have to pay the first full mortgage payment without the help of board checks from out new clients.

Our Construction loan was to expire and our new business loan was to start in June 2006. We were finally there. Our guys who were building our barn were just about done and had been paid in full. After we paid them the amount that was due, the main builder came to us and told us they wanted more money! They were figuring out their hours and since it took a little longer at the end they wanted even more. We couldn't believe it. This time we put our foot down and told them NO! That was not what we had worked out and it was not in the contract. It was over. They drove off and we never heard from them again. The guy who was in charge apologized and told us this sometimes happens and not to worry about it. It all seemed a little strange to me but since we had never built anything before we didn't know better.

From the beginning of this project I have always felt that people look at the size of our building and they assume we must have money or a money tree. It seemed like everyone we came in contact with during the building process wanted more money than was originally agreed upon. This was something that I wish we would have been more educated in as far as our legal rights when you hire a builder.

IF I EVER DID THIS AGAIN

If I was ever to do it again (which I'm not thank goodness) I would hire a lawyer to look at every contract from every person involved before we started the building. If I could give any advice to anyone before they start to build a barn, make sure you have a good lawyer that you trust and pay the money to have him look at all the contracts before the first stone is turned over. It could save you tens of thousands in the long run.

We were so incredibly busy trying to get everything done and David decided to take a walk through and look at everything very close to see how it was all built. Until David started taking a walk through the barn and checking on all the workmanship, we didn't realize how sloppy some of the work was done, especially when installing all the huge doors in arena and to all the aisle ways. David is a perfectionist and as he looked at everything he got more and more upset. Many things were put together in a hurry and you could see it. I am not sure why we didn't put the responsibility back on our builder for fixing all the mistakes. I think at this point we were done and exhausted to the point of no return and didn't want to deal with it any more. David would spend the next eight years fixing things that he didn't think were built correctly. I guess you get what you pay for. Another lesson we learned the hard way. The building was completed and I think David and I were too exhausted to be excited.

Because our debt was many tens of thousands of dollars more due to all the extra costs to get the barn up and lawyer fees, we were hoping to recoup some of that money. Our lawyer said it would be okay to try but we needed very detailed information about the whole building project. The project was at the end for our builder and he agreed to help us out with all the paperwork and numbers for the lawyer. We would be in contact with him a lot over the next year. We thought the water was calm and the storm was over but the final tidal wave was coming and it was a big one.

~18~
THE BUILDER AND THE REST OF THE STORY

As we got through our first year of boarding horses in the new barn it was a whirlwind to say the least. Our barn was complete for the most part. Beside learning how to run a business and learning to deal with boarders, David and I were both back to work full-time and trying to raise a family in the mix of all of it.

The longer the year went on and the more I realize how much debt we were in because of this whole mess, the more upset and angry I became. David and I had to pay out more money to defend ourselves to get the lien off of our property. On top of it we were in debt for tens of thousands more than what the original loan was for.

A year had gone by and after many letters back and forth between our lawyer and the first builder's lawyer we thought we were at the point where it was all coming to an end. We had told our lawyer that we were not going to let up and we thought we could win but the cost of hiring a lawyer is not cheap. Our attorney fees were already unbelievably expensive and we were accumulating more debt due to those fees as well. After much communication between both parties involved and the lawyers we knew it was over. We would be spending too much money that we didn't have to begin with and end up with nothing. We were informed that they would release the lien on our property. That was good news but the rest was not.

After much thought and prayer we decided to let it go. We really had no other options and we were going to have to start fresh and work extra hard to make sure we could pay the bills. We told our lawyer of our decision and moved forward. The lien was taken off of our property and it was over.

David and I drove home from our lawyer's office once again and very little was said. He handled it again much better than me. I felt robbed and cheated again and I had to give it to the Lord. This would turn out to be one of the biggest challenges I have ever had in my life. I knew if I didn't let it go it would eat me up and destroy David and me. We took it one day at a time.

We got home and I called the second builder and told him of the outcome and not much was said. I thanked him for all the extra help he did to put this all together and we would keep in touch. David and I were so thankful for all the extra work he did for us putting all the paperwork together. That chapter was over and now to get on with running our business. I figured that would be the last time we talked to the builder that finished our barn. I was very wrong.

The days got back to normal between taking care of the farm and all the horses and the daily job of learning to run a business. David was still working and so was I. Every day was the same exact schedule. Chores, kids, off to work, chores, kids and finally sleep. We didn't have any breathing room financially now due to all the money we owed so we couldn't hire anyone to help us. I just kept hoping as the years went by that things would get easier and David and I would both be able work at home and not have to go to another job during the day. The months had gone by and life was a blur. Everything was going good but it was far harder running a boarding facility than I could of ever imagined.

THE PHONE CALL AND OUR 2ND BUILDER

Then one day I was in the house taking care of the girls and my phone rang. I picked it up and it was the builder that had finished our building. He was extremely nice on the phone and wanted to talk. After about two minutes I realized he was asking for more money! He had told us that he had calculated all his hours that he had worked on all the numbers and paperwork for the lawyer. He wanted to be compensated!

If you could have seen my face you would have known easily that I was in total shock. I remember telling him that we did not owe him any more money and we truly appreciated all he did but he had been paid in full. I don't know where he thought we were going to get the money to pay him more. We were completely tapped out to begin with but even so we didn't owe him a penny more. He told me to talk to David and he would get back to us and we hung up.

I was keeping busy with the girls, making dinner and finishing up chores but my head was spinning and I was panicking inside. We were broke and our business had only been open a short while. How were we going to come up with more money? Wait, we didn't owe him anymore money! All these thoughts kept popping into my head and they started to become irrational. I couldn't go through another lawsuit and come up with more money for the lawyer. Why was this happening to us?

I looked out the window and David was finally driving in. I waited in the house and as he walked in the door my mouth flew wide open. I told him who had called and what he had said. I was waiting for David to make me feel better but that never happened. He was more upset than me for a moment. I think he was in shock also and we decided to call our lawyer the next day and tell him what might be on the horizon for us.

I started to calm down and thoughts started to pop in my mind that this barn and business was a huge mistake. We should have never built this barn. Everything we had gone through with the first builder was hard enough. Now the thought of going through it all over again with the second builder was overwhelming and exhausting to think about. The evening came and sleep was a welcome relief from real life for a few short hours. The next day I called my lawyer and told him of the phone call. He was always reassuring and calm and told me not to worry and just wait. Maybe nothing would come of it and the builder would just stop calling.

I WAS SERVED PAPERS!

Another month had passed and our new life of running our business kept us busier than ever. I was in the barn and had just finished bringing horses in for the evening. It was a warm day and I was talking to a couple of boarders in the aisle way and feeling pretty good about the day. All of a sudden I happen to look down the aisle towards the front of the barn and I saw a young guy coming down the aisle. I didn't recognize him and he was coming straight towards us. I asked him if I could help him and he asked to see the barn owner. I told him I was the barn owner and he handed me a letter. I looked at the writing on the front of the envelope and I am sure my face turned as white as a ghost. I had just been served papers from the court system!

I opened the letter up at the house and another nightmare was beginning. The second builder was suing us for a huge amount of money! I couldn't believe it. Did he think we had extra money just lying around? He knew better than anyone how much this building project cost us and he even sat in the lawyer's office with us and knew how much more we had to borrow. I was utterly speechless again.

David got home and here I was with the letter in hand waiting for him to read it. I am sure by the look on my face he knew we didn't just win a million dollars. After he read it there really wasn't much to say. I would again have to call our lawyer in the morning and see what the next step was.

My daily routine changed overnight when all this happened. It started to look like this; chores, kids, work, call lawyer, chores, kids and finally sleep. I talked to our lawyer and set up a meeting and the second round began. I was sick worrying about money but thank goodness we were able to make payments to our lawyer. We met with him and went over everything that had happened from the very beginning with the second builder. I asked our lawyer how it is possible that he can sue us and he simply stated that anyone can sue anyone for anything even if it is not right.

Well after several meetings with our lawyer, we were going to try to settle out of court otherwise it could cost us a lot more money in the long run and we didn't have any. Either way it was costing us a lot already so the best advice our attorney gave us was to make it short and sweet and get it over with.

To make a long story short we decided not to fight further and have this lawsuit go to court. It would only cost us more money of which we had zero. We settled out of court for a lot less money and everything was dropped after that. It did end up costing us thousands of dollars more to pay for the settlement and lawyer fees but it was done and we were glad.

LESSONS LEARNED IN BUILDING OUR BARN

One of the reasons I really wanted to write this book was to be able to help others so they don't end up in the same mess we ended up in.

Before I wrote this book I had never heard of this happening to anyone. After I wrote this book I found out how much it does happen to people who are uneducated like David and I were. It truly can make a difference between a successful business and one that falls apart due to all the debt that is often accumulated during the building process.

The biggest mistake David and I made through our entire building process was the fact that with both builders we didn't have our lawyer look at any of the contracts. There were many things missing from both contracts so we were not protected at all. IMPORTANT-You cannot depend on the banks or Title Company to cover everything. If they miss something it will still fall back on you. You need to take the responsibility yourself and hire a lawyer to make sure you are protected throughout the entire process.

We did get the barn finished and we learned a lot about hiring builders and what to look for in a builder. We should have checked references and we never did. I highly recommend that if you are going to hire someone to build for you, check their references. Do your homework and make sure you have every part of the building process written down in a contract with signatures from everyone who is involved.

Here is our barn now.

The backside of the barn where the hay and grain are stored.

THE YEARS FOLLOWING THE LAWSUITS

Over the next six years we rarely talked to anyone about the builders and all the financial problems because of the lawsuits. We never talked to the boarders about it and we thought it was better not to say much at all to anyone. Looking back I know we were both very embarrassed of what had happened and we both felt stupid at times for getting into such a huge mess. We knew it was time to move ahead and run our business the best way we could.

One last thought—I hope you see now how truly important it is to have a lawyer look at everything before you start a business or build anything. Any changes that happen during your building process should all be written down on paper and signed by both parties involved and that includes any change in amount of money to be paid out. If you have any changes that occur during the building process, make sure it is all written in an updated contract and your lawyer looks it over before you sign it. Spending a little money ahead of time to have your lawyer look over all your contracts and paperwork could save you tens of thousands of dollars if something goes wrong. I wish we would have had someone tell us these things before we started to build.

So much can go wrong in a blink of an eye. David and I take full responsibility for what happened and for not having our lawyer look at all the contracts and fine print first. Over the years I have had many people ask, what is the most important part of any building project? Without a hesitation, I always tell them to find a good lawyer and make sure he is part of the whole process all the way to the end. You will never regret it.

~19~
BUSINESS INSURANCE FOR A HORSE FARM

It was June 2006 and there were so many things to think about before our opening day at our barn and with thirty-five new horses coming in possibly all at the same time, it was overwhelming. We still had not put our automatic waterers in and that was the next project David was going to tackle in the coming week. The stalls were finished and all the rubber mats were put into place in each 12 x 12 stall. We had to purchase six large rubber mats for each stall and if you multiply that times 27 stalls, that is a lot of rubber mats! If you use rubber mats in your stalls you will understand when I say that was an exhausting day. They are extremely heavy and very awkward to carry! Thank goodness we had much needed help from friends.

We needed to make sure we were fully covered with the proper insurance because our construction insurance had come to an end. We had home owners insurance and during the construction of the barn we needed construction insurance. But now it was time to get insurance for the horse farm and Care, Custody and Control insurance for the horses. Having liability insurance is so important and the risks are great when you are involved with horses. As you know anything can happen when working with horses and you need to make sure you are covered properly.

It was amazing to me that when I was shopping for insurance many insurance companies would not touch a horse farm. Over the years I have switched insurance companies three times and each time I have learned many new things I didn't know before.

An Insurance Company That Understands the Business of Horses

A couple of years ago a friend told me about Excalibur Insurance in Wisconsin. They only deal with horses and horse businesses and she told me I should call them. When I talked to the person on the phone I felt for the first time like he understood my business and he was going to give us the appropriate coverage for our facility. After he looked at our declaration pages he realized that we were paying for things we didn't need and we didn't have enough coverage in other areas. He came out to our barn and took a walk through and it was done. We had new coverage and for less money. It was one of the best changes I have ever made regarding our business.

The insurance company I use now is wonderful and deals mainly with equine and farm coverage. The other two insurance companies I had used in previous years were nice companies but didn't understand the horse industry at all and I would end up having to explain things to them on how the horse industry works. They didn't specialize in the equine industry and now I only recommend a carrier that does. My insurance is less now than it was five years ago and I have much better coverage.

Trainers and Insurance

I also want to share a few thoughts on insurance for trainers working out of your barn. First of all make it mandatory that they carry their own liability insurance. So much is riding on the line when they are working out of your facility and if they make a mistake and a person or horse gets hurt, someone will come after them and if they don't have insurance then they will come after you as the barn owner. Trainers should carry insurance if working out of your barn and they need to give you proof of insurance. They either need to give you a copy of their Insurance Binder or a Certificate of Insurance. Nothing else will do. It is very easy to get worn down by a trainer that keeps telling you it's in the mail and it's even harder when they are a very nice person. I have had trainers tell me that they couldn't afford insurance and asked if I could please make an exception. You need to keep it professional because you have too much to lose if something goes wrong. Remember, if they are in the business and are truly a professional then they will understand this and have no problem giving you the proper documents.

When starting your business no matter how big or how small get insurance! I can't tell you how many people I have come across over the years that don't carry any insurance for their equine businesses. I know it is not cheap but it is not worth the risk. Why take a chance and lose everything. All it takes is one mistake.

Care, Custody and Control Insurance

If you are taking care of other people's horses on your property-**Get Insurance!** You want to make sure you have Care, Custody and Control insurance. This insurance is for people who board or train horses or are responsible for other people's horses in any other circle of the industry.

The Equine Care, Custody or Control insurance is an essential coverage for all horse operations which involve non-owned horses including boarding, breeding and training.

This coverage fills the void in your regular business insurance and is coverage in case of injury or death of a non-owned horse because of your negligence. If you have a lawsuit brought against you then this insurance will cover the defense cost. This coverage does not apply to horses that you own.

When you talk to your insurance agent he will ask you many questions to find out exactly what kind of operation you have (boarding, training, breeding etc.) and then he can write up the proper Care, Custody & Control insurance for your needs.

I can't stress enough how important Care, Custody & Control insurance is for your equine business. Above all else make sure you have the correct coverage for the type of equine business you are in and most importantly make sure your insurance agent knows the equine industry better than you do. You won't regret it.

~20~
ESTIMATING HOW MUCH EVERYTHING WILL COST

Up until this part of the book you have read about my family's journey into the world of building our barn and becoming business owners. I hope through our mistakes I shed some light on what to look out for. Now the real story begins. The rest of this book is about what it takes to truly run a horse business. I will talk about everything from money to the day to day life of running our farm and the emotions that go along with running a horse boarding business. This is real barn management.

I didn't have any clear numbers on what our net income was going to be every month when we first opened. We knew if we had a full barn we would bring in so much per month but we really had no idea what our expenses were going to be each month. At this time we didn't know how much our gas and electric would be for our barn and how much gasoline we would use on farm equipment for the month. Shavings were a huge guess in the beginning. We were going to start with bag shavings and we did use them for a couple of months but the expense was too much and the labor was unbelievably hard! It is a lot of work opening bag after bag for 27stalls each day. We switched to bulk and to this day we only use bulk.

It was extremely hard to know how much shavings we would need in a month. It took us about six months to get that under control for 27 stalls. To feed forty horses for a year was also a huge undertaking and we really had to do an educated guess that first couple of years. We always would purchase extra hay just to make sure we didn't run out in the middle of winter. Years later, I still buy more hay then we need just so I don't have to worry about running out during our cold Wisconsin winters.

WE ESTIMATED TOO LOW IN THE BEGINNING

Looking back we really estimated too low in how much it really cost to operate a boarding facility. David had worked on a dairy farm for many years but he did not own the farm so he had no idea how much the owner was shelling out each month for the entire year for expenses. It took us about three years to really get a grasp on how much it all cost to keep everything in full operation.

One of the areas we completely underestimated was the cost of fixing equipment. If you own a farm then you realize and understand that your equipment is going to be used almost on a daily basis and through all types of weather. Winters here can be very hard on machinery and we have had lots of extra expenses through the years fixing tractors and skid loaders and anything else we use. We were not prepared for this in the beginning.

When you start your business it will be a guessing game for quite a long while. With each season comes new expenses and wear and tear on everything. If I can offer any advice, put money away for a rainy day because they will come. Make a fund just for repairs on equipment. The rainy day fund may sound "old fashioned" and you can call it what you want but there is nothing worse than owing the bank an enormous amount of money and then having to borrow more to fix stuff. I have seen too many people get themselves into financial trouble because they are already in debt and then they keep borrowing to fix things around the farm. I've talked to other business owners that tell me that they can just use it as a "write off" on their taxes. What they don't seem to understand is that yes you can write it off on your taxes but now you have another monthly payment. If you need to borrow money to begin with then it would be safe to assume that your rainy day fund is not in place.

Also another problem I have seen business owners get themselves into is increasing debt to the point where they can't pay all their bills each month. They keep borrowing because they have this false sense of security because they own a business and at the time it might be doing pretty good. Be very careful because if you own a horse business you will have plenty of unexpected bills and you don't want to become over your head in debt. It is just something to think about.

I was planning on working for the next couple of years after we opened but the plan was for David to stay at home and run the farm. After all that is why we started this business. After about a month of going over how much money we thought we would be bringing in and guessing how much expenses would be, and now of course the larger mortgage payment because of the building disaster, we were starting to get the feeling that David was going to still have to work part-time much longer than we had planned. We were not sure how long he would need to but at this point we didn't think we were going to have enough money to cover everything. He agreed that after the barn was full in the summer of 2006 he would still work part-time. I think his heart was broken a little but we didn't have a choice and we were thinking it would be only for a short while.

I thought David and I worked hard now but I never dreamed about how hard we were going to have to work to keep our business up and going. To this day I am so blessed to call this man my husband and he still amazes me on his work ethic and never giving up even during the darkest days.

~21~
THE FINAL PUSH BEFORE THE HORSES ARRIVE

It was the end of June 2006 and our barn was full. Every stall was taken and all our outdoor board spots were filled also. We were extremely happy and relieved. The first horses were going to come in the early part of July. I had been talking to a friend of mine and I was telling her that we were full and she gave me some great advice. She told me to be glad all thirty-five plus horses were not coming all on the same day and be very happy they are staggered throughout the month. She told me it would be a lot easier to get settled in a few horses at a time and learn their personalities. Then you can decide what herd you want to put them with instead of trying to do all of them at the same time. That would be a disaster and completely overwhelming. I learned very quickly that was excellent advice.

David was finishing up with the automatic waterers and making sure they worked correctly and the tack rooms were just about done. I felt like we had just been through nine months of labor and we were just about ready to give birth. I know it sounds corny but that is exactly how I felt. I am sure David's description would be much different.

Another area of the business I needed to learn about was contracts and liability forms. I was not sure where to go to find boarding contracts and I did get some samples from other boarding facilities but I wanted to modify things and have one that fit our barn. I looked online and purchased a contract for horse boarding for the state of Wisconsin and modified it to what I wanted on it. I was amazed at how many different contracts different barns have. I would strongly urge you that if you are going to do anything with horses professionally have a lawyer look over your contract first to make sure you are covered. As the years have gone by I realize how important this is.

I also recommend that you have liability forms for every person that is in contact with horses on your property that do not board there. Anything can happen at any time and it will. Cover yourself! I will go into more detail about our boarding contract and liability forms in a later chapter.

Checking to See if We Are on Schedule

Our banker had been in contact with us every couple of weeks just like clockwork to make sure everything was on schedule and I am positive he wanted to make sure we were able to fill our stalls. He understood why we would be opening a month later than scheduled. I also told him that David would continue to work part time for a little while until we financially caught up on things.

The interesting thing about a business loan vs. a home loan is once you sign your papers and get your keys for your home you never see anyone from the bank again unless of course you are late on a payment and then they start calling. It is so different with a business loan. You are in constant contact with the loan officer for many years to come. I didn't realize that until after the first year went by and he would stop by or call just to make sure everything was going good and making sure we weren't having any new problems.

Every spring after taxes are done your bank will want to make sure you filed and will ask for a copy of everything from tax paperwork to a business expense sheet. This was part of the business world I had to learn on the job. David and I assumed it was just like buying a home but it's not. Now I completely understand with such a huge amount of money on the line. To this day I still think we had a great loan manager and I am sure we gave him a few grey hairs during those first couple of years.

I had a job for the school system so it helped tremendously that I had summers off. I was putting in full time days seven days a week trying to get everything finished before the first horses came and David was still working full time and coming home and working hard trying to get it all done. I can't even tell you how many hours I spent giving tours and explaining every part of how our barn was going to run and how we did things. I had become a salesperson overnight and didn't realize it. I still needed to become a business person with a business mindset but that didn't come for a few more years.

Most of the time, I would get your basic questions about how we take care of the horses on our farm. How we feed and what kind of hay we used were common questions but once in a while I got a question that I had never even heard of before and I didn't know how to answer it.

Often in the beginning I stumbled through many things trying to act like I knew it all when it came to horses. I was very insecure in my knowledge and I was trying to sell myself and what we were selling in our facility. It was not a good way to start off a business relationship with my new boarders.

Before our barn opened for business we had only taken care of four horses on our property. I was used to only taking care of my two ponies for my girls and two boarders horses. Things were getting ready to change and I thought I was prepared but I guess you really never know what to expect until it happens. Going from four horses to forty was going to be a huge jump and a bigger shock on top of it. It was truly going to be a roller coaster ride for the next few years.

~22~
WE ARE FINALLY OPEN FOR BUSINESS!

Here they come! It was early July 2006 and our first two new horses were coming into our barn. By the end of the first week of July we would have ten horses in our new barn. I couldn't believe it, our barn was open for business and we were officially business owners of Vinland Stables in Neenah, Wisconsin.

I still remember the day the first two horses came. It was an absolutely beautiful summer day and the owners of these horses were excited and also nervous. I spent quite a few hours out in the barn that day just getting the people and horses acclimated to everything. I felt like I needed to be there for everything and was closely watching the horses and their owners for any sign that they might need something. By the end of the month I had spent countless hours with our new boarders and horses coming in.

NEW FEELINGS AND OVERWHELMED

The feelings I got the first week were overwhelming. For the first time I realized that we were in business now and I just couldn't take off like I used to. I had many animals to take care of two times a day which meant even if I left with the kids during the day, I would need to be back for the afternoon chore time. After much time thinking about this and wondering why it was so different now than when we had just our two ponies and two boarders, I believe the reason is because it was now our livelihood. This was how we were going to make our living and everything was riding on keeping our barn full with happy horses and happy people.

All of a sudden I felt this huge responsibility. I would be lying if I told you I didn't feel a little sick to my stomach that first week over the heaviness of responsibility we had overnight. You can think you are prepared but you never really are in the beginning. I believe now it takes a few years of working on the job day in and day out to really know what running a horse farm is truly all about.

I had always felt like we had taken great care of my own horses and my two friend's horses but there was never any pressure. They would come and help feed the four horses if I wanted to go somewhere with the kids. It was always so casual. This was much different now. It wasn't casual at all and I was experiencing my first business owner/boarder relationships. My life was going to change forever. Owning and running a boarding stable is a way of life twenty four hours a day and 365 days a year which I was about to learn and live on a daily basis. I have told people many times that you can work at a horse farm for many years (which I did at different times in my life) but you still get to go home at the end of your shift and have days off. It is completely different when you own the farm. I didn't realize the difference would be so vast.

Through the month of July and August while the horses were coming in, David would stay at home and we would get the horses out early in the morning and then we would clean stalls together and then off to work he would go. I would finish up the water and everything else that needed to be done. Things started off pretty smoothly and I had and endless amount of energy. David never seemed to get tired and we thought we had arrived as new business owners. I thought this was the perfect life.

~23~
MANY FIRSTS TO COME

Did I say my life got busy? With the opening of our horse boarding business things got crazy busy! The month of July went like a flash. New horses were coming in all through the month and all of a sudden I had to learn their personalities and behaviors and which paddocks and herd of horses I thought would be a good match.

With each horse came their supplements and grain and each with special instructions. Here at our barn we lead each horse out to the paddocks in the morning and bring them back in for the evening. Each horse had their own individual personality and ground manners were lacking in quite a few of our new tenants. We even had a couple with some very bad vices. My brain was on overload a lot just getting to know thirty-six new horses all in the same month. Some of the horses loved people and some clearly did not. I wanted to make sure each one was adjusting well to their new surroundings and of course David and I wanted to be safe when we were handling them.

Over the next five years there would be many firsts to come. I had thought about the first time a horse would have to be put down at our farm. It had never happened but I knew it would in the future sometime. How would I handle it and what would be the best way to comfort the owner of that horse and their great loss? There would be the first time a horse colicked. I would hope it would never happen but unfortunately even with the best care it does sometimes. The first time a horse was really hurt. How would I handle the horse herds when clearly two horses don't get along? How would I handle the owners when the horses don't get along? The first time someone falls off their horse and we need to call the ambulance. The first time I have to call the parents or husband of a person that was hurt. The first time someone leaves our farm because they were not happy. The first time boarders didn't get along. The first time I would have to deal with drama in the barn. The first time I lose my temper and have to apologize. I would have so many "firsts" over the years to come and with that I would learn how to handle each situation better for the next time.

THE REAL LEARNING WAS JUST AHEAD

I thought I learned a lot about business during the first year of building our barn and all the construction problems we had. I believe I did but the real learning was just ahead. I would be learning more about people and horses in the first year of business than any college could teach me in a class. I think college courses are wonderful to take in equine management. I would highly recommend anyone that is going to run a horse business to take these classes. But I would say now that nothing can compare to actually operating your own business and your learning curve will go through the roof during the first couple of years. I definitely run my business differently now, than I did when we first opened.

Our barn was full with many different breeds of horses. I have always loved diversity and welcomed the different riding disciplines into our barn. The barn was alive with all kinds of action. It was a very active barn. We had been only open a couple of months and we were having beautiful summer weather but it was almost time for me to go back to work. So far things were going along pretty smooth and everyone seemed excited and getting along. I had spent the last month really getting to know the horses and the herds were doing pretty well. We would have to move a couple of horses around a few times until we found a herd that better suited them but it seemed to be working out real well. I was learning at an accelerated pace about horse behavior and people and the unique combination of both.

David and I had settled into a routine for the summer months that would stay the same until the first of September when I would have to go back to work fulltime. At this point we thought we could handle any problem that would come up. We knew we couldn't hire anyone to help us and we had come to terms with the huge financial increase in our loans and we were going to do whatever it took to pay it down as fast as we could. We had no idea yet what the true monthly cost of keeping our barn up and running throughout all four seasons would be but we just knew we were going to be fine with hard work. We were pretty optimistic still at this point. We were still planning on David quitting his job after a year or two and staying home full time on the farm.

Our Daily Routine for Chores

I have had many people ask what our day looks like so I thought I would share a little about what our day looks like on average. Each barn will run differently but we like to get up early and get a jump on the chores. During the summer our daily routine would run like this. We would be out in our small barn (the dairy barn) at 5:30am and I would feed grain and supplements and David would feed all the hay. Afterward, I would put the horses stalled in the small barn out for the day. Then off to the big barn I would go. I would feed grain/supplements and any medicines that needed to be given and he would feed hay outside. Then we would walk 27 horses outside. After they were outside for the day we would clean the stalls. If David and I cleaned we could usually have them done by 9 or 9:30 in the morning and then shavings would be added and then we topped off all the water buckets for the day. When you are working at a job where the public comes in to use the facility it is nice to be done with the work before they come in to use it. It is much easier to get the feeding done and stalls cleaned when you are not working around the customer.

It All Sounds Good on Paper Doesn't It?

Most of the time things would run pretty good but I also had two little girls that I had to keep checking on in the house and I had to help them with whatever they needed. Many times, it would be much later when we were done. When winter came morning chores started taking much longer. We were not prepared for how long things would take once winter had settled in. I truly believe now that it does take a couple of years of completely running a horse farm through all four seasons before you can really grasp the magnitude of all the work involved. I had no idea how much work needed to be done on a forty horse farm. It is much different when you are the hired help for everything.

David and I had talked a lot about how he was going to do all the morning chores when I went back to work. What normally took two of us to do in about five hours, now he was going to have to do by himself. I was already starting to worry that it was going to be too much for one person to handle. We decided that I would still go out with him every morning at 5:30am and do all the grain and supplements for all the horses and if I had time I would also walk some horses out before I had to get back in the house to get the kids ready for school and be at work by 7:45am. David was going to clean all 27 stalls by himself then go to work afterwards. I would get home by 3:15 pm and I would do all the evening chores. We were planning on only doing this for a year or so at the most. With me having the summers off I could take over in the summer and David could take care of other things that needed to be done. We didn't know at the time we would struggle so much financially because of all the extra financial debt from the lawyer fees and building problems and this would be our way of life for many years to come. Looking back I don't know how we did it. I still ask myself that question every now and then.

During those early years we were truly blessed to have a couple of wonderful boarders who would volunteer to help with cleaning stalls every once in a while during the week and help on the weekend with chores sometimes. I still feel indebted to those people. We would always make it clear that we couldn't pay anyone at the time but they were so kind and I think they loved being out at the barn. Blessings come in wonderful ways.

~24~
CHANGES IN OUR FIRST YEAR

When you think of starting a business, you will already have a preconceived idea of how you think it should run from the very first day of operation. Everyone does this and most new business owners get a real wake-up call after they are open for a while. The fun part of starting a business is the planning of every detail. I have been to many horse farms over the years and there were things from each farm that I absolutely loved and wanted to do at our farm. And of course there were things that I wouldn't do. I know it would be the same if someone came for a tour of our place as well. That is a very normal thing we all do.

What I didn't realize when we started our horse boarding business was that so many of the things I wanted to do at the beginning of our business venture, I have now changed or modified. We have simplified certain things that we made too complicated in the beginning and only with time can you really tell what is going to work and not work on your farm. I thought a chapter about some of the changes we made the first year would be appropriate because it will definitely happen to you if you start your own horse business.

CHANGES WE MADE IN THE EARLY YEARS

Bedding for our stalls was one of the first changes we made early on. I had been looking at many different companies that supply shavings. Many farms in the area use bag shavings and they would tell me, "You never know what you are going to get with bulk." After talking to a few different sales people we had decided to go with a company that had beautiful "quick pick" shavings in bags. We had talked to companies that sold in bulk but the salesman for the bag shavings was a very good salesman and told me I would be so much happier with bag shavings. It would be less of a mess storing them and they would be so much easier to clean in a stall. I thought I would give it a try. The company delivered them to our home. I think our first delivery was about a thousand bags of these very pretty shavings in pretty bags. When the truck came they unloaded all the bags and stacked them nice and neat in our hay room. It was perfect. We put a couple of bags in each new stall to start and then after all 27 stalls were filled we would use them each morning when we were cleaning stalls. I learned very fast that when you have to open 27 bags every day or even half that amount, it is exhausting! We would have to wheelbarrow the bags down the aisle and it was very time consuming. Then on top of it we had plastic bags everywhere. It was a real pain and very labor extensive.

Using bag shavings when you only have a handful of horses is easy but when you have a huge barn full of stalls that need bedding I found the bags created far too much extra labor. I decided I was going to try bulk shavings after the bags were gone. I know now that bedding 27stalls is so much faster when using a wheelbarrow and bulk shavings. I found a guy that sold bulk shavings and when I had him deliver the bedding I saved five hundred dollars right at the start! He has been our shavings guy for all these years now and we have never run out of shavings.

It is true that when you order bulk shavings sometimes the shavings are a different consistency, but as long as they are not dusty I would recommend this way to do it for saving money and time when you have a barn with a lot of stalled horses. We have never had a problem but if money is not an issue and you have employees at your farm then bag shavings might be your preferred choice. If on the other hand you are the person doing all the work like myself then I would highly recommend bulk to save you a buck and your back!

CLEANING STALLS SEVEN DAYS A WEEK

Another thing we changed after about a year into opening our business was stall cleaning seven days a week. At the beginning we thought we could do it all and we wanted to be the best barn in the area and try to accommodate everyone. We offered stall cleaning seven days a week which most places did not do. Most barns in our area don't clean on Sundays. We thought it would set us apart to clean stalls on Sundays and it did but with a huge price tag. Because we could not hire anyone to help us, we would be out there even on Sundays cleaning and it is amazing how fast you can get burned out. I can still remember our first winter. We had a bad snow storm and it was on a Sunday and we were not able to get the stalls cleaned due to the storm. I can remember panicking because I thought our boarders were going to be so upset. They weren't at all. But looking back, I put so much pressure on myself and I felt like I was a slave to our business in this area.

As new business owners David and I were slowly killing ourselves working so hard and we needed to prioritize. I wasn't spending any time with my kids and I was exhausted when I had time to spend with them. I finally woke up one day and realized it would be okay to tell the boarders that we were only going to clean six days a week and not on Sundays. They could clean their own stall on Sundays if they wanted to. That was extremely freeing and I felt like a weight was being lifted off of my shoulders. We would still do the normal chores including turnout on Sundays but just the idea of not cleaning stalls on Sundays took off all the pressure. We never lost a boarder over that decision.

Changing our Barn Hours

Another change we made in our business after we were open a full year had to do with our barn hours. As a new business owner we wanted to please everyone that boarded at our barn. I thought at the time it was possible. That tells you how naive I was. There is so much that goes into the decision of setting up barn hours. You are probably asking why barn hours are so important.

Here are my thoughts on the subject. When we first opened in the summer of 2006 our barn hours were 8am to 10pm, seven days a week/twelve months a year. Because I was fresh and had endless energy it was fine that people were out riding until 10pm at night. Each evening David or I would make sure the tack rooms were locked, every stall was secure, horses had water and lights were out. Everything was to be put back in its place. This seemed like an easy enough thing to do for a while but it soon became very hard. Because we had been up an out in the barn by 5:30am, we were tired by 8pm. David or I would stay up so that one of us could shut the barn down. We didn't feel like we could go to bed unless everything had been double checked.

It never failed that a light was left on somewhere or tack was not put away. We would find manure was left in the aisle way or arena and often the barn was a mess. We had even come out a couple of times and found a stall door that was not shut completely and one time the owner forgot about their horse and the horse was tied to the ring at the back of the stall late at night. He had left and completely forgot about his horse. Many times the arena lights were left on and the barn would be completely dark except for the lights. When you get the electric bill each month it hits home very fast when you realize the meter has been running and no one was using the arena. Because we were new we were not sure what our electric bill was going to be each month and we had to watch it very closely. I started posting signs and reminders everywhere. This was something I never thought I would have to do.

By the time David or I got in every night it would be 10:30pm or so and then we would be up again at 4:30am. This became very hard for me very quickly because I am not a night person at all and I need a lot of sleep. I love the early mornings but they came way too fast. We were burning the candle at both ends. I know a lot of people wouldn't bother going out to close down the barn and that might work for them but it didn't work for us. I couldn't sleep unless I knew it had been checked and the horses were safely secure in their stalls.

After a year we realized the hours were killing us. I remember walking through the barn in the late evening in the summer time and I was crying because I was so tired. If you are like me, anytime I get over tired I either cry a lot or I end up getting sick. It was not worth it anymore. We decided to inform all the boarders that our new barn hours would be 8am-8pm during the months of September through May. The summer months of June, July and August would be 8am-9pm. We were not sure how everyone was going to take it but it worked out great and we never lost a boarder over the hours. I know it was hard on a few people that worked late but we needed to do what was best for us and our family. We have never regretted that change and it is truly amazing the difference two hours can make.

DO WHAT WORKS BEST FOR YOU

If you are going to open your own horse business, do what works best for you. It doesn't help the clients at all if you get sick or are grumpy all the time (and I was many evenings) and it is bad for business. I believe many horse businesses go downhill because the owners try to please everyone and end up exhausting themselves and then hurting their clients. I love the phrase "Slow and steady wins the race." I truly believe you have to pace yourself and it is okay to say "No, we can't do that here." You will be surprised how many of your clients will appreciate your honesty with them. Also remember you can't please everyone which took me about five years to figure out!

We are blessed to have an amazing group of boarders now and they respect us and our barn decisions and we love having them here. I don't worry half as much as I used to. It took years, but the boarders we have now I believe feel an ownership to our barn and go way beyond the call of duty to help and make sure things are where they should be at the end of the evening. This is something that doesn't happen in the beginning with a new business. It has to develop and grow and it could take a couple of years for that bond to take place between everyone. It has to be nurtured at times during the infancy stage of a new business.

A BARN OWNER'S RESPONSIBILITY

I have had other barn owners tell me through the years that they don't have to come out in the evening because they have wonderful boarders that shut down the barn and make sure everything is good before they leave. Here is my thought on that. We also have wonderful boarders and they do turn off lights and lock the tack rooms in the evening, but it is not their responsibility to check every horse (which there are forty) and make sure they all have water, stalls doors are completely shut and horses look good. That is not why they pay board. They pay board so they can come out and enjoy their horse without all the barn chores that go with it.

One last side note-I have boarded at many barns in my earlier years that had very late barn hours. It was great. If you live in a state where the weather is extremely hot then you will find that many people ride in the very early morning or late in the evening when it finally cools down. Here in Wisconsin it is so cold in the winter, very few people ride in the late evening. Depending on where you live in the United States, barns are going to do things differently. Weather will play a big role in barn hours. If you are going to run a business and do not have employees to help with some of the things like closing the barn in the evening, then your situation will be a little more like ours. If you have employees then you can have an evening person close down the barn and make sure the horses are settled in for the night. The great thing is, you can set this up anyway you would like and you can make changes as your needs change.

~25~
THE EARLY YEARS OF RUNNING OUR BOARDING STABLE

When I think of those first five years and what David did to keep our business from going under I am just amazed. Because of all the debt we had and nothing had been reconciled yet, we had no choice but to keep going. After I would leave for work in the morning, David would get all the rest of the horses outside and begin his daily job of cleaning 27 stalls! Monday through Friday he would clean stalls by himself because we could not afford to pay anyone. We were so totally blessed to have a wonderful boarder that would come out in the morning after that first year and she would help a couple of days a week with stalls for no charge. Thank you so much Deb!

David would finish with stalls and top off the water buckets and off to work he would go. This was not the way we wanted to run our business but it was the best we could do in the beginning. During the weekdays there would be about three hours where we were both not at home. I would have a very hard time with that because of all the horses at our farm and I felt someone should be there during the day in case something happened to one of them. We both felt a heavy responsibility and as you know, it only takes a second for a horse to get into something and get hurt.

During those early years I didn't have my own cell phone so my work phone was ringing off the hook. I felt like I was being torn into two and it was very stressful. I was constantly having boarders call me at work (which was not their fault) and I am sure my boss was getting annoyed with me also. The blessings kept coming because my boss was a very understanding woman. I am sure most supervisors would not have been so easy.

Often the stressful times seemed magnified when both David and I would be at work and I would get a call that a fence had been torn down or a storm had come up fast and I needed to get home to get the horses in. To this day I don't know how I didn't get fired from my job because I know I had to leave to go home and take care of things at the barn quite often. The same thing was happening to David on his end. If it was something serious I would call him at work and he would have to leave. This was definitely not a good way to run a business! I would have to say those were dark years for us. We never knew if we were coming or going and even though we both worked on the farm we never saw each other. We had taken being tired to a whole new level. I believe now it was only with God's grace that we made it through those first few years. We believed that we would only have to do this for a couple of years then David could stay at home and run the farm the way it should have been run. The hope that things would get easier kept us strong and going.

Afternoons were always crazy because boarders would want to talk to me and have questions and I would be doing evening chores and bringing in all the horses at the same time. It was also a strain on me because I had to constantly keep checking on my girls in the house because they were so young still. Again, we were so fortunate to have another boarder who would come out in the evenings when she could after work and help me with evening chores even though she knew I couldn't pay her. She was an amazing help to me and I am forever indebted to her also.

I worked for the school system so it helped that we had certain days off during the school year including Christmas vacation and spring break. Before I knew it June was here and I was off from my day job but full time at the farm for the summer. We made it through our first year and summer was wonderful. I truly enjoyed cleaning stalls during the summer and to this day I still find it therapeutic. After all these years of business I still clean stalls five days a week.

JUST HIRE MORE HELP

I know some of you that are reading my book are wondering why we just didn't hire more help right at the beginning no matter what the cost? The one thing about a brand new business is that it can be very hard at times to hand over the reins to someone else. To let them be in charge when you have worked so hard to get everything up and going. We were learning so much about running a business and we didn't want to take a chance that something would go wrong with someone else handling the horses or feeding the wrong grain. It was so important (and still is) that everything be done right and with great consistency for the horses. We were brand new with no reputation good or bad yet. We had to earn the respect and a good reputation from our boarders and community and it doesn't happen overnight. I now believe it takes a couple of years to earn that. We were doing the best we could at the time, the only way we knew how to. Also money was a huge factor and because we were so tight on money, we didn't have any extra at the time to pay employees.

I have learned so much from that first year of owning our own horse boarding business and the work load can seem daunting at times for any new boarding stable owner. I encourage you to make it a priority to form a strong foundation for your business and be open to changes because there will be many during the first couple of years. It happens to everyone.

~26~
THE EVER CHANGING WEATHER

When I started to write this chapter about weather and running a horse boarding stable, I wondered if I would have enough material to warrant doing a chapter on the subject. Then I remembered that I live in Wisconsin! The weather will determine the daily activities on your farm and will be a huge factor on how you do your daily chores and turnout for the horses that you take care of. Remember I am a California girl, born and raised in Los Angeles County. The weather almost always stayed the same. Sunny and more sun coming! I can remember when I lived there every once in a while I would get so tired of the sun and wish we would get some rain for a change. I can tell you now that it never happens here in Wisconsin. My father-in-law used to tell me, "If you don't like the weather just wait ten minutes and it will be different."

It is amazing to me how many different and often stressful situations we came into the first couple of years of our business and many of them had to do with the weather. Each year through each season things would change all the time. What worked the year before all of a sudden needed to be modified the next. Weather was and still is one of the biggest hurdles we have to deal with on a daily basis each season here in Wisconsin and especially when dealing with horses – your clients horses. That is when it becomes challenging.

Because I had only four horses on our property before we opened our stable, it was very easy to quickly run out and feed them and make sure they had water and run back in the house. Believe me, many times I did run especially when it was extremely cold. I never really gave the weather much of a thought because I didn't have to be out in it for many hours at a time. Not until we opened our business. Things changed in my life more than I would have ever imagined.

THE FALL CAME AND SO DID THE MUD!

As we moved into fall 2006 the weather changed and lots of rain came our way. Because our paddocks were on the farm land that had been used to grow vegetables for many generations the ground was very soft. We never realized until we put horses in the new paddocks and you add a lot of rain what it does to the ground. Our dry ground turned to extremely deep mud in a matter of days! It was a mess like I had never seen before. Horses could hardly walk in it and very quickly boarders were telling me that they didn't want their horses to go outside in it. The fall temps were cold and the ground could not dry and it was not safe for horses to be in it at all. They were pulling shoes left and right and I was much more concerned that one of them would pull a tendon. All of a sudden most of the horses were staying in even on sunny days because the paddocks were not drying at all. It did not help at all that our soil is a clay base soil with very poor drainage. Because it rains so often in this part of the country all we could hope for now was for the ground to freeze so we could get the horses back outside. It was truly a mess and a very stressful situation that we had not expected.

David and I felt it was our responsibility to fix this problem but it was too large to fix overnight. We would walk into the barn and I knew our boarders were disappointed that their horses had to stay in a stall because our paddocks were too wet and muddy. It was especially hard when you drove around and saw other farms with all their horses outside for the day. I would get a sick feeling inside every time.

A NEW PROBLEM WITH WATER

We also had a new problem. The drain tile we had put in earlier to get the water away from the paddocks was too small and couldn't handle the large amount of water that was draining from the fields and away from the barn. When we would get a large storm and a lot of water in a short amount of time, our paddocks would flood. I can remember one time taking my girls out for lunch and the weather was sunny with some clouds coming in. During lunch we had a huge storm come in with high winds that were not in the forecast. David was at work and I rushed home with the girls to pull into our driveway and see three paddocks completely underwater with horses standing in knee deep water! I was in shock. I dropped off my girls at the house, put on my muck boots and out I went to bring in all the horses standing in deep water. The horses were quiet thank goodness but it was not good for business at all. We ended up losing a couple boarders after that one.

It was very hard because I live in a small town and I would run into a neighbor or another horse owner and they would say to me something like, "Looks like you have a drainage problem." or "How do your horses like swimming?" It would cut me to the core. We were not off to a good start trying to earn a good reputation. Running our own business was turning out to be much harder than I ever thought it would be. As soon as the next summer came we had the excavator put in a drain tile ten times the size of the original one along with a new drainage ditch and culvert. That came with a huge price tag but it was worth it.

Looking back now I completely understand why those boarders left our barn. We had offered certain amenities at our facility like daily turnout and the horses were inside more often than they were turned out due to our water issue. We still can get muddy here at our farm in the fall and spring but not anything like we did during that first couple of years of business.

If you are designing your paddocks on virgin land, my advice to you would be to watch very closely how the water flows when heavy rain passes through. It will tell you a lot about how your water is going to flow in your paddocks and it will help you in designing them. I never realized how the slightest grade can make a huge difference in a well-drained paddock or a paddock that stays continually wet and muddy. We underestimated how much the water flowed in certain areas of our property. Unfortunately it didn't flow very well in the areas where we put up our fencing. That was a big mistake we made. It is much easier to do your homework ahead of time then to go back and take down fencing and try to do it all over again after you already have horses on the property.

~27~
OUR FIRST WINTER SEASON RUNNING OUR HORSE FACILITY

Winter in Wisconsin. Do I need to say more? As I am writing this chapter today we are experiencing the coldest temperatures we have had in decades the weatherman said this morning. Dealing with horses and winter in Wisconsin was something brand new for me when I moved here twenty-four years ago. Like I had mentioned in an earlier chapter, I worked on a horse farm the first year or so that we moved here and after going through a winter working with horses, I thought I would never own another horse as long as we lived here. As you can see that did not happen.

When we opened our barn doors for business I had already dealt with many winters here and we also had four horses on our own property. This was another situation where jumping from four horses to forty was a whole new experience when it comes to dealing with winter. I was going to learn real fast the difference between having a hobby farm and having a horse boarding business. After we had got through the mud and wet of fall the ground started to freeze. We were very glad to have this happen so the horses would not be in mud up to their knees. When we started putting horses out again we were already running into a new problem. Because we had the horses in the mud they had made huge divots and holes everywhere and now it was frozen and very hard for them to walk on. We had not experienced this before on such a huge scale and I did not feel it was safe to have them out there. I was extremely worried one of them would twist a leg or even worse break a leg.

David and I would look at all our paddocks with disgust and have to think of a way to fix it. We would walk out in our paddocks and it was even hard for me to walk. It was rough beyond anything I had seen except for the farm fields after they plow them up for winter then they freeze. David had an idea to smooth them out. Of course this meant more work for him and he was already extremely busy. He spent many hours and days out in his skid loader scraping all the dirt and divots and smoothing them out. He would come in and his hands would be frozen.

It worked good but very slow and time consuming work. Another thing we did not realize was that because of the extreme weather changes David would have to fix the paddocks in the fall and spring. It was never a one time and its done project. It would be a way of life for years to come. This was not in our business plan of running a horse barn. This was something we had never even dreamed we would have to do. Again we were getting on the job training.

Another problem that was new to us that first winter was snow. The snow wasn't the problem at all and the horses absolutely loved the snow. Everybody loved the snow. But we would get a lot of snow and then we would get very warm temperatures and the snow would melt and freeze again as the weather changed. All of a sudden we would have an ice skating rink everywhere which was extremely dangerous for the horses. The snow would melt and because the ground was frozen underneath, the water had nowhere to go and then it would sit on top of the ground and then freeze overnight when the temperatures dropped. This was the worst possible thing to deal with. It would be glare ice by morning.

A LITTLE MANURE GOES A LONG WAY

I don't know what I would have done without David. I am so glad he loved farming and knew what to do. He would take his old tractor and manure spreader and load up the spreader with hot manure and cover every paddock and path with a layer of hot manure. This was another job that took many long hours. He would let it sit on the ice overnight and it would melt the ice just enough that as it froze back up it would be stuck to the ground. It worked fantastic and made it completely safe for the horses to walk on. This was also another very time consuming job on the farm for David but it worked and worked great. We have done this practice every year since the first time and it has been a lifesaver. Sometimes he has to put manure down a couple times a year depending on the weather. It may not be that pretty but by the time spring comes it all blends together and you never even knew it was there. We always thought winter time would be slower and a time to rest a little more on our farm but that turned out not to be the case. It was just as busy and the work can be much harder because of the cold temperatures.

I know some of you reading this chapter probably are wondering why we went to all the trouble. Why didn't we just leave the horses in their stalls until we could finally put them out? At this rate all the horses would have never gone out. We didn't want that for the horses and the owners didn't want that either. Each boarding facility does things their own way and this is what we wanted to do for the horses. I truly felt it was healthier to get them outside as much as possible. They were happier when they were outside for the day and quieter at night when they were in. It was always a matter of keeping them safe.

Many Different Opinions

We were experiencing new situations that we had not thought of before. Another issue that was coming up our first winter was the difference in opinions of when the horses should go outside. I didn't realize I would have boarders that would be upset that we put the horses out and boarders that would be upset that we left them in due to weather. I was being pulled in two different directions with a lot of pressure from both sides.

I ended up sitting down with a friend of mine who helped me write up some guidelines of when we would put horses outside and when we wouldn't due to inclement weather. We had one of these sheets for all four seasons. We passed them out and I would always make myself available to answer any questions our clients would have.

In the beginning I would be intimidated by boarders that would tell me very quickly how other barns did things. This was hard for me because I didn't want to be like other barns and I also felt I knew how to take good care of horses. The biggest fear was I didn't want to lose any boarders. We were a very young business and had already gone through major obstacles and a few boarders had already left. I was constantly trying to find a balance. Looking back, those early years were terrible because I had not learned to be confident in my decisions I made about the horses. Fear was my boss and also the constant fear of losing boarders was always in the back of my mind. I was worried we wouldn't be able to fill an empty stall if someone had left. It was a very difficult time for us as new business owners.

The temperature always seemed to be the biggest conflict for boarders. Because they were cold they would assume their horse would be cold also. I spent much time talking about breeds and horses with heavy coats vs. a thin coat horse and blanketing. This is still the main topic of discussion each winter. I am just now ready to answer questions with a much more educated answer than in the beginning of our business. I am also more confident of myself and not afraid to express myself and what I believe works well in keeping horses healthy through extreme cold temperatures. This was something that took years for me to learn and much experience with horses and wintertime. I believe now you can only learn to solve these business problems when you are forced to as the business owner. That is where the buck stops. You can work on a horse farm for years and know how to do it all but you will not learn to problem solve with clients until you have to do it on a daily basis. I was getting on the job training every day.

HERE COME THE BLANKETS

Because we had a barn with great diversity (which I absolutely love) with that came all different types of breeds and riding styles. In the summer it was very easy. No one blanketed. We opened in the summer when the weather was absolutely beautiful so we didn't have to worry about this. As the days got colder more and more horses were getting blankets on. We had boarders that put light weight blankets on and graduated to medium weight and then heavy weight. We also had boarders that doubled up on blanketing and then we had boarders that would not do anything until it was extremely cold out and then would put a heavy weight on and leave it on until spring.

I believe that when you have a boarding facility, the owner of the horse should decide what they want to do as far as blanketing their horse. The only time I would intervene is if I saw a horse sweating because they are too hot under the blanket or shaking because they are too cold and need a blanket. I have seen both these situations several times at our stable and I had to learn how to discuss these issues with the boarders without hurting their feelings.

This is a very sensitive issue and I never want to make anyone feel stupid but sometimes no matter how you say it, they are going to be upset. I was not ready for that since I was just trying to help and educate them if they didn't understand how to blanket. You need to remember that the horse comes first. If you see a horse that is stressed out because they are too hot because the blanket is too heavy for the temperatures or the horse is cold and is shivering and needs a blanket, you need to tell the owner and it doesn't matter if they become upset. They need to know so the horse doesn't get sick or colic. You are going to have clients that just don't know what to look for and don't even know what their horse would look like if they were stressed. It is your job as the barn owner or manager to walk them through that and hopefully educate them as you go. I have had boarders at our barn that were truly happy that I told them about their horse and the condition the horse was in and I have had boarders that didn't care or were even annoyed that I bothered them. You will need to be prepared to deal with both types of people and the bottom line is it's your barn and you don't want a horse getting sick or worse due to mistakes made by the owner of the horse. Trust me when I tell you that if you are running a boarding facility these situations will come up. They do every winter for me.

Dealing with the difference of opinions on when to put horses outside in the cold weather was becoming a common occurrence. The horses loved the snow and loved to play in it. If the temperature dropped too low or it was a windy day and the wind chill was too cold we would leave the horses in. I was finding boarders that would become upset if we put them out and boarders that were upset if we kept them in. We would have boarders drive over in a rush just to go outside and bring their horse in because they thought they were cold. We couldn't understand why they would bring them in when the horses seemed so content outside. At this point I had not been able to stand my ground yet on the subject and I didn't want to upset anyone or even confront them about their reasons for bringing their horse in. Sometimes it would be an awkward silence when I would walk in the barn and sometimes I was not prepared for how many calls I would receive wondering why we made the decision we made on any particular day.

LACK OF TRUST

Between the blanketing and all the other questions about winter and horses, I believe now it all came down to the fact that we had not earned the trust of our boarders. They did not truly believe we would put their horses first and make sure they were not too cold. It was very hard for David and me when a boarder would come to the barn and say, "I just drove by blank farm and their horses are out" or "I just drove by blank farm and their horses are in today" and it would be the opposite of what we had done for the day. That happened a lot in the beginning. I was going to need to toughen up and feel confident of our decisions we were making but it would take me years before that confidence would come. I needed to be a leader and let them know we knew what we were doing. Some of the boarders were looking to me for guidance and I was not ready to give it back then. They didn't want to be told what to do but they wanted someone to guide them through their decision making on the care and well-being of their horse. Wow! This was something I had not ever thought about when wanting to own a horse business and it was a lot of pressure for me at the time.

I was so naïve and I just figured people would do their own thing and it would all be good. That was not the case at all. Don't get me wrong, I truly enjoy helping people now, but years ago I was not ready for that. Like I said, I didn't have the confidence and I believed at the time others knew more. It was becoming so complicated and a little out of control and I was not the owner I should of been back then. I was actually letting people tell me how things were going to run in the barn. Isn't that crazy! David and I were not leading and I was seeing frustrated boarders every day when I walked in the barn. Those first couple of winters were very draining for me and not fun at all.

As I am writing this we have had all our horses inside for the last week due to extremely cold temperatures. I am sure it has been a little stressful for everyone here as well as other barns. Years later I still every once in a while have a boarder that gets upset at a decision we made on whether the horses go out or stay in due to the weather. Sometimes our choice is not the popular one but at the end of the day I have to do what is best for the entire farm and I have to stand by my decisions. It will never be perfect because the weather is not but we sure do try as hard as we can to give the best care for these amazing horses we have the honor of taking care of at our farm. I could write a book alone on dealing with horses and winter here in Wisconsin. I won't but there is a lot to talk about on this subject and running a horse boarding business.

The bottom line is if you want to have a horse business and are going to have clients, then be ready for all different types of opinions. Remember that at the end of the day, you have to do what works best for your business and you will find the right boarders for your type of facility. We sure did and even though things come up every now and then, people trust David and me now and it is so much easier and less stressful then those early years. I never really realized there was so much debate or opinions on the care of horses in winter until we opened our stable.

One More Thought on the Subject

There are so many different ways to run a horse boarding stable. I am not saying that our way is the only way. I am just trying to give you a glimpse into our life of starting a horse boarding business from nothing and give you an open window into the heart and soul of what it took to get this business off the ground and the transformation we needed to go through in order to become confident and successful business owners. I can say that most of it was not easy in the beginning. The only way we learned was through trial and error and there was a lot of that. Most importantly just because I have a business doesn't mean I was instantly a business person. So much of it is experience and how you mentally deal with it but it doesn't happen overnight. For David and me it took many years to where I believe now I can truly call myself a businesswoman and run my farm like a business. I feel confident with the decisions we make every day with the horses on our farm no matter what season we are in. We still have differences of opinions from clients now and then and that is perfectly fine because I am much better equipped to handle those opinions.

~28~
BOARDING CONTRACTS AND LIABILITY WAIVERS

Talking about contracts between the barn owner and the client is not the most exciting topic but it is one of the most important parts of running a horse business. I am surprised at how many people don't use boarding contracts at all but after building our barn and having both the builders sue us over a period of five years, I see now how absolutely crucial it is. You would be crazy not to have a contract with your clients.

As the owner of a large boarding facility I wanted to make sure I had a contract in place. I wasn't sure where to go when we started so I went online (which is how most people do it) and looked at boarding contracts for the state of Wisconsin. You can purchase a contract online, download it and change whatever you want on it. It's a great starting point but like everything else make sure your lawyer has looked at it to make sure you are completely covered. Many of the contracts you find on the internet may sound good but many of them are not accurate in their wording. Also each state will have their own laws regarding the equine industry so make sure your contract is accurate for your state. The boarding contract or any contract between you and your client is there to protect you. If you are in the business long enough, eventually a situation will arise where you will be glad you have a contract in place.

TROUBLE COLLECTING BOARD PAYMENTS

One of the questions I get asked often is "Do you have any trouble collecting board payments from your boarders?" I have been told so many times from different people that they have a very hard time getting paid from their boarders. Just think of that. You work all month and only get one pay check and now it doesn't come. Would you stay at that job? Of course not! But now you have to because you are the owner of the business and you are stuck working for free because you can't just walk away. It will feel like you are working for free and unappreciated if your boarders are not paying you on time.

When we started our business this was another situation where I was so naive. I did have my contract in place and because it was signed and dated I assumed that my boarders would follow everything on the contract and of course I would be paid on time. Yes you can laugh a little if you want right now! I am chuckling as I am writing this because that is what I truly thought way back then.

Our original contract had stated that our board was due and payable on the first of each month. I also had in the contract that the client was allowed 10 days after the first of the month to pay. It was a 10 day grace period. In the beginning I didn't think anything about the "ten days" that was stated in the contract. I assumed most everyone would pay on the first and once in a great while I would have a client that would need to wait until around the tenth due to financial reasons. Being the optimist that I am I didn't see any problems with this.

Pretty quickly after we opened I realized that my boarders were going to use the ten days grace period as a normal payment plan. What I didn't figure into the equation was the fact that most of my bills including my business mortgage were all due on or before the tenth of each month. Things were quickly becoming stressful each month because I would have checks float in on all different days all the way up to the tenth of the month. I did have a lot of great boarders that paid on the first of the month but because our budget was so extremely tight it didn't give us any breathing room. Most businesses are financially tight during the early years and most new business owners don't realize how financially tight things can get until they are deep into it. I never did either until we started our own business.

My contract also had in it a paragraph that states that if the board is overdue on the tenth of the month the stable had the right to add a finance charge from the tenth of the month at a rate of 5% per day. It all looked so good on paper. I was a woman trying to run a business with zero business skills so when it came to collecting the 5% finance charge on the late board I was scared to ask for it. I would take a minute and talk to the boarder about the overdue payment and they would tell me their financial woes and I would buy right into it. Not a good way to run a business at all!

This would go on for the next couple of years and I would get very frustrated each month to the point where it was causing stress between

David and me. I had to change how I was doing things. We were working harder than we ever had our entire life and now we were having a hard time getting paid for it.

Time for some serious changes

I was going to change how I ran this business when it came to getting paid. I can still remember the first time I called a boarder and told them over the phone that they needed to add the 5% finance charge to the overdue board and it needed to be paid as soon as possible. This time I was nice but firm and told them per their contract it would accumulate every day that the board was late. It was the hardest thing for me to do but I did it and sure enough the board came right away with the 5% added on. It was baby steps but I soon began calling each boarder that had not paid by the tenth day of the month and sending out a reminder that the board was due by 8pm the next day and if it wasn't paid there would be a 5% finance charge added on. Things started to change. I started getting paid by everyone in a timely manner and the stress level started to go down.

The next thing I needed to change was the amount of days I allowed for a grace period. David and I talked about it and decided we would change the time allowed from ten days to five days. I am sure some of the boarders were not thrilled but we were having a very hard time making our bills on time and I didn't want them to be late. I never realized that it would be so difficult for some people to pay their board on time and that I would have to ask people for the board payment each month.

Since the time when we made these changes, our boarders know and understand I will be calling or texting as a reminder when they are close to becoming late on the board. It still is not fun when I have to do this but I treat it just like a business and I do not get wrapped up in all the emotion anymore. Getting paid is much less stressful now. I still get a late check now and then and the five percent is always added. I have had some crazy excuses on why a client couldn't get out here to pay the board but for the most part we have been lucky and it runs pretty smooth.

Remember that many of the boarders at your stable most likely have come from other barns and it might not have been a big deal if the board was late. So if the client is used to paying the board whenever they feel like it then you will have to show them how you would like it done at your barn. I will be honest and tell you that in the beginning it will probably be stressful but it will get easier the longer you do it. Change doesn't always come easy especially when dealing with people and money.

OUR BOARDING CONTRACT

Our boarding contract has been updated through the years as I have realized things I wanted to do differently. Our contract is four pages long and most of the time the boarder doesn't read it when they sign it. It will become your job to make sure they understand what they are signing. I have had boarders upset at me for one thing or another and the first thing they want to do is look at their contract to see what their rights are. That is completely fine and I am glad they do. I never want to make a boarder feel stupid but if they are going to threaten me with my own contract then I believe they should know what the contract says. Once they read the contract they usually quiet down pretty quickly. If they are that upset then they will most likely give their notice anyway. Remember it's not personal, it's business.

This was a very hard concept for me to embrace during our early years of business because I was taking everything personal in the beginning. There was a very emotional part to the whole equation of the relationship between me and my clients and it took me some time to look at it differently. Even after all these years I still struggle with this area in certain situations when I have to talk to a boarder about a problem that has come up.

Please remember above all else that when a boarder comes into your facility they are always very happy to be there at first. At the beginning they seem like they are going to be the perfect boarder and then something happens and they get upset. Be prepared and protect yourself. I truly believe people are good people with the best intentions but when it comes to their horse, if something bad happens, there are people out there that will want to blame someone and if they don't have anyone to blame then most likely it will fall back on you. You want to be protected. I can't stress this enough.

In this chapter I am going to share what is in my Vinland Stables LLC boarding contract. You will want to modify your contract to fit your business needs and that is very easy to do. You can find contracts on line for boarding, training, breeding or anything else in the equine industry. **Remember, after you have your contract worded how you would like it to read, spend the money and have a lawyer look at it to make sure you are covered for the state you do business in.**

It is very important to remember that if your contract is not accurate with the laws in your state and you find yourself in a situation where you have to go to court with a client, there is a very good chance your contract will be void and you will lose the case. I can't stress enough that you will want to protect yourself. Each state has different guidelines and you will want to make sure your contract is current with the laws in your state for equine businesses.

VINLAND STABLES BOARDING AGREEMENT:

Here is a sample of what is in our contract. The bolded paragraphs are the wording we have for our contract. After each paragraph I will explain what each section means.

Your opening paragraph of your contract should be the paragraph that you have your date (when the contract starts) and the name of your business and address. The date will be blank until you fill it in but must be filled in. Ours reads like this.

***WITNESS THIS AGREEMENT** this _____ day of _____, 20___, by and between Vinland Stables LLC, hereinafter referred to as "Stable," and the individual or individuals undersigned, hereinafter referred to as "Owner." Address of Stable is 2588 County Road GG, Neenah WI. 54956.*

1. Fees, Term, and Location.

Owner acknowledges and accepts those terms set forth in the rate schedule as posted by Stable. Whether said rates be daily, weekly, or monthly. Payment shall be due in accordance with that rate schedule on a timely basis. In the event the subject animal is removed from the premises for any reason and returned, this agreement shall be deemed reinstated at said rates. Stable reserves the right to notify Owner with fifteen (15) days of the horse's arrival if the horse, in Stable's opinion is deemed to be dangerous or undesirable for Stable's establishment. In such case, Owner shall be solely responsible for removing the horse within seven (7) days of said notice and for all fees incurred during the horse's presence upon the premises. This Contract shall be deemed terminated and concluded upon the payment of all fees.

This first part of my contract is to set the perimeters of what my rights and protection are for new horses coming into our facility and also to set the guidelines for the monies involved for payment. Believe it or not we had a situation where a horse had come on our property to be boarded and within three days I had to tell the owners of the horse that the horse needed to be removed from the property. The owners of the horse were very nice people but the horse was extremely dangerous and David and I did not want to deal with the situation. The people needed to find a facility that was better situated for such a horse with a trainer that could help them work through all the extreme aggressive behaviors. This happened during the first year we opened and we didn't have a good trainer at the time that was willing to work with this horse.

You hope this never happens but be prepared in case a situation like this does. Protect yourself.

The next paragraph is about collecting board rent.

"The boarding fee is due, in advance, on the first of each month. All other fees and charges are due on the first of each month following the date of the invoice. All outstanding boarding fees and all other outstanding invoiced fees and charges are subject to a finance charge from the fifth (5) of the month at the rate of 5% per day, 1825% per annum, until paid in full. In addition, Stable shall be entitled to enforce a lien against said horse and Owner's property on the premises as further described below. The initial monthly boarding fee and charges applicable to the services as set forth below shall be $_____per month, plus tax." Owner acknowledges and agrees that Owner shall be responsible for all

costs of repairing or replacing all property of Stable damaged or destroyed by Owner's horse and shall timely make payments as set forth above.

This will be one of your most important parts of your contract. You don't know how many times over the years I have talked to someone and they always ask me if I have trouble collecting rent from a client. This happens more often than you might expect.

Years ago we did have one person leave with their horse and not pay board and I lost a month's pay. I decided it wasn't worth going to small claims court over the whole thing so we just ate the cost. I only had one other time when a wonderful boarder who had been at our barn for a long time lost his job and couldn't pay his board for several months. I truly felt bad for this man and we ended up working out a deal that I would help sell his horse and then I could recoup the money that I had lost on the board.

This situation was so unfortunate for the owner but we kept communication open and we sold the horse and I was able to recoup my money. The horse went to a great home and we are still friends with this man. Most of the time good communication and a little patience work the best. The last part of this paragraph is equally important. It has to do with the owner's horse causing damage to your property. If you have horses they will break things. Make sure you have a part of your contract that covers this so you are protected and you have the legal right to get reimbursed for damages done by a boarder's horse.

2. Description of Horse(s) to be boarded.

Owner agrees to submit a fully complete Owner Information sheet for each horse boarded upon execution of this agreement. The terms and conditions set forth herein shall be applicable to each and every animal boarded by Owner.

What I have found easiest to do is type up your own BOARDER AND HORSE INFORMATION FORM and have one for each horse on the property. It will be your contact information for emergencies. I have the owner's information on it and emergency contacts and numbers. I have a section for Horse Identification. There is also a section for Choice of Veterinarian and any additional Information and Services Desired. This will be the sheet you go to the most when you have a problem with a client's horse. I suggest you keep them in a place with your contracts where you can get to them easily. I keep them in numerical stall order in a file cabinet next to my desk. You will be surprised how often you need to contact one of your clients.

What is great about this form is that you can design it however you want. I then staple it to the contract so it is easy to find. I will have a sample sheet at the end of this chapter.

3. Feed, Facilities, and Services.

Stable agrees to provide adequate feed and facilities for normal and reasonable care required to maintain the health and well-being of the animals. Owner acknowledges and Owner has inspected the facilities and finds the same in safe and proper order.

This paragraph protects both you (the barn owner) and the boarder. You just want to make sure they have seen the facility and accept the condition and care ahead of time.

4. Risk of Loss and Standard of Care.

During the time that the horse(s) is/are in custody of said Stable, Stable shall not be liable for any sickness, disease, astray, theft, death or injury which may be suffered by the horse(s) or any other cause of action, whatsoever, arising out of being connected in any way with the boarding of said horse(s), except in the event of negligence on the part of Stable, it's agents, and/or employees. This includes, but is not limited to, any personal injury or disability the horse Owner, or Owner's guest, may receive on Stable's premises

This is an important paragraph. As long as you are the owner of a facility whether it is boarding, breeding or training, there will come a time when a horse gets hurt or worse dies due to injury or sickness. When this happens there is no way anyone can predict how the owner of the horse is going to respond. You can always hope for the best but the worst can happen.

We had a sad situation years ago where a boarder's horse lived with my horses in the same paddock. My husband was gone for the weekend and I was taking care of the farm. I was feeding evening hay to the horses and when we went to feed my horses we noticed that one horse was standing very still and not baring any weight on one leg. We quickly realized that he had either broken his leg or shoulder. It was absolutely heartbreaking. The owner of the horse happened to be at the barn and before we knew it the vet was there. The horse ended up having to be put down that evening.

It was extremely upsetting and the biggest challenge and what everyone wanted to know was-how did it happen? None of us had seen it happen and I could tell by the conversation from the owners of the horse that they wanted an answer which is completely normal under these circumstances. I am sure I would be the same way. The veterinarian told them there was no way to know how it happened and we would never know in this particular situation.

As the barn owner I was very glad that a Veterinarian had been on the site and helped calm the situation but I was also relieved that I had a signed contract in place with this client. You always hope for the best but under bad circumstances you never know how things will turn out.

The next part of this section reads:

The owner fully understands that Stable does not carry any insurance on any horse(s) not owned by it for boarding or for any other purposes, whether public liability, accidental injury, theft or equine mortality insurance and that all risk connected with boarding or for any other reason for which the horse(s) in the possession of, and on the premises of Stable are to be borne by the Owner. Stable strongly recommends equine mortality insurance be obtained applicable to the subject horse(s) by Owner.

I have had boarders ask us if we carry insurance and yes we do. We do carry insurance to cover the death of a horse if we are negligent and the horse dies. What some horse owners don't understand is if their horse dies on the property and it is an accident then the barn owner is not responsible and they should have had mortality insurance for their horse. New horse owners might need to be educated on this. This is an important section of your contract and I would discuss this with your insurance agent along with your attorney. Make sure you have the right insurance coverage for your business. We will talk more about this later on.

5. Hold Harmless.

Owner agrees to hold Stable harmless from any and all claims arising from damage or injury caused by owner's horse(s), to anyone, and defend Stable from any such claims. Owner agrees to disclose any and all hazardous or dangerous propensities of horse(s) boarded with Stable.

You are going to want to ask the new boarder coming into your barn if the horse has any bad habits or bites, kicks, is aggressive at feeding time or has a problem walking through gates etc. We have seen all of this over the years and we have even had people knocked over or kicked because of behaviors. If the owner of the horse is aware of a bad habit or aggressive behavior, they need to disclose it at the beginning. It doesn't mean they always will but in most cases people are pretty honest.

6. Emergency Care.

Stable agrees to attempt to contact Owner, should Stable feel that medical treatment is needed for said horse(s), but if Stable is unable to contact Owner, Stable is then authorized to secure emergency, veterinary, and blacksmith are required for the health and well-being of said horse(s). All cost of such care secured shall be paid by Owner with fifteen (15) days from the date Owner receives notice thereof, or Stable is authorized, as Owner's agent, to arrange direct billing to Owner.

Be prepared because it will happen sometime during your career in the equine industry. A horse is going to need medical attention and you are not going to be able to get hold of the owners or they are out of town on vacation. This means you will need to make the call on what to do.

It is Murphy's Law-if the owner goes away on vacation their horse will need the vet!

This has happened to me several times over the last few years. Thank goodness even with a colic case we had a happy ending without having to decide on surgery. When the new clients are signing their contract with you make sure they understand this part of it and find out exactly what they want you to do in an emergency.

STABLE SHALL ASSUME THAT OWNER DESIRES SURGICAL CARE IF RECOMMENDED BY A VETERINARIAN IN THE EVENT OF COLIC, OR OTHER LIFE-THREATENING ILLNESS, UNLESS STABLE IS INSTRUCTED HEREIN OR ON OWNER'S INFORMATION SHEETS, BY OWNER THAT THE HORSE(S) IS/ARE NOT SURGICAL CANDIDATES.

Owner agrees to notify Stable of any and all change of addresses, emergency telephone numbers, itineraries or other information reasonably necessary to contact Owner in the event of an emergency. In the event Owner departs for vacation or is otherwise unavailable, prior to departure Owner shall notify Stable as to what party is authorized to make decisions in the Owner's place with regard to the health, well-being, and/or medical treatment of the horse(s).

These paragraphs cover all the bases for emergency situations. You hope you never are put in the situation where you need to make the decision of what to do with a sick horse but if it does, this protects you.

I had a boarder once leave out of town and never told me and I couldn't get hold of her for days. When I finally did, she was in another state! When she came back she had a vet bill but thank goodness her horse was going to be fine.

7. *Limitation of Actions.*

Any action or claim brought by the Owner against the Stable for breach of this Contract or for loss due to negligence must be brought within one (1) year of the date such claim or loss occurs.

This is a pretty straight forward paragraph simply putting a cap on the time allowed that a boarder can come back at you for damages or loss of life. It protects you the business owner so that someone can't come back two years later and try to sue you.

8. Hoof Care/Shoeing, Vaccinations, and Worming.

Owner agrees to provide the necessary hoof care of the horse(s) as is reasonably necessary, at Owner's expense. Owner agrees to provide Stable with all health records with regard to the horse(s). Owner agrees to have the horse(s) vaccinated on a regular schedule, and in the event same is not accomplished and proof of the same presented to Stable within thirty (30) days from the date of such services or veterinary treatment, Stable is authorized to arrange for such treatment, but not obligated to do so; such expense shall be the obligation of Owner, and upon presentation by Stable of the bill for such services rendered, including service charges, any bill shall be paid with fifteen(15) days from the date the bill is submitted to the Owner.

There have been a couple of times over the years where I have had to call a boarder because their horse's feet were extremely long or severely cracked to the point that the horse looked like he was having a hard time walking. There are people out there that really don't care if their horse's feet ever get trimmed. It becomes a very sticky situation and I had one extreme case where the owners of the horse would not return my phone calls and another boarder was so upset about the condition of the feet on this particular horse that she was willing to pay for the farrier. The entire situation became very stressful.

Each horse will grow hoof at their own speed and some horses grow hoof much faster than others. It becomes negligent when the horse can't walk properly. You will also run into different views of what is appropriate timeframe for hoof care. I have boarders that get their horses feet trimmed every six weeks like clockwork no matter what time of year it is. I on the other hand let my horse's feet go a little longer in between trims in the winter because their hoof grows much slower in the wintertime. It depends on the horse.

As the barn owner you will make the final judgment on when to call the boarder if you feel he is not taking care of his horse's feet properly. Sometimes it is as simple as just educating the person. Sometimes they just don't know and then we need to guide them a little.

When it comes to vaccinations for a client's horse, this is cut and dry. They need to take care of it. You will most likely have one or two people that will put it off due to money issues but at the end of the day it is your facility and they need to follow the rules of your barn.

Owner will deworm horse(s) on a regular rotation schedule. If Owner does not deworm horse(s) as printed in the rotation schedule and falls behind, Stable will deworm horse(s) and the cost of deworming will be added to the board for that month and it will be Owner's responsibility to pay the fee for deworming that will be billed on the next board invoice.

This is also pretty straight forward. Your deworming protocol and schedule for your stable should be provided to the client at the time the boarding contract is signed so they know upfront how you want things done.

9. Ownership-Coggins Test.

Owner warrants that he owns the horse(s) and will provide proof satisfactory of Stable of the negative Coggins test upon request.

This is also pretty straight forward and you would think you wouldn't have any problems with this part of the contract but you most likely will at one time or another. I have always made it clear that when a new horse comes to my stable that they need to have a current Coggins and it has happened several times over the years where the owner's bring the horse and they forgot the Coggins! It can be a little maddening.

I have even had one extreme case where a boarder that had a horse at my barn, left with the horse in the morning and came back with a different horse and put the new horse in their stall and didn't let me know they were switching horses until I came out later to do chores. On top of that I didn't see the Coggins until the next day because they forgot it. I hope that never happens to you.

10. Changes or Termination of This Agreement.

It is agreed by the parties that this Agreement may be changed or terminated upon thirty (30) days' notice, regardless of the rental period. All notices must be issued in writing unless otherwise agreed upon by the parties. The posting of updated rate schedules in a conspicuous or open place in Stable's office shall constitute notice of any and all rate changes or regulation changes as may be deemed appropriated by Stable.

This short paragraph protects you the barn owner for when you need to make a change at your barn or raise your board fee. I always give a thirty day notice for most situations except in the event of raising my board rates. Then I give a sixty day notice. I want to make sure I give the clients enough time to prepare for the rate increase. Sometimes it can be sticker shock to raise the rates so it gives the boarders plenty of time to find a new facility if they feel they won't be able to afford the rate hike. I try to make it as easy as possible on everyone. Your clients may not like the rate increase but they will appreciate the fact that you had enough respect for them to give them plenty of notice. It is the little things you do that will set your business apart from other boarding stables.

11. Rules and Regulations.

The Owner agrees to abide by all the rules and regulations of the Stable. In the event someone other than the Owner shall call for the horse(s), such a person shall have written or verbal authority by the Owner to obtain said horse(s).

Following the rules of your barn should be a no brainer but sometimes it doesn't happen. Either for the reason that people just plain forget or sometimes they might actually think your rules don't apply to them. For whatever the reason, this protects you. It happens a lot at our barn where someone will lease out their horse and it is important to make sure the person leasing the horse also gets a copy of all the barn rules.

12. Right of Lien.

The Owner is put on notice that Stable has a right of lien as set forth in the laws of Wisconsin, for the amount due for the board and keep of such horse(s), and also for storage and services, and shall have the right, without process of law, to retain, said horse(s) until the amount of said indebtedness is discharged. However, Stable will not be obligated to retain and /or maintain the horse(s) in question. In the event the amount of the bill exceeds the anticipated unregistered value of the horse(s), in the event Stable *exercises Stable's lien rights as above-described for non-payment, this agreement shall constitute a Bill of Sale and authorization to process transfer applications from any breed registration as may be applicable to said horse(s) upon affidavit by Stable's representatives setting forth the material facts of the default and foreclosure as well as Stable's compliance with foreclosure procedures as required by law. In the event collection of this account is turned over to an attorney, Owner agrees to pay all attorneys' fees, cost, and other related expenses for which a minimum charge of $250.00 will be assessed.*

This paragraph protects you if you find yourself in a situation where you have a client that is not paying their board bill and you are not able to collect any money for overdue board. I have heard many stories over the years where barn owners have had boarders that have up and left the horse at the stable never to come back and have left outstanding bills on top of it. This contract protects you in this situation and gives you the legal right to hold the horse until all bills have been paid. In the worst case scenario you will be able to sell the horse to recoup your finances as long as you go through the proper steps according to the laws of your state. I would always first contact your attorney if you find yourself in this situation and he will be able to tell you what steps you need to take if you decide to pursue further action against the client.

13. Property in Storage on Stable's Premises.

Owner may store certain tack and equipment on the premises of Stable at no additional charge to Owner. However, Stable shall not be responsible for the theft, loss, damage or disappearance of any tack or equipment or other property stored at Stable as same is stored at the Owner's risk. Stable shall not be liable for the theft, loss, damage, or disappearance of any tack or equipment taken to horse shows or clinics. Vehicles and horse trailers stored upon the premises will be subject to a $_____/day storage fee.

We do not charge our boarders to keep their horse trailer at our barn. I know there are a few places in the area that do and that is a personal business choice. I can truthfully say we have never had a problem with theft at our farm and I am proud of that. Usually what happens when something turns up missing is that the owner has misplaced it. You just want to be protected in case you do all of a sudden have a problem with theft at your barn.

14. Inherent Risks and Assumption of Risk.

The undersigned acknowledges there are inherent risks associated with equine activities such as described below, and hereby expressly assumes all risks associated with participating in such activities. The inherent risks include, but are not limited to the propensity of equines to behave in ways such as, running, bucking, biting, kicking, shying, stumbling, rearing, falling or stepping on, that may result in an injury, harm or death to persons on or around them; the unpredictability of equine's reaction to such things as sounds, sudden movement and unfamiliar objects, persons or other animals; certain hazards such as surface and subsurface conditions; collisions with other animals; the limited availability of emergency medical care; and the potential of a participant to act in a negligent manner that may contribute to injury to the participant or others, such as failing to maintain control over the animal or not acting with such participant's ability.

Basically the client is agreeing that they understand all the risks involved with horses under all circumstances. When you are designing your contract you want to make sure you cover all areas when it comes to the risks involved and make sure you have your lawyer look at this.

Over the years since we have been open we have had an ambulance at our barn two times and three other times we had had to take riders to the emergency room for injuries. They all were fine but it still is peace of mind when you have a signed contract in place.

Owner also understands that they MUST WEAR A HELMET at all times while riding a horse if under 18 years of age.

Any and all riders other than Owner MUST SIGN a Release of Liability PRIOR to riding.

Owner also understands that APPROPRIATE RIDING SHOES MUST BE WORN while riding. To clarify, appropriate riding shoes must have heels. Riding in tennis shoes is not allowed.

These last sentences are pretty easy to understand and pretty straight forward. I know a lot of barns do not make kids wear helmets and that is their choice. Remember that I am sharing a little of what our contract contains. You can design yours with any rules you would like.

One of the last paragraphs in our contract reads;

UNDER WISCONSIN LAW, AN EQUINE PROFESSIONAL IS NOT LIABLE FOR AN INJURY TO OR THE DEATH OF A PARTICIPANT IN EQUINE ACTIVITIES RUSULTING FROM THE INHERENT RISKS OF EQUINE ACTIVITIES. Wis. Stat. s 895.481

You are going to want to find out exactly what the correct wording is for your state when it comes to liability and injury or death.

Our barn contract has gone through modifications over the years and you will want to make one that fits your facility. I really wanted you to see what some of the core elements are that you will want in your contract if you are taking care of other people's horses. If you are training or breeding besides boarding horses then you will have more to include in your contract regarding those parts of the business. If you do it correctly in the beginning it will save you time and money in the long run.

EMERGENCY INFORMATION FORM

Here is a sample of what my form looks like. You can modify yours to whatever works best for your stable.

Vinland Stables LLC Boarder & Horse Information Form:

Personal Information

Name _____

Address_____

City_____ State _____ Zip _____

Phone H _____ W _____ C _____

Emergency Contact C_____

Horse Identification

Horse Name _____ DOB _____

Breed-_____ Color-_____

Sex-_____

Distinctive Markings_____

Date of Arrival-_____

Date of Departure-_____

Veterinarian Information

1st Choice-_____ Phone_____

2nd Choice-_____ Phone_____

Additional Information/Services Desired

_____

You can add as much information to your emergency form as you would like. Each one will look a little different depending on what kind of operation or business you are running. If you are a trainer or breeder then you will want extra information that would be important to breeding or training.

One more thought-when you have a client that is filling out one of your forms, make sure they give you at least two contact numbers. I have been in a couple of situations over the years where I had a sick horse and when I went to call the owner all I had was one number and I couldn't get hold of the owner at all. I really needed a second person to contact but didn't have one. Now I always make sure I have a second person to get hold of incase the owner is out of town or doesn't answer their phone. Be prepared for the unexpected because it will happen.

LIABILITY WAIVER

A liability waiver is a legal document that a person who participates in an activity may sign to acknowledge the risks involved in his or her participation.

When writing up your liability waiver you will want to make sure you have your lawyer look at it to make sure you are fully covered for your State of operation. Each State will have some modifications so if you print one off the internet make sure it is for the state you are doing business in.

I keep our liability waivers in the lounge so that people coming to our facility can find them right away and sign them before they go into the barn.

~29~
TRAINERS AT OUR BARN

During our first couple of years boarding horses we were consumed with many new problems that needed solving. One of the newest problems we were starting to have to deal with involved trainers and boarders. I bet I caught your attention now!

Because we were a brand new boarding stable we didn't have an established trainer at our barn. I am not a trainer and I will never be a trainer. I am very happy with cleaning stalls and managing a barn. I wanted a barn that allowed the boarders to choose who they wanted to take lessons from. I thought this would be a very positive thing for our barn because many barns in our area do not allow you to bring in your own trainer. Most of the barns in our area are owned by the trainer and they make their living from their lesson program. I am sure this is common in all parts of the world and I completely understand the reason if you are the barn owner/trainer combined. It is purely a smart business decision and that is how trainers make their money.

For David and me it would only benefit us to have trainers here helping our boarders. I truly believe we should always be learning and growing and guidance is a very good thing. We opened our business and in came many trainers. We had only been open eight or nine months and problems were already happening. Because we had many different riding disciplines and philosophies on training and riding, I was getting calls from different boarders that were upset because they didn't understand what a particular trainer was doing to a horse in the arena. Sometimes it would be that a boarder thought the trainer was too harsh with the horse. Other times I would get calls that the trainer was taking up too much of the arena or asking people to wait out in the stall area until they were done. The issues started to escalate from there.

First of all we have a huge arena and there is plenty of room for two trainers and several horses to be in the arena at the same time. I found myself spending too much time trying to talk to these trainers and come up with a solution on how we could all share the arena. I needed to come up with a list of what was allowed during lessons and what was expected from the trainers. I was also having a big problem with trainers not following the regular rules of our barn. I actually had one trainer that would use other people's tack without their permission and then forget to put it back! Also they needed to know this was not their barn and they didn't make the rules. I was very willing to listen to them and find a way to make it work for everyone but I was dealing with some very strong personalities and during that first couple of years I was very intimidated by them. They were used to giving instructions not taking instructions. During my first conflicts with a few trainers, I would write up new notes for them and at one point it got so bad with a trainer that he started showing everyone my notes and making a joke of it. That was extremely upsetting. I could not figure out how it got so bad at my barn so quickly. I had to learn fast how to be the business owner and not the door mat.

TRAINERS NOT DOING THEIR JOB

Another problem I was dealing with was an upset boarder because she had paid so much money to a particular trainer to work with her horse and the trainer was not coming out or when she did she hardly did anything. We also had trainers that were telling clients that they were here at the barn on certain days working with their horse and charging them for it and David and I knew they had never even come to the barn on those days. Sometimes we wouldn't see the trainer for a couple of weeks but they were charging the client for it.

I know some of you are wondering why I even got involved with all of this. First of all it is hard not to get involved when the boarder comes to you and ask how many times you have seen the trainer. I was not going to lie and I wasn't going to stand there and say nothing. That to me is just as bad. This was all new and unexpected for me and this was not the way I wanted our barn to run. David and I felt it was a bad reflection on us and what we believed in if we let this dishonesty continue.

The worst part was about to come. As the barn owner I wanted an honest barn with an honest reputation. I learned real fast how much power a trainer can have in a barn and how they can very fast set the tone for the barn. Because our boarders were so dependent on their trainer and didn't see the problems that David and I were seeing, if we were to question a trainer or even ask them to leave we would risk losing boarders that would follow with them. Eventually this did happen. It was another very low point for me and the stress was more than I could imagine. We lost boarders and money all because of what a trainer wasn't doing and we wouldn't allow at our barn.

The Seeds of Transformation

Looking back, I have to say it was a life lesson and I believe one of the seeds of transformation for David and me into business owners. It was very painful but I don't think we would have grown or learned anything if we didn't go through those trials. If I had to do it all over again, I would handle the situation with the trainers back then much differently. There were many times in the beginning of our business where I let the trainer run the barn and I was too intimidated to stand firm on how things should run in my barn. If you run an honest business with honest and positive trainers then your barn will earn a great reputation. I have seen so many people ripped off from lazy trainers that do not spend the time with a horse that they should and still take the full payment. I never realized there would be issues at all with trainers but there were and I am sure if you start your horse business you will come across some of these situations right from the start. Don't be afraid to stand your ground for your boarders, for yourself and for the reputation of your business.

I have learned not to be a door mat and it opened doors for a wonderful trainer to come to our barn and make this her home. She has been here for years now and it has been a blessing. We still and always will allow other trainers to come and work with their clients and it always seems to work out just fine. We don't have any of the drama we used to and now I am not afraid to talk with a perspective trainer coming into our barn for the first time and let them know what we expect here at our barn. I am also not afraid to ask them to leave if I need to.

Charging a Trainer Fee

I have had many other barn owners ask me over the years if I charge the trainers a fee to work out of our barn. The answer to that is no. I never have and I don't ever plan on it. There is only one exception to this. I believe that the boarders should not have to pay extra to have a lesson at the place they board and if I charged the trainer to give lessons out of my barn for our boarders then it would automatically trickle down to the boarder. Without a good trainer and lessons, I believe there would be many more accidents on and off the horse.

The only time I charge a lesson fee is when the trainer that is working out of my barn has a client that trailers in or comes in for a riding lesson on a lesson horse. If they do not board at our barn then they pay an arena fee. I have always charged a five dollar flat fee for this but I am sure it will vary depending on where you live. Without having a good trainer at your barn your job as barn owner or manager will become much harder because you will always have boarders that need help. I believe it is a win/win situation for everyone involved.

One last thought. If you find a trainer that has the same philosophy about the care of horses and clients and you both respect each other, they are worth their weight in gold! I think one of the biggest assets a boarding barn can have is a good trainer. If you find one don't lose them.

~30~
BARN AND ARENA RULES

Setting up barn rules is really not a fun subject to talk about but if you run a barn you will need them. When I had boarded my horses out in California many years ago, I don't ever remember receiving a copy of barn rules. Once in a while you would see a sign posted about this or that but never any formal rules. I had not even thought about barn rules until a friend of mine had mentioned it a few months before we were to open our doors. I thought to myself, what could possibly go wrong at our barn? This is another part of the book where I give you permission to laugh! I would be laughing after reading this paragraph also.

Because we had only two boarders before we opened our business, if there was something that needed to be addressed, I would simply just go up to that person and we would talk about it. It really never happened. Things were about to change in a huge way and I was not prepared for this part of barn management.

I decided I would type up a sheet of barn rules that I thought would be important for boarders to know and pass it out to every new person at our barn. I can remember sitting at the kitchen table trying to think of rules. I was blank. I could only think of a few at the time.

Here were a few of the ones I thought of for my first set of barn rules:

No Smoking on the premises

Please keep off the grass if it has rained a lot.

No dogs allowed in barn at all.

Please wear correct footwear when riding.

Riders under the age of 18 must wear a helmet at all times when riding

As you can see it was pretty short! I made copies and passed them out to each new boarder that came to our barn. I thought that would be enough and everything would go as planned and everyone would follow the rules. I was in for another new life lesson!

We were well into our first year of business and we were excited about our barn and had great boarders. Then problems started to occur in the barn in many different areas. We had a brand new barn and we were so proud of it and wanted to keep it clean. It was very hard for me and even harder for David when we would walk into the barn and find horse manure left in the aisle way and the boarder was in the arena riding and never bothered to clean up after their horse. This also became a problem in our arena. Manure was left everywhere. We were having problems with people putting their horse in someone else's clean stall while they cleaned their own. Then they wouldn't clean up the other stall or top off the water after their horse had drank half the bucket. We would have kids running up and down the aisle yelling and spooking horses. People were not cleaning the wash stall after they used it and it would be a disaster for the next person to use. These were just a few of the things I was dealing with. What made my life even more stressful was that I was getting phone calls from boarders complaining about what each other was doing.

Now understand not everyone did this. Most of the boarders were great and cleaned up after themselves but it only takes a few people to ruin it for everyone else. No one wants to put their horse in a crosstie area with a bunch of manure, mud and hair on the ground for you and your horse to step in. I also did not want to be the clean-up police. This was even harder for David because he likes everything clean and in its place so he was shocked at how people often left our barn a mess.

Keeping everything in its place will help keep your barn clean and safe.

We also started having problems with safe riding in the arena and what was allowed and appropriate. We decided we were going to write up "Safe Riding Rules." Again I had to go into unfamiliar territory as a barn owner. It was a whole new learning experience being on this side of the fence. Because we had so many people coming from different barns and stables, their idea of arena rules were much different depending on their previous experiences at other facilities. We were going to have to decide what we wanted for our arena rules.

I realize now everyone has a different idea of what is clean and appropriate in a barn and also what is okay to do in a barn. The margin is extremely wide on practices that have been allowed in stables and practices that are not allowed. I have never found two barns that are alike. **You might find some similarities but you will find more differences if you look close enough.**

I was going to need to rewrite our barn rules and make them much more specific. My list of barn rules all of a sudden became much longer. I no longer could leave it up to the boarder to decipher what was appropriate and what was not. I had to be extremely clear. There was not going to be any reading between the lines.

OUR FIRST BARN MEETING

This was very hard for me because I didn't want to become a drill sergeant and I didn't want people to think we had too many rules. I wanted it to be a casual and fun atmosphere at our barn and I was trying desperately to find a balance. It was much harder than I thought.

Over the last few years when I have talked to other barn owners, many have always used that expression, "It is my way or the highway." I didn't want to have that attitude but we needed to have rules and I wanted the boarders to understand why we had the rules we did. All I could do at the time was hope that each boarder would understand why we put so many rules in place. If they didn't understand or didn't agree with the rules then this probably was not the right barn for them.

We decided to have our first "barn meeting." Because our business was so young and we were all of a sudden making so many changes in the first year, we thought it would be better to have a meeting with everyone and explain our vision for the barn and our rules and goals and this way they could ask us any questions they might have. It was also a great way for our boarders to get to know David and me better since none of them knew us at all when they decided to move their horse to our barn. The response was great. We had almost everyone that boarded at our barn come to the meeting (which was held in our indoor arena) and I believe it was a very positive experience for everyone. I had many people tell me that they had never been to a barn that took the time to have a barn meeting and they really appreciated it.

If you are going to run a large facility then I would recommend having a barn meeting every once in a while. It's a great way for everyone to get together and it will make your clients feel important and feel like they are part of something. I valued the input people gave at our meeting and used many of the ideas that were suggested. It was definitely good for our business.

Now years later, our barn rules are much longer and I think very appropriate for our facility. I have to update them every now and then but for the most part they have stayed the same. I have had on a couple of occasions had a boarder that complained because they thought we had too many rules. They usually leave and find a barn that better suited them and I am perfectly fine with that. I truly believe you have to find the right barn that best works for your needs. If you want a barn with fewer rules I am sure there are plenty of them out there. If you want a barn with more structure then our barn as well as other barns might be the right barn for you. I have learned that in the boarding business it never stays the same and horses and clients will come and go and it is okay. I want people at our barn that truly want to be here. I don't want to be a last resort because everything else is filled up. I want to be their first choice. We will always strive for that.

Whether you are planning on building a small barn or a large barn like we did, rules are so important to keep everyone safe and easier for the barn owner and manager. If you build on a small scale you probably won't need as many rules but if you have forty horses like we have here, it can get pretty crazy in a minute and that is when accidents happen. We set our goals high even though I know with horses nothing is one hundred percent perfect but we keep trying.

Vinland Stables Barn Rules

Here is a list of our barn rules and arena rules we have had over the years to give you some ideas and a place to start. It truly all depends on the type of barn you have and size plays an important role in it also. At the end of the day you have to do what works best for your business. This is just to give you some ideas.

Vinland Stables Barn Rules
1. No Smoking on the premises

I have found out that you will need to be very direct and cover all areas with your barn rules. Even with the rule of no smoking on the premises, you don't know how many times I have found cigarette butts on the ground on our farm and even once in the barn. Always remember that 99% percent of the people that come to your farm will follow the rules but there will always be that one percent that you will have to talk to.

2. No Dogs allowed in the barn at all. You may bring your dog out to the farm and walk them but they need to stay on a leash.

To this day I still have someone once in a while bring their dog into the barn. Many horse facilities don't have a problem with this and that is great. I just found out early on it was much easier to have "no dogs" in the barn at all because some people's dogs are never around horses and it can become a safety hazard very fast. You will need to find out what you feel comfortable with when it comes to dogs and your horse stable.

3. Riders under the age of 18 must wear a helmet at all times.

This is definitely a personal preference but you will want to check with your business insurance carrier. Our insurance agent let us know right from the start that we needed helmets for kids under 18.

4. Correct Footwear with a heel must be worn while riding. No Sandals or tennis shoes at all while riding.

You might think that this would not be an issue but it has been an issue many times. I have seen trainers in the past come to teach lessons in flip flops! I have also had to talk to a boarder once in a while because they would come to ride in closed toe sandals with no heel. It is a very hard decision to make when I finally decide to talk to a boarder. The kids are always easiest to talk to then the adults when it comes to footwear. With the kids I can tell them the rules and they need to put boots on and it is over. When I have had to talk to another adult, I have found it uncomfortable because they are usually around the same age as me and it can be very hard to remind a boarder and friend of the rules. We will talk more about this later in the book.

5. No Running or yelling in barn at all, as this could spook a horse.

It may seem like a no brainer but you need to have this in your rules and you will find yourself reminding kids about this from time to time.

6. Observe barn hours:

Winter hours: September 1ˢᵗ–May 31ˢᵗ -8am to 8pm

Summer hours: June 1ˢᵗ–August 31ˢᵗ -8am to 9pm

Barns all have different hours of operation depending on each owner's situation. You will be able to design your hours to what best works for you. Be prepared because if you don't have the barn hours in your barn rules, you might find people at your barn during all hours of the day or night! If you are okay with that then that is great but if you want to have barn hours then you need to put them in your rules.

Just for an example - I know one barn in the area that is open until 9pm every day but is closed at 7pm on Sundays year round.

7. All Friends/Visitors must sign a waiver release form prior to riding on the property.

You will want to have liability waivers in a place where visitors can get to them easily and sign them before they go into the barn.

8. Absolutely no riding in any stable aisle ways.

We have this rule because we have cement aisle ways in both of our barns and we have had people try to ride their horse in the aisle way with horses in crossties which is dangerous. You might not need this rule depending on how your stable is set up.

9. Never leave your horse unattended in crossties.

Horses and crossties can be an accident waiting to happen if the horse panics or spooks and gets turned around. I encourage you to make it a rule that a horse is never left unattended in crossties in case something happens.

10. Never tie your horse to any stall grills at all. The ring on the back wall of each stall is for tying your horse. If you tie your horse to a stall grill and they pull and bend it, you will be responsible for paying for the repair and replacement of the damaged grill.

I have this rule because I have walked into so many barns over the years and you see lots of badly bent stall grills due to a horse pulling back when tied to the stall. Remember, your stalls cost you a lot of money and you want them to last a very long time. Boarders will come and go but your stalls will still be there and if they look terrible because of years of damage it will decrease the value of your barn.

Simple rules like this will help keep your stalls and barn looking great for many years to come. I have had many people comment on how nice our stalls look even after all these years. I truly believe it is because we don't allow people to tie their horses to the stall grills. Your stalls will already take a beating from horses living in them. Why add to it by having bent grills that look terrible and decrease the value of your barn.

11. If you get your horse out from the paddocks or pasture, please make sure all gates are securely locked.

You wouldn't think you need this rule but you will! You will need help create this good habit to get into so horses don't get out.

12. Clean up after your horse, BEFORE YOU RIDE. This includes sweeping up the crosstie areas and placing the sweepings in the muck bucket. Clean up ALL manure in arenas after use. We have a great barn and lets all work together to keep it clean.

The reason I have this rule of sweeping up your mess before you ride is for the courtesy of the next person that wants to use the cross-tie area. No one wants to tie up their horse in a filthy area and have to step in another horse's mud, hair and manure. I will tell you right now that if you don't put this rule into your program then you will have people that don't sweep up.

When you have your business you will find clients that keep everything very clean and are wonderful and then you will have clients that are messy and never sweep up until they are told that they need to. It just comes with the territory so make your life easier right from the start. It truly does make it nicer for the next person using the crosstie area and it will make your job much easier. It can get very old cleaning up after people day after day. This simple rule really works to help keep the barn clean.

13. Adult supervision required for all young children at all times.

This is important! You are going to have parents that will drop off their young child and then go and run errands. You will also have some parents that are at the barn but are not watching their very young children and that is when things can happen. You will need to decide at what age a child can be left alone at your stable.

14. If you deworm your horse please make sure to clean up any droppings of wormer that may fall to the floor. It is toxic to dogs. If your horse is not good when it comes to deworming then please deworm them in their stall.

A lot of your clients will not be good with deworming their horse and some of them will not know how to do this. That is when you will find dewormer all over the place. If a boarder is learning how to deworm their horse or the horse is difficult to deworm then I would have them do it in their stall. And yes it is toxic to dogs!

15. Do not put your horse in another person's stall without that persons consent. If your horse messes in the stall or drinks the water, clean the stall and fill up the water bucket. Leave the stall just like you found it.

Believe or not I had a problem with this a few years ago. I would come out to the barn and find a horse in a different stall than the one that was assigned to them. I really never did understand why a person wouldn't use their own stall but for some reason they would use other stalls and then leave without cleaning it. This soon became a problem in the barn because the person who was leasing the stall would come out to the barn and find a dirty stall. I had to put a stop to this fast.

16. During spring when your horse is shedding or if you are clipping your horse please put all hair (if a lot) in trash can back in grain room. If you have just a little hair it can be put in muck bucket. Do not use trash cans in tack rooms or lounge at all.

This may not be an issue at your stable but I had a problem with people putting horsehair in our tack room garbage cans which mice love! They would use it to make nest. I found it is better to have a designated garbage can or muck bucket for horsehair.

17. Clean the wash stall immediately after you are finished using it. Be sure to sweep up all debris and put into muck buckets to prevent clogged drains. You also must empty the drain of all hair and mud. If water gets out into the aisle, take a broom and brush back towards the drain. Please make sure water is turned OFF after use.

Some of these rules might seem like no brainers but let me tell you that if you don't put it down in your rules then it won't get done. Over the years we have had our wash stall flood two times and had water back up into our bathroom toilet and shower because boarders were not cleaning the drain after each use. We have had to call a plumber out once already and it was the weekend! That was not cheap. It is amazing how much hair and dirt can come off of one horse and now you multiply it by many horses and you will have problems. It is much easier to get everyone to start cleaning up right after each use then to try to fix the problem later.

18. Wash Stall & Mud - If your horse has a lot of mud on his legs because the paddocks are muddy, please use the hose outside to wash the mud off. After most of the mud is off then you can use the wash stall. This will help keep the drain from clogging.

This is a good protocol to have during the wet and muddy season when the horse's legs are muddy.

19. When bringing horses into the barn from paddocks please stay on path especially in spring and fall. If you walk horse on the grass when the ground is soft it will tear it all up.

We have this rule of walking horses on paths because in the spring and fall it is very muddy at our farm and people will try to avoid the mud by walking their horse on the grass. I will come out to the barn and find the grass all torn up. If you want your lawn to stay nice then you will want to have some of these simple rules in place. Your boarders may not be thrilled with this rule but it is all part of having horses and a good pair of muck boots will do the trick!

20. Turn off the lights if you are the last one to leave the barn. Helping conserve electricity will help keep fees down.

You are going to feel like you are repeating yourself often especially in the beginning when you are trying to get everyone in the habit of turning off the lights. You will have to send out a few reminders but stay consistent and eventually most of your boarders will make this a great habit to get into.

Now that you have read a few of our barn rules and why we have them, I hope it gives you some ideas of what you would want to have in place for rules at your facility. Every horse boarding stable will have different rules depending on what works best for them. With this many horses and people, if you don't have rules, things can get out of hand in just one day. Remember that, at the end of the day it all falls back on you and if you want a little less stress in your life then you might want to think about barn rules for your stable that work for you and your family.

One more thought - if a boarder leaves because they feel you have too many rules then they probably were not the right boarder for your barn anyway. Once you are established, the right people will come to your barn and will stay because they like the way you run your facility and they like the rules.

VINLAND STABLES ARENA RULES

We decided to have a separate list of Rules for Safe Riding and Arena Etiquette. We realized very quickly that people were coming from all different places to our barn to board their horse and it became crazy and unsafe at times in the arena. We had people that had never boarded before and had no idea about safe riding practices with others and had never had to share an arena with someone else. Our arena is very large and once in a while we still have near collisions because someone isn't watching where they are riding. Even a couple of times through the years we have had riders get into arguments in the arena about space and riding. I know it is hard to believe but it happens. It was time we needed to get arena rules in place.

Here are a few rules we have to get you thinking about your arena rules. This is just a starting place for you to decide what you would like to have for arena rules.

1. When entering the INDOOR ARENA, be sure to announce your entrance WELL BEFORE you enter the arena. Call out "COMING IN" and listen for a reply. Riders inside the arena will say, "OK" or "STOP, WAIT A MINUTE." Do not enter until you have heard a reply.

Believe it or not we have had two accidents over the years where a person had just walked right in the arena without saying anything at the same time that a horse and rider were coming by. The horse spooked, jumped to the side and the rider fell off. This happened because the person coming into the arena did not announce to anyone that they were there at the door way.

2. Lunging Horses-Only two horses are allowed to be lunged at a time in the arena. If you come in and two horses are already being lunged you will need to wait until one is done. Also, please be aware of where you are lunging your horse. If other people are already riding or having a lesson and you come in, please ask them "Where would be a good area to lunge my horse?"

When horses are being lunged they take up a lot of area in an arena with the lunge line and it makes it very hard for people to ride around them. Please communicate with each other.

3. The INSIDE of the arena is toward the center. The OUTSIDE is by the wall.

4. When passing another rider from behind and they are close to the wall, ALWAYS pass on the inside (not between the rider and the wall). When meeting another rider coming toward you, pass so your LEFT shoulders meet.

These may seem like simple riding practices and you might even think riders will automatically ride this way. That is not the case. When riders are out in the arena they are concentrating on their horse and not paying attention to what is going on around them much of the time. Sometimes we can have five or six horses in the arena at the same time and the riders really need to pay attention to where they are riding. These simple rules help keep everyone safe.

5. Please let other riders know if you are going to be traveling across the diagonal of the arena or need to do lateral exercises on the wall. Communication is key.

6. Stop your horse and stand still whenever a rider is having trouble controlling their horse.

7. Do not stop in the line of travel of another rider. If you need to stop/dismount, please make sure it is clear in both directions.

8. Please be sure to talk to each other. We are all equal in this arena and are all here to help one another. The best thing to do if you are unsure is to ask.

When writing up your Safe Riding Rules much of it will depend on the disciplines and styles of riding you have in your barn. If your barn is a hunter/jumper barn then you will most likely have added rules for jumping. The same would also apply for speed horses. Your rules will change a little depending on disciplines but the core safe riding practices will stay the same no matter what type of barn you have. I hope these few examples I have given you will help you with the foundation of what you want for your barn.

~31~
THE MULTI-DISCIPLINE BARN

Having a multi-discipline horse barn was the type of boarding barn I wanted when we decided to start our business. I loved the idea of having many different breeds and styles of riding all at the same facility. I really enjoy going to many different types of horse shows to see how other people ride and compete in different riding disciplines and I always leave with a great appreciation. I find that I am always learning something new when I watch a different discipline other than the ones I am familiar with. I never dreamed it could cause any problems in a boarding barn as was the case for our barn.

At our barn we have a wonderful group of riders. We have people that trail ride, ride western, english, hunter jumper, saddle seat, dressage, driving horses and lots of youngsters (I mean young horses that are not broke yet). We have many people that show and people that don't but love to come and watch and support the ones that do at the local horse shows. The same would go for the breeds. We have everything from Miniature Horses to Quarter Horses and Warm Bloods and everything in-between.

As I am writing this chapter, I can with confidence tell you that our barn runs very smoothly now with all these types of breeds and styles of riding but it wasn't like that in the beginning when we opened. We were so lucky to be completely full when we opened our doors and I rented each stall out as a first come first serve basis. I would always ask the person that was coming for a tour what kind of horse they had and what discipline of riding they did but after that I never gave it another thought. I had boarded my horses at barns back in California that had all different styles of riding and as a boarder I loved it. There never seemed to be any problems back then and I could not see any problems in the future here at Vinland Stables.

Complaints and More Complaints

We were in the middle of our first year of business here in Wisconsin and because the winters are so cold the only place for anyone to ride is the indoor arena and ours was used heavily. We have a huge arena and even with all the room we started to have problems among the boarders. I was starting to get complaints about how the dressage people needed the entire arena to practice their tests and the saddle seat rider's only road on the rail and the western and hunt seat riders were all over the place. There were riders that wanted to practice patterns and then of course I had the carts and horses that seemed to cause a frenzy among a few. There were people that wanted to set up a trail course and they were frustrated when others wanted to set up jumps to jump!

Now I am exaggerating a small bit but these were real complaints that I was getting from a handful of people that I had never thought of as a barn owner and now all of a sudden I had to deal with it. On top of it came the different personalities of the people. Some of our boarders had strong assertive personalities and opinions on this subject and others kept very quiet and were not happy. I was not prepared for handling these kinds of issues. I was going to learn very fast.

During that first year I spent much time talking with boarders and working out ways for everyone to get along and ride together. I had boarders that would not ride if a horse was pulling a cart in the arena. If the horse and cart would come in the arena and they were riding they would leave or tell the person driving to wait until they were done riding. That became very stressful dealing with both parties. I believed that it was good for a horse to get use to all different types of equipment and that included carts and I needed to be a strong barn owner and talk to the boarder that was having issues. I know now this wouldn't be an issue but back then I let people turn little issues into big issues. A huge part of it was people understanding each other and learning to speak up and learning to share the arena. Communication was the most important part of the whole equation and it did take a long time to smooth out. Understanding each other's disciplines for some boarders that had never seen any other style of riding other then what they rode was something they needed to do in order to make it work.

During the first year or two of our business we did lose boarders that felt it was not the right barn for them and wanted to go to a barn that strictly did the discipline that they rode. I respected their decision to do that. Other wonderful people came in and as new potential boarders would come to tour our barn I had learned to explain to them what type of barn we had and make sure they understood that we had horses that pulled carts and horses that jumped and everything in-between. I wanted potential boarders to think about it before they gave notice at the place they were currently boarding at.

Not All Disciplines Work

I also now have learned how to tell a person coming for a tour that this is probably not the right barn for them if they do speed events. I love watching speed events but we have a general purpose arena and it is too shallow for reining horses or speed horses and I don't want a horse getting hurt here at our barn because the footing was not good for what the owner was doing with the horse. I have found it so much better to be up front with potential boarders.

A few years back we designated a block of time on Sundays for a couple of our boarders to set up a full jump course if they wanted. That worked out very well and they could practice jumping a full course. During those times when they would jump others would come to watch and ride afterwards. I have learned to be very flexible and realize that from year to year you will have more of one discipline than another but I try my hardest to make everyone feel important here at our barn. We still have a great diversity of riding styles and it works! What makes it work more than anything is the great communication between boarders and respect for each other's style of riding. We did not have that for the first couple of years and now that we do the atmosphere is much better in the barn.

A multi-discipline barn is not for everyone but for me and my family I wouldn't have it any other way. I think our boarders would agree also. Variety is the spice of life!

~32~
Extra Charges for Services Done

We were moving right along through our first couple of years in business and another area I had not thought much about was the extra charges for services done beyond our regular boarding agreement. I knew there would be a few services I might charge extra for but for the most part I gave it very little thought. As I was remembering back to when I boarded my horses, I don't ever remember asking the barn owners to administer medications or blanket my horse or even hold my horse for the farrier. I was always there to do those things and I really never paid attention to what other boarders did.

Before I knew it I was doing all kinds of extra services. I started to realize fast that it was taking up a lot of my time and even at times putting me behind on other chores. I started looking at how other boarding barns handled extra services and then I needed to decide what I was going to do at our barn. This was another one of those areas that I found out every barn does differently.

One of the biggest factors that play a role in extra services provided from a barn is how much a barn is charging for boarding to begin. Another key to the equation is to decide if your barn is a full service barn or not. We clearly did not charge enough at our barn for it to be a full service barn but I couldn't keep doing all these time-consuming services anymore without being compensated for it. This put me in an awkward position because we didn't start off charging for many extra services. Again I was not prepared for this part of owning a business.

Charging for Services

One day I started writing down on a piece of paper what services I thought I needed to charge for. I came up with a list and then I had to come up with a price for each service. This was very hard for me and looking back I am sure I did not charge enough but I had to start somewhere.

Our board rate is not the highest in the area but it is not the lowest either. We are on the higher side and that also made it harder for me to charge for extras. I didn't want people to leave simply because they couldn't afford it. Finding a balance in the beginning can be extremely challenging and to this day I sometimes still have a hard time charging someone for something they needed done, especially if it is a medical emergency. With each situation I have to look at what is going on and my time involved in the whole thing. There have been a few times that I have not charged for medical emergencies even though I may have been with the horse for a few hours. My heart always goes out to the owner and the horse when this happens. This I know is a situation where sometimes my business sense goes out the window. If I were to give advice to someone about charging for medical services I would tell them to charge a fee but find a balance. It takes years of learning through each situation and how you want to handle emergencies and your time and fees.

I found out very fast during the first year that putting on and taking off blankets is very time consuming and whether you have five horses or twenty-seven horses that need blankets put on, you have just added a lot of extra work and time to your day. This was a service we decided to charge for in the beginning but I had no idea what to charge. I know my fees in the beginning were too low for the amount of work I was doing. I also added to the list a holding fee for the farrier if I needed to be out there because the owner could not be. I don't charge for simple medicating in the morning or afternoon but if I need to do any medicating during the day then we charge. Other services we would charge for were a walking fee, hosing fee, bandaging fee and private turnout. When I was done writing up my list for the boarders it really was not that long.

I typed up a letter explaining the changes here at our barn and why we made these changes regarding services and handed out a copy to everyone. Because I was making so many new changes in the first year or two of our new business I knew people were not happy. Deep down inside I waited for people to give their notice because I figured they were going to be upset enough to leave.

Looking back I really was running a business purely on emotion that first couple of years which is very dangerous. You make poor decisions when you base it on emotion. I was learning every day on the job how to be a business owner and it was rough most of the time. We did have many people leave the first couple of years because of all the changes we were making and I had to deal with it and move on. I now can understand years later how they were annoyed at all the changes because that is not what we offered when we opened. We made promises we couldn't keep. It was painful to watch horses and people leave but again we were so blessed to have wonderful new horses to fill the stalls and with those horses came nice people. It was a big learning curve to say the least.

One of the biggest things I had never realized before we opened was how long everything took with a barn this size. And with any added chore or service it could really make it an even longer day. Because we didn't have employees at all we needed to do all those extra services ourselves and now I know the saying is true, time is money in the business world. To some people it might sound harsh or cold but it is just a business reality. I also can't be out in the barn twenty-four hours a day. Sometimes it is hard for people to understand that.

Over the years I have modified our extra charges a few times. In fact I am in the middle of changing it again. During the early years our list of services we charged for became very long. Now years later I am actually taking a couple of things out that I don't feel I need to charge for. It is always changing and you have to be willing to change with it. I have learned now it never stays completely the same and often change can be a good thing.

One of the most important things I want you to remember as you start your boarding stable is the fact you can't please everyone. If a boarder doesn't like the charges be prepared because they might let you know it and it is okay. Let them share how they feel but in the end you need to do what is best for you and your business and if you are exhausted or miss an appointment you might of had because you have been walking a horse for two hours then you should be compensated for it. If you want to do that service for free that is completely up to you. Remember that if you offer services for free then you will be asked to do many extra things. If you charge for extra services then you will find out that you will be asked a lot less and you will make money for the services you do perform. You have the wonderful choice to design your horse business any way you like. Just don't let it burn you out like it almost did for David and me. It's your business and running it like a business will keep you in control of your time and your life!

I have written up a sample list of our "Extra Charges" that we have for our barn. I am giving you a list of what we have done throughout the years. It is just to give you some ideas and each barn will be different. Always remember that what you start out with most likely will change down the road. Be open to change and always remember that it is a business and time is money. You need to have a life also.

If I am going to be completely honest and tell you that there are some "Extra Services" that I don't want to do at all. It is not worth the money to me. There have been times throughout the years when I have told a boarder that I would not be able to provide the service they wanted and they would need to find someone else that could help them. It almost always works out and they find another boarder that can help them and make a little money on the side.

In some cases depending on the unique situation I might charge extra if I am asked to do something for an extended length of time that is not on my list. It doesn't happen very often but you will want an area on your extra charges for services" sheet that allows for miscellaneous services and TBD *(To Be Determined)* pricing.

I have written down some of the things we charge extra for at our barn. These are just some ideas for you to think about and things that might come up in the future if you are running a boarding stable. Some of these services I have never had to do but a few of them I have done at least three or four times a year. Again, this is just to give you a starting point. Remember that what you start with will most likely change over the years. As your barn grows and evolves so will some of the things that you want to charge the boarder for. There are even a few things we now do for our clients for free that we used to charge for.

Here is a list of things we charge extra for and also I have included things we used to charge for that now we do for free.

VINLAND STABLES EXTRA CHARGES FOR SERVICES
1. Private Turn-Out -$10.00 per week

2. Stall Fans-$10.00 per month. Fan must be approved before it is hung up.

We do not charge for fans anymore. We had always charged each boarder for having a fan up during the hot months because of the electrical cost. I really wasn't sure how much more the electric bill was going to be and I wanted to make sure I was not losing money. After a few years I have realized that it really doesn't take a lot of electricity to keep a fan on so we decided to cancel the fee for fans. We no longer charge for fans and this has been a real positive perk for the boarders. I think they appreciate the fact that we are not trying to nickel and dime them to death.

3. Boots (on/off)-$15.00 per month

4. Blanketing (on/off)-$2.00 per time.

Please note-if we have to put on a blanket or take off a blanket because the straps are broken and we have asked you to fix them and they were not, you will be charged. If your horse gets soaked because of rain and your blanket is not water proof and we have to pull it the charge also applies.

5. Fly Mask (on/off)-50 cents per day.

We don't charge for putting fly mask on anymore. We used to because I envisioned having 27 fly masks to put on each day and I did not want to do that. It turns out only a hand-full of boarders ever ask me to put a fly mask on or take it off. I do let the boarders know that if the fly mask becomes muddy it will be their responsibility to wash it out. I will not put on a muddy fly mask.

6. Holding Fee (Vet/Farrier) -$10.00 per time.

7. Extra Shavings- We charge $5.00 per extra wheelbarrow of shaving.

Every barn does shavings a little different. We use to charge extra and allow the boarder to have extra shavings. We no longer do that because I feel we bed the stalls with plenty of shavings and when it comes down to it, the heavier the stall is bedded the longer it takes to clean it. This is something that is going to be different at each barn. I always make sure our new boarders understand this when they first come to our barn.

The only time we will bed a stall heavier is if the horse is hurt with a leg or hoof injury. Then we will add extra bedding and we do charge the boarder.

8. Giving Dewormer-$10.00 per time

I give the boarder a choice on our deworming program but it must follow what the Veterinarians are recommending as guidelines. I have had boarders that do not want to deworm their horse themselves and prefer me to give the dewormer and I am happy to provide the service for a fee.

Extra Charges for Rehabilitation/lay-up Fees (Veterinarian Prescribed)

1. Simple Medicating-Any medication given at times other than scheduled feedings-$2.00 per time.

2. Walking Fee-$10.00/per walk (10-15 minutes)

3. Hosing Fee-$10.00/per session (10-15 minutes)

4. Bandaging Fee-$2.00 per leg

5. Misc. Fees-TBD depending on service

6. Material, Supplies, Medication Fee-TBD

Again, here are some ideas of what you will be dealing with and what services you might want to charge for. Remember, you can always try something and if it doesn't work or is taking up too much of your time you have the power to change it depending on each situation.

It took us a couple of years to figure out what worked and didn't work. You might find that some request are not worth your time no matter how much you charge. That is when you will need to be honest with the boarder up front and tell them that you don't offer the service at your barn.

A perfect example of this is with our outdoor board. For the horses that are boarded outdoor, we only do grain in the morning. I will feed supplements with grain but it needs to be given in the morning. I have had several people over the years that want their horse grained in the evening and have offered to pay me extra to do this service for them. I could do it and make extra money but it is not worth the money and time to me. I am so busy as it is and I would need to bring the horse into the barn and feed them and then take them back out and I don't want to do that when I am taking care of so many horses. In those times the boarder has always found another person at our barn to feed their horse the grain in the evening. It works out great for the boarder because they get what they want and the person providing the service makes extra money at the same time. It is a win/win situation for everyone.

In most cases they will find someone in the barn to do the service for them if they want to stay at your barn.

~33~
BARN AMENITIES–TRYING TO PLEASE EVERYONE

Be prepared because people will compare barns. Designing my own barn and then building it and watching your dream come true is an unbelievable experience. When we opened our doors David and I couldn't be more proud. We felt we had so much to offer and who wouldn't want to have their horse in a brand new barn! I had much to learn about people.

The people that boarded at our barn for the most part seemed very happy. One of the biggest surprises for me in the first couple of years of having our barn was how quickly boarders would tell me what other barns had for amenities and what we should think of getting in the future. Wow, it caught me off guard and even though they were not trying to hurt me I have to admit it stung a little. I am sure I was just too sensitive but at the time we were trying to please everyone and now I know that is impossible to do.

When we opened for business we had wonderful indoor arena and a small outdoor arena. We have some areas to ride outdoors but not as much as other facilities in the area and we really didn't have trails for trail riding. As time went on I would get a boarder that would ask me now and then when we would get a round pen. We were asked if we would be willing to put up a jump course out in our field. I was starting to feel inadequate about our barn when this was happening and would put pressure on my husband to build and buy the things our clients were asking for. I realize now I put a lot of pressure on him in those early years and it created a lot of stress between us that I couldn't see back then. I should have been proud and satisfied of the amenities we had and build on what we have instead of what we didn't have. Don't get me wrong, it's not bad to grow and add on but it doesn't have to be done overnight and don't borrow to do it.

The second summer we bought a round pen and put it up because we had a few requests for one and we believed it would be an asset. By the third year he had built a huge 100 x 250 outdoor arena on the back part of our property. Now we had two outdoor arenas and I thought that would be enough. Then the next year I was ask if some of our land could be used for an outdoor jump course. I loved the idea but when would we have time to build a jump course and how much would that cost? We were already so much in debt. I was feeling a lot of pressure to give the boarders anything they wanted and that was not a smart way to run a business at all. I think deep down inside I believed if we gave them those amenities they would never leave. Another hard lesson about running a barn and business was quickly coming for me.

Giving False Hope

Another thing I found myself doing was giving the boarders or potential boarders false hope. If they asked me about something we didn't offer at our barn, I would always make it sound like it was going to happen in the future. I was not strong enough to just say we don't offer that here. I wanted to have the all-around ***perfect*** barn and if we did then we would never lose boarders. It is really a stupid way of thinking and a terrible way to run a business. I can remember sitting in my home after a couple of boarders gave their thirty-day notice and wondering why on earth they would leave when we had a brand new facility. I didn't see the big picture back then about people and running a business. I was taking it personally and that was the wrong thing to do. You can't run a healthy business if you are trying to fulfill every desire of a customer at any cost and you can't make it personal.

I have learned so much from those early years. The first thing is you can't please everyone with everything. Such a simple idea and it took me years to learn. The second thing is no matter how nice your place is, people get bored or things always look greener on the other side of the fence. Many clients will leave looking for the perfect barn and that is okay. Sometimes after they leave they come back and realize how good they had it at your barn. I now can be proud of what we have and I am very comfortable with telling people what we have and what we don't offer at our barn. I now will even tell them about other barns that have great trails for trail riding if that is what they are looking for. I want our boarders to be happy and completely satisfied with the amenities we offer and not come to our barn with the false hope that we will build whatever they want in the near future.

SMALLER STABLES ARE NEEDED!!

One last thought-If you are a smaller stable, build on that. Many people are looking for a smaller boarding barn with less people. They want a quieter barn where they can ride with just one or two other riders at a time. That can be a great asset. We have had boarders that come to our barn who were very nice people but after a while they felt our barn was too big and busy for them and they left. I totally respect that and their honesty. Then I get a lot of people who like a big barn and love all the happenings of a big barn and that better suits them.

The horse industry is growing and more and more people are getting horses. I believe there are plenty of people looking for a good caring facility for their horse. Size doesn't matter. Build on great care because that is what matters most. What people want more than anything is to have a place where they don't have to worry about their horse and know they are being taken care of. A barn could have all the amenities in the world but if the care of the horse is not good then what good are all the amenities? Put your personal care as your biggest asset and build off of that. The rest will come in time. Don't push for more stuff like I did in our early years of business. It was bad for business and very hard on my husband and our marriage.

~34~
WHEN THINGS GET BROKEN WHO PAYS?

When David and I had our two ponies and two boarders at our barn, every once in a while you would find something broken. Either a horse would kick and break some wood or one of them would chew on the wood to the point where it needed replacing or even bust a heated water bucket. Occasionally one of them would go through the fence. David would fix whatever was broken and all was good. It was never a big deal. When we went up to forty horses, the things that needed fixing had multiplied many times over! We both could not believe how destructive these beautiful animals could be at times. We were shocked at how often something was getting broken either in the barn or outside. It was so very hard to watch because our barn was brand new and we would walk into the barn and something new would be broken. It's like buying a brand new car and it is perfect and then you get the first ding in it. It really hurts. Now multiply those dings several times over. Not Fun!

Many of the things that have been broken over the years were the boarders fault and of course many times the horses were the culprits. There were also times when we never knew who broke what. We love them but the truth is they are very large animals and all it takes is a little kick, bite or body slam and all of a sudden you are fixing something.

During the first year or so of our new business we did not charge for things that were broken by an owner's horse. After fixing and replacing everything from corner feeders to broken wood in the stall and everything in-between, we realized it was costing us a lot of time, labor and money to fix everything. It was never just a once time deal. It was happening a lot. With this many horses the odds of something getting broken had risen very high and we were fixing fences and replacing items often. We needed to start charging the boarder for these items including time and labor. This was another area where David and I were getting on the job training about running a business.

WHERE DO I START?

I wasn't sure of the best way to start charging our clients in this type of situation so I checked with a few people I knew that boarded at other facilities and asked them how their barn received payment for something that had been damaged from an owner's horse. It was interesting to me that a few of the barns I checked with had different ways of collecting payment. Around our area it was common for barns to charge a deposit when you first bring your horse to their barn, to cover the cost of damages that you would get back when you leave that barn as long as your horse did not do any damage. It would be similar to putting down a cleaning deposit when renting an apartment. Other barns had people pay up front when the damage happened.

I decided for our barn and myself it would be too hard to remember what a horse had done or not done over the course of a couple of years and when it came time to give the owner back their money, it seemed to me like there would be disagreements on what the damage actually was at the time. I know I could keep a log of everything through the stay of each horse and then figure it out but that would be more work for me and I can almost guarantee that the owner of the horse will not remember either. I also didn't want to run into a problem where the owner could not remember and then would disagree with me. I have heard of that happening in other barns and I didn't want this to happen in my barn. Above all else I didn't want the person leaving to be angry over the situation.

I decided for us it would be the easiest to charge the owner at the time it happens and add it on their invoice for the next month. Our invoices are itemized and it would be clear for everyone. It would be fresh in the owners mind and since we started this practice I have never had a person upset about paying us for the item that needed fixing. Usually they feel bad and are very happy to pay. I still to this day have a hard time going up to a boarder and letting them know that their horse broke something and we need to charge them to fix it but it is something that needs to be done and it is all part of running a business.

This is one of those areas that I can gladly say we have never had a problem with if we know which horse did the damage. Now unfortunately there have been quite a few times over the years that we have found something broken and no one has come forward. It is frustrating but it is a part of having a business and we just deal with it.

We have also had situations where a horse has broken something and the boarder will come and fix it themselves or help David fix it. That is wonderful especially if David is gone to his other job and I truly appreciate those boarders that have done that through the years. In those situations I have never charged the boarder unless I had to buy materials.

When you are running your business you need to remember that the boarder will most likely feel terrible that their horse has broken something. Getting upset with them does not fix the problem and in every case will make it worse. If you take the time to discuss the problem with them they will most likely be very happy to do whatever you need done to get the item repaired.

~35~
INVOICES AND BILLING

I wanted to share a little bit about invoices and billing. When we first opened our barn I did everything by hand. I would hand write out the invoices. The time that it took was unbelievable. I didn't know any other way. We were fortunate to have a person at our barn that had a business and they set me up with Quick Books and taught me how to use it. It was one of the best decisions I did. They would come over once a month and teach me how to do my invoices and now that I can do it on my own it saves me hours of time. Quick books can keep track of each invoice and you can itemize for each boarder and make changes at any time. It is very easy to read and also takes care of the sales tax. I would recommend it for anyone that has a small business. I am sure there are other similar computer programs like Quick Books. Find a program that you like and I guarantee it will make your life much easier.

If you have a lot of clients at your farm then find a place where you can put your client's invoices. I put our invoices in each stall pouch so that it is private. If you don't have stall pouches then make a designated spot where the public does not see the invoices and other notes for your clients. I always fold them in half and write their name on the outside. To make it easier for everyone, I have a locked mail box in a **private** room in our lounge where my boarders can drop their board checks and not have to try to find me.

I also believe that every detail of your business including your billing or invoices should look professional. I feel that if you have a printed invoice for each client it makes your business look more professional and stand out. You will have clients that want to keep their invoices for the entire year and some of them might even use them for their horse business and tax write-offs.

If you are going to run a horse business, then run it as professional as you can even when it comes to the paper work. Paying the board or training bill is a private matter to most people. You might not realize this but you are showing the client respect by not leaving their paperwork all over the place for others to see and I believe they will appreciate those little details in how your run your business.

SETTING YOUR RATES AND WHEN TO RAISE THEM

When we were first deciding on what our board rates would be for stall board and outside board we had no idea what all our monthly costs were going to be. I had checked all the barns in our area to see what they offered and charged for board to give me a starting place. I didn't want to be the lowest but I was very nervous to be the highest also. Years later I know that our rates were too low to start.

I was so worried that we were not going to be able to fill all the spots so at the last minute before we started advertising, I lowered my rates by twenty dollars per horse! This was something I never should have done but I was so insecure and I felt like every other farm was nicer than ours. After a few months of our monthly bills coming in, I very quickly realized that we were not bringing in enough money. Lowering our rates in the beginning was a huge mistake based all on emotion.

It is extremely bad for business to raise your rates after a couple of months of being open so we were stuck. I didn't have a clear view of money that was coming in or going out each month. If I can give one large piece of advice, before you start your business or if you have an existing one, sit down and write out your complete budget. Include all your costs for the entire month and make is as detailed as possible. You need to be diligent with this for a few months to get a full grasp of where the money is going. In a perfect world keeping good financial records all year would be the optimal especially when going through all four seasons. Our expenses are much higher in the wintertime.

When you are setting your boarding rates do not be intimidated by what other barns are charging. Find out what they offer for amenities and where there location is and **stop**. The part of the puzzle that is missing is the fact that you will never know what their debt load is. That can make a big difference on how they set their rates. You need to find a board rate that will work for your barn and your finances.

A HUGE MISTAKE

One of the biggest mistakes I made in the beginning was that I wanted my two boarders that I already had, to stay at any cost here at our barn. I knew our rates were going to go up dramatically and I thought they would not be able to afford the new rates. Believe it or not that had some influence on me and the financial decisions I made in the beginning when I set our board rates. I wanted them to be able to afford the board and that was a VERY BAD BUSINESS DECISION. I was all wrapped up in the emotion and not acting like a mature business owner. Successful businesses do not operate on emotion. Remember they are successful because they run like a business. I knew our board was going to be too expensive for some people and I was going to have to get over that. It does no one any good if you go out of business because you can't pay your bills so remember that when setting your rates.

Raising rates is another tough part of owning a business. As I said earlier when we first opened, our board rates were too low and now I couldn't raise them right away. The first time I raised our board it was very stressful for me. I had no idea how people were going to take it and I was so worried people would leave. I have always made it a policy to give my boarders a two month notice so they have time to find a new place if our barn is going to be too expensive for them. I have in the past usually only raised the rates every couple of years but there have been times when I raised them two consecutive years in a row. To this day it is not easy and I really try to raise them as little as possible. You need to remember that the cost of living is going up each year and you will need to adjust your fees accordingly. It's not fun but it is how successful businesses work.

I truly believe you can make it in the horse industry, but to do that you need to have a very clear understanding of what everything will cost on your farm and keep an extremely good record of all money coming in and money going out. Once you truly know what your budget will be then you can set your rates accordingly.

One last thought-you will always run into clients that will tell you they can't afford the board. Don't take is personally and the right people will come that can afford it.

~36~
How much hay do we need?

How much hay do we need to feed forty horses for the year? That was the big question for us as we opened our business. You can talk to ten different people about hay and what kind of hay to feed and they will most likely have different answers. Should it be grass hay, alfalfa hay or a mix? Do we use small squares or the large nine hundred pound squares? Would round bales be the best way to go? These were just a few of the questions David and I were trying to figure out as we were getting ready to open our doors. Something that was so simple when we only had four horses to feed now became very complicated because it would affect how much time and labor was involved.

Because the winters are so cold and long in Wisconsin, above all else we wanted to make sure we didn't run out of hay. That would be a nightmare with this many horses. We were already buying small bales from a farmer down the road but he only made small bales. We wanted the large bales to keep in our new barn because we thought it would be less labor intensive to stack. We had filled our old dairy barn with about six thousand small bales.

David had a good idea of how much hay we went through in a year's time for four horses. He kept track on paper how many small bales we used for the entire year before we opened. Then he would multiply that many times over to feed forty horses. We were going to estimate on the higher side to be safe. Next I had to figure out approximately how many small bales would equal out to one large bale. It was a lot of math and talking to farmers that make hay but we finally came up with a starting number. I found it very interesting that even the farmers we talked to had different answers for me on hay. No two answers were the same.

Moldy hay delivered

I was looking in the local paper and saw an advertisement for a guy up north selling the large bales and he would deliver. I called him up and to our farm he came with a massive truck load if large bales. We bought about one hundred large bales that first summer we opened. We unloaded the hay and I paid him and he drove off. We didn't know this guy at all but he assured us that if any of the hay was moldy he would come and replace it.

The easiest way for us to run our operation here at our farm was for David to feed the small bales outside each morning in separate piles and when the horses came in for dinner, the hay from the large bales would already be in their stall. One by one we started to open the large bales and as we got into the bale we were starting to find mold and lots of it. I couldn't believe it. Right away I called the guy who delivered the hay and he told me he was out of town and would call me when he got back in town. He never returned my call! I called several more times and got his voice mail. I was so angry and I was getting worried that we were going to be stuck with this bad hay. We had just spent thousands on hay and every large bale we would open would have some mold somewhere in it. David spent much wasted time over the course of that first year separating the hay and pulling out the bad hay to throw out. It was a nightmare. I must have called that guy ten times and he never returned my call. I think we must have had sucker written on our foreheads. We were already in debt up to our eyeballs and now we had to save as much hay as we could from those crappy bales. We never did get hold of the guy we bought the hay from and we lost a ton of money that year on hay. We were very lucky to have a lot of small bales to help get us through winter.

Our reputation was at stake also. I wanted our facility to be known for feeding great quality hay and it wasn't. I can remember walking to the back room where we keep our hay and two of our boarders were looking at our hay and when they saw me they just stared at me with a blank look. I should have talked with them about the hay but I didn't know what to say and I guess back then I was embarrassed. They didn't know David or me and we were a brand new business. I am sure the word was spreading about the poor quality hay we were feeding. I would handle the situation much different now and talk to anyone that has concerns about our hay.

We also ran into a few other problems in our early years regarding the hay. We had a boarder bring their own hay because they didn't like ours. I can remember being told right to my face that they went out and bought *good* hay to feed on top of what we were feeding. Talk about a blow. I was learning firsthand about people and how bold they can be. I was speechless in that encounter with that boarder and having to figure out what we were going to do about this situation of someone bringing their own hay in. It really made us look bad and I was sure that if the other boarders saw this person bringing hay in they would also start to question our hay. David and I didn't know who to talk to about this situation and for a while we just let her do what she wanted. That is a terrible way to run a business. She did eventually leave our place and my confidence was growing and I was becoming a stronger businesswoman every day to be able deal with tough situations like this one.

THE NEXT YEAR WAS MUCH DIFFERENT

The next year was much different. We have a neighbor who is a farmer and grows hay and he said he would make large bales for us. I told him what I wanted for hay and told him it could not have mold. The great thing with him was the fact that if I had a bad bale, he would take it back for his cattle and switch it out for better hay for our horses. We have been buying hay from him ever since and it has been wonderful hay. He knows I am picky and he gives us what we want for the horses. It is a great business relationship and I think one of the most important business relationships you will have when running your stable. Having the right business connections with people you trust makes all the difference in the world. Here is a word of advice. If you don't know the person you are buying hay from (or at least someone that knows him) then I would be very careful and get references if you can. You don't want to get stuck with bad hay like we did our first year.

Another problem we ran into during our first couple of years was the difference in opinion of what type of hay we should be feeding. We did have a lot of boarders that were happy with our hay but we also had one or two that didn't think our hay was good enough and we started to have problems. This was something I never dreamed would be an issue.

During the summer when we were making hay we would fill our barn with first cutting hay which usually consisted of grass hay with some light alfalfa. Our second cutting hay was grass hay with heavier alfalfa. Because we had two different types of hay and the alfalfa was so rich in the second cutting we decided to feed the grassier hay outside each morning and the second cutting hay in the stalls in the evening. The second cutting hay is more expensive and with all the alfalfa can be richer. We definitely did not want it to go to waste at all. We have always mixed our hay and fed both types and it works out fabulous. But when we opened we were having problems with a couple of boarders that would go into the back hay room and open bales of hay that they liked the look of so they could feed more of the alfalfa. We would also have boarders that would pick through the hay looking for the hay they thought was the best. I would walk into the hay room and find alfalfa bales opened up. I can remember one time having three bales cut open at one time because a boarder was going through our hay! I couldn't believe it and it caught me off guard. I had never dreamed of doing something like this when I boarded my horses and so I never thought it was something I was going to have to deal with. We quickly had to tell people they were not allowed to cut open bales or pick through the hay. This was something that was happening with both the large bales and small bales and in both barns.

At this point David and I were so new at this whole business thing that we just moved on and thought it wouldn't happen again. Were we wrong! It kept happening and on top of it we were feeding the horses very well in their stalls. We would always find a couple of stalls where the boarders had put in much more extra hay in the evening after we had already fed and by morning the hay was all over the stall and completely wasted. I would try to talk to the boarders that were doing this but back then I was not very confident and had a hard time taking control of the situation.

I now believe that the reason some of these people were doing this was because they came from barns where their horses were not fed enough and losing weight and they were scared it would happen at our barn also. I hear about this so much now when I talk to someone that is looking for a new place to board their horse. At the time we had not earned the trust of our clients about how we fed the horses. We had to prove ourselves and prove that we would take good care of their horse and make sure above all else that they were being fed enough. Years later this is no longer a problem and people do trust us now and we have a great reputation for feeding the horses well but it took time to gain that reputation and some heartache along the way.

Those early years were tough and it didn't help that our first huge purchase of hay was moldy throughout most of it. I am much more careful now when I go to purchase hay. It can make you or break you in business. I am also much more confident about what kind of hay we feed. Once in a while I still will talk to someone that has a different opinion on what hay we should be feeding and in that situation I try my best to assure them our hay is very good quality. But if they keep disagreeing with me then I politely let them know this might not be the barn for them and they need to find a barn that better suits their individual feeding and nutritional needs for their horse. It works so much better to be up front right away.

I also want to make something clear. I truly believe people are allowed their opinions on what they would call "good" hay. If they have their own place they have the wonderful choice of whatever hay they would like to feed their horse. When running a huge operation like ours it can make things extremely complicated and it only brings more work when you have many different people wanting different types of hay for their horse. Sometimes you have to just say, "I'm sorry, we don't offer that here at our facility" and it's okay.

I believe one of the reasons boarding barns goes out of business is because they underestimate how much you really need to feed a full size horse to keep their weight up especially during the cold months or if the horse is in heavy work program. If you are going to start a horse business then make sure the hay is at the top of the list of importance. I have learned through the years that it is not the case for many stables and they end up going out of business because they were not prepared financially when it comes to purchasing hay year round.

One last thought. If you do not have the land to grow your own hay and you have to buy it, hay will most likely be your biggest expense. I truly believe if you spend a little more and buy good quality hay you will save money in the long run and you won't have the waste you find when the hay is poor quality. Poor quality hay is cheaper for a reason. Do your homework and check the hay as it comes in to your farm.

~37~
GRAIN AND SUPPLEMENTS

Feeding grain and supplements to forty horses twice a day can be very time consuming if it is not organized. We have some outdoor boarded horses that only get grain in the morning and if you board a larger number of horses you will probably have a couple that don't get any grain at all. So what is the big deal? Those are the exact words I said years ago before we opened. I was used to only giving grain and supplements to four horses before we opened and I really wasn't prepared for how time consuming it would be. Even after working at a few barns I still didn't get it. Remember that working for someone else at their stable is much different than doing it all yourself. Whether you are paying employees or doing it yourself you want to make this part of your business a priority.

I checked around with a few other barns to see how they fed grain twice a day and how they gave supplements and every place did it differently. I had to decide what would work best for our barn and for me. I didn't realize at the time that this area of our business would also change throughout the years. What we did when we first opened is now much different.

I decided to hang up two very large dry erase boards in the back where we keep the grain and write down each horses name and what they get each morning and evening. For our big barn I purchased twenty-seven buckets and put numbers on them to match with the stall numbers.

Dry erase boards are great for keeping track of grain and supplements.

Every boarding facility in our area included grain as part of the feed included in the board price. Well I figured I would have to follow suit to keep up with the other facilities otherwise people would ask me why we don't include grain like other barns do. Back then I really didn't think too much about it and did the same thing everyone else was doing. If other barns included grain then it must work and I never bothered to look at what they charge for board at those facilities and I never really checked on how much this would cost me each month. Boy did I need to take a business class!

We decided for our barn grain we would feed a nice all-purpose grain from the local feed store. I was able to get a little discount on it because I was buying so many bags at once. It was not the top of the line and it was not the bottom. I was going to give our boarders the choice. They could use our grain or bring their own. I would include up to four pounds a day of our grain. If they brought their own grain they would need to bring a garbage can to keep it in. This seemed to work out real good at first. I believe I had about three quarters of all the boarders using our grain. The others brought in their own.

Next were the supplements. I had decided that if a boarder had more than one supplement they needed to put them in containers or baggies. With this many horses I could easily be opening many containers of supplements which would take me a long time. Putting supplements in small containers or baggies was the perfect solution. We have been doing this since we opened and it has worked well.

GRAIN SKYROCKETS IN PRICE

Very little changed the first few years with how we were doing things with the grain. Back in 2006 grain prices seemed pretty low and we were able to afford most of grain we were including in our board. It was tight because we had made our board rates too low but we were making it work with the outside income from our other jobs. I would notice a small price increase at least once or twice a year but I thought we could handle it. We didn't want to raise our board the first couple of years so we had to eat the cost of the increase. We were managing until four years later when all of a sudden grain prices sky rocketed. I was paying almost double the price for the same grain. With the huge increase and also the gradual increase of everything else it takes to run a horse farm we were losing money in every area. I didn't know how other stables did it but we were struggling financially with all the increases.

We decided to make a huge change at our farm and I knew it was not going to be a popular one. I also expected boarders to leave after I announced the change. Since we had half the boarders buying their own grain I didn't think it was fair to those same clients to have a board increase while the other boarders were getting their grain included. How was I going to make it fair for everyone across the board? I decided that we were not going to be able to include grain as part of the feed here at our barn anymore. I didn't know of any other barns doing this practice but we were going to do it. I had talked to a friend of mine and she advised me against it and told me to be ready because we might lose people. I thought about it for a long time and then decided to go forward with the change.

The more I started really thinking about how other barns do it the more I began to realize for the first time that they were not including the grain for free. That would be a terrible business practice. Their board was more than ours and they were including grain as part of the board but the boarders were still paying for the grain. The advertising of their barn and amenities was just packaged differently. People were willing to pay more for board at these barns and having grain included was a perk like buying a fancy car with extras. The extras are never free. They just make you feel like you are getting extras (like grain) for free. The truth is businesses would all go under if they gave everything away for free.

Marketing Our Grain in a Different Way

I was going to offer our package to our boarders in a different way. I was going to give the boarder the control of what they wanted for their horse. I was still going to supply grain (a top quality grain) and give it to the boarder for the same price I get it for. I was going to offer a senior grain and good quality grain for the working horse. It would save the boarder from having to get the grain and bring it to the barn. It would save them time, labor and gas and most importantly, it would keep the board down. They could also choose to bring whatever kind of grain they wanted me to feed just like before and I would feed it.

It was a big chance but I was willing to try it. I wrote out a letter explaining the change and also gave everyone a sixty-day notice of the changes we were making. Then I set up for a nutritionist to come to our barn and answer any questions anyone had on grain and supplements. It worked out great. Many of the boarders came to the clinic with the nutritionist and got a lot out of it. We were so very lucky that we only lost one boarder due to the grain change. I was so happy that our boarders wanted to stay even if it was going to cost them more each month. We have been doing this now for years and it has worked out just fine. I am not sure what other barns include in their boarding but for us it was the right thing to do. At the end of the day you have to do what is best for your business.

Remember when setting up your business and how you want to run it, grain and feed will be a major part of it. Don't be intimidated by what other barns offer in this area. I was at first, and I was trying to do what they were doing and it was not a good financial choice for us. If you want to include grain as part of your feed program then make sure you keep close tabs on price increases and how much it is truly costing you each month to feed grain to the horses. It got away from me very fast in the first couple of years because I didn't have a clear picture of the total cost each month. Whatever way you decide to do it at your farm is fine but I found it much easier to know the exact cost of grain each month when I sell it as a separate item. It takes all the guessing out of it.

If you do include it as part of your board, then you will need to keep very good records on how much each horse is eating per day and total that out each month. I do believe boarders like having the grain included as part of the board and it does become a perk for them. Just be very diligent in keeping good records so you don't lose money. It can happen overnight as grain prices increase.

GIVING SPECIAL SUPPLEMENTS

I have a couple more thoughts for you to think about when you are setting up your barn and figuring out how you want to do grain and supplements.

When you open for business you will have every kind of supplement under the sun. I have forty horses and almost all of them are on different supplements. Many of them are powders and pellets and some are Smart Paks. These all work out great but in our early years I had a few boarders ask me to give a supplement in a liquid form. A lot of joint supplements come in a liquid form and they have the consistency of syrup and can be sticky. Trying to give a horse this liquid supplement became problematic for me because I didn't want my buckets sticky and it would attract insects in the summer. I also realized in the winter that it would freeze if you don't have a heated barn and it is extremely hard to get the liquid out of the container. When you are setting up how you want to feed grain and supplements, take the time to really think about liquid supplements. I realized years ago that I didn't want to give liquid supplements anymore. I had to ask boarders to change what they were giving and that was very hard. Think about those things before you announce what you are going to offer in your amenities so that you don't have to go back and change it like I did.

Anytime you are dealing with any supplement or grain and have to add water it can be a mess and in the winter it can freeze very fast. It made my job much harder and so years later I have simplified how we feed supplements. The only time I deal with anything of a liquid form is when it is a medical prescription and it is temporary. These are suggestions and things I never gave any thought to when we opened our barn and I hope these ideas will help you with setting up your boarding business.

~38~
NOT PREPARED FOR SPECIAL REQUESTS

When we opened our barn doors for business at our new facility I never dreamed of all the things I would learn in the first couple of years. You can never truly be prepared for what people are going to ask you for. All the special requests for the horses at our barn was something I gave zero thought to before we opened. I had boarded my horses for years back in California and I never asked for anything more than good hay (and enough of it) and fresh water and a clean stall. I lived pretty simple. Things are much more complicated now in the world we live in.

When Vinland Stables opened things were about to change in a crazy way for David and me and I was truly going to get a lesson in *barn management*. As all the new horses came in during that first summer so did the special requests. Remember we were a multi-discipline barn so we had a wonderful group of people but they all came from different barns and different ways of doing things. David and I were fresh and ready to take on anything that came our way and we were in a service orientated business now and we were here to give the customer what they wanted. We did not know how much more work and problems those special requests would create.

ONE OF OUR FIRST SPECIAL REQUEST

One of the very first requests we received came the summer we opened. We were asked right away to leave two horses (that were normally in a stall at night) outside all night and only bring them in if the weather turned bad. This particular boarder owned both horses and told us that this was a common practice at her previous barn. These were horses that were stalled in our new barn and all those horses came in every evening.

David and I said no problem but we told her there was no shelter out in the paddocks and storms can come up fast here in Wisconsin overnight. She said she was fine with that. David and I had not really given this much thought at all. I truly believe outdoor board is the best for some horses but you also need proper shelter so they can get out of a storm if one comes up. We went ahead and gave it a try. We brought in all twenty-five other horses and left her two horses outside. Then we fed them hay and then had to go get grain pans to give them grain. I ended up having to stand out there and keep them separated from each other's grain. It was already becoming more work. As we watched the two horses, they never settled down that first evening. They ran up and down the fence for a couple of hours until they were heavily lathered up! The owner of the two horses was gone and when I called her to tell her about the problems, it didn't bother her and she told me to keep them out. Four hours later both horses were a complete mess and the other boarders were getting upset at what they were witnessing. I had no idea how to handle this.

David had watched the weather to see what it was going to be for the evening and they said a possible rain shower might come through. Well if you live in Wisconsin a possible rain shower could have thunder and lightning and be two inches of rain! We decided to bring the horses in. They were sweaty and very stressed out. I did not know these horses at all and did not know the boarder at all either. When I called her to tell her we were bringing them in she got upset with me on the phone and asked me to try again tomorrow.

Because we had not learned how to say no at this point in our business, we did the same exact thing again the next night and the same exact thing happened. I started realizing very fast how much time this was taking me. The second night it was very late and I brought the horses back in again. Now I had fed outside and had to feed again in their stalls because they did not eat all the hay outside. It was double the work. I called her again and told her we brought them in and again she let me know she was not pleased.

David and I had a long discussion that second night and decided we were not going to do this at our barn. We were going to have every horse come in every night. No exceptions. This way we would not have to worry about the weather or stand out there while they eat their grain or anything else. This was one of our first decisions we had to make about not giving the boarder everything they ask for. We wanted to please everyone but we were quickly realizing it came with a high cost at times. The boarder was not upset that her horses were stressed out but I was extremely upset.

Now I know there are a lot of horse farms that keep their horses outside all night in the summer and bring them in during the day. I believe if it works for your barn then do that. At our place without shelter we didn't feel comfortable leaving them out all night. It is a personal preference for the barn owner. We were not prepared for anyone to ask us for that request. I just assumed that because they were paying for stall board they would want their horse in a stall at night. We did have a few other people in our early years of operation ask us to leave horses out at night and bring them in during the day so their coat would not fade from the sun. We said no to this request right from the start. I was learning quickly as you can see.

LIGHTS AT NIGHT

Another special request we had at our barn had to do with lights. We had a couple of people that showed all the time and in their particular show setting it was common to have lights on your horse to help keep their coats short. We had outlets in each stall already so David thought it would be fine and easy to do. The owner of the horses went out and bought lighting and up it went. I still remember thinking to myself how bright it was but the lights were on a timer and we thought it would work out fine.

Pretty quickly we started to get complaints. The way our barn is designed made it possible for the lights to shine into the stalls on either side of the lighted stall because there are grills between each stall and the horses can see each other. In simpler words, it is not a solid wall. We had boarders who came to talk to me and had valid concerns. They didn't want the lights shining into their horse's stall at night. My head was spinning as I was trying to figure out how to fix the problem and make all people involved happy. What was happening was the clash of different horse worlds in my barn and there was not going to be a happy ending to this. I completely understood and felt they were valid concerns and we were going to have to make a choice. Back then we didn't want to lose a boarder over this so we tried moving the horses with lights to different stalls which of course affected other boarders and their horses. It never worked out and eventually we had to make a difficult choice and tell this particular person that we were going to say no to lights. Our barn was just not set up for it and it was making an extreme amount of work for David and stress for both of us. We had to do what was best for the barn.

Today at our barn we do not allow boarders to use lights at all. I have nothing against them and if a barn wants to do that I think it is fine for their facility. It just doesn't always work in every stable area. There are many barns that offer special lights for their show horses and I think the boarder will find the right barn to fit their needs.

These special requests that I have mentioned might not seem like a big deal at all. It's not a big deal until you are in the driver's seat and running the entire barn. Every request you get will take your energy and time. I love when I can tell a boarder "Yes we can do that." It makes me feel good to give them what they want. It just took me many years to find out what we can and cannot do at our barn. The same will be true for your boarding stable.

I am not saying there is a right way or wrong way to run a horse barn. I am saying you need to find what works best for your barn and what you can handle as a job load. All the requests you will get will be time consuming and stressful at times and you will need to find a balance otherwise you will be in the barn twenty-four hours a day. Now after all these years, I realize how important it is to be able to say "We don't offer that here," or "Sorry but we can't do that here." It will change your life and how you do business for the better.

~39~
HERD MANAGEMENT

Herd management on a horse farm is a subject that you could have endless discussions about. There are countless variables that go into the whole equation of each individual horse farm and how they group their herds. A boarding barn like ours can have even more opinions and variables because you are also dealing with all the owners as well as their horses. I had to think for a long while on where to start this subject.

I believe the best place to start is at the beginning back in California. I grew up with horses in Los Angeles County but horse boarding is completely different as far as turnout for horses. There really isn't any turnout for most. There is not enough land in the city so most horses are stalled in large pipe stalls and they stay in that stall until you come to get them out. Some facilities will have little turn-out pens that you can turn your horse out for an hour or two but most places do not have large paddocks to turn out groups of horses on a daily basis. Growing up through my twenties I didn't have access to large herds and an understanding of herd management. I really didn't learn about it until I moved here to Wisconsin years ago. It was an eye opener because I had never seen so much open land accessible for horses. Open fields everywhere with herds of horses everywhere you go. I loved it! I started learning fast at the horse farm I worked at about turnout with many horses together. I learned more about horse behavior and herds that first year I worked at that farm then all my early years in California.

Now fast forward a few years. When David and I decided to build a barn and run a forty horse boarding operation we only had two paddocks back then for my two horses and our two boarder's horses. They all got along really good (except for the occasional scuffle usually started from my mare Lou). Our herd was mixed (geldings and mares) and it was not a problem. The geldings were pretty mellow and not interested in the mares. It worked out good. Things usually do on a very small scale.

When we were in the building process and designing our paddocks we decided early on that we would only have three horses living together in each paddock for our "outdoor boarded" horses. That would be the maximum. Our shelters were big enough for three horses with extra room so they could get away from each other if they needed to.

For our new barn that housed twenty-seven horses we built five large paddocks to start and then built a sixth one the next year. We also added four private turnout areas. We were not sure at the time if geldings or mares would be coming in so we would have to wait and see what we got. Our plan back when we opened was to not have any more than six horses in a paddock. To this day we have never had more than six horses in any paddock but in a few of the paddocks we only have two or three at a time and our private turnout is always being used.

Soon we opened and the horses came. As each horse came I would always ask the owner some questions to get to know their horse. What kind of breed was their horse? Were they on top of the herd, in the middle, or always on the bottom? Were they easy going or not. I found out quickly that many of the boarders did not know if their horse was dominate or submissive so we often had to start from ground zero. I spent a lot of time watching horses and their behavior to see if we had any red flags. With this many horses coming in the odds were high that we were going to get a couple aggressive horses and I would have to make sure they were placed in the right herd. My plan from the beginning was to always keep things consistent with the horses. If a herd was getting along good then I was not changing a thing.

Putting horses together in herds that get along can be work at times.

Looking back all those years I have to say this was the most difficult part of the job. I worked very hard to put horses in groups where there personalities meshed but it didn't always happen and since all of them were new to our barn within a month's time it became very stressful at times and even exhausting on certain days. No one likes to come see their horse and find a new bite mark or cut from another horse or even worse, lame due to a kick. This became magnified during the first couple of months.

I truly believe now you could read many books on herd management and behavior but when you have to do it yourself it is another story. When you need to watch the horses and move a horse from one herd to the next because you see a problem that is not going away, there is no better classroom. During this time we did have bite marks and kicks and everything else and I was going to have to learn how to deal with this and the upset boarder. That subject will be in a later chapter.

After all these years of boarding horses we still once in a while have a horse come to our barn that is either aggressive or has been on the show circuit and has lived his whole life in a stall. When that happens he then must learn to be outside with other horses and this can take a long time if he has never been in a herd situation. I have seen horses become depressed and stand in the corner of a paddock for weeks trying to adjust and learn to be in a herd when all they have known their entire life is living in a stall twenty-four hours a day. I had one horse in particular that had never been with other horses his entire life and every time we put him with a herd he didn't know how to act and he would constantly try to attack every other horse in his paddock. I would go out there to watch him and all the other horses were in a corner just watching him as he was trying to be tough and act aggressive towards them and they would just walk away as if they were saying, "What is his problem?" Sometimes it can be hard watching a horse that is having a difficult time adjusting to his new surroundings. As the barn owner you will need patience and a strong understanding of what is going on because the boarder will look to you for reassurance. On the bright side I had a show horse come to our barn a few years ago and he had never been with another horse in a herd setting and he adjusted wonderfully. He is one of the biggest players in his herd now and he is constantly playing all day with the other geldings. I truly love when I see a horse that is happy and acting like a horse.

There also have been a couple situations over the years where I have had an extremely aggressive horse that is continually going after other horses (and making contact) and does not let up all day. In those cases I have tried everything I possibly could think of with those horses. As a last resort I have had to put the horse on private turnout. It is not what I wanted to do because I truly believe these animals need to be with each other but I had to look at what was best for the entire barn and each herd. I have always felt bad in those situations and it is heartbreaking for the owners. It is one part of the job that is not fun at all.

If you are going to work in the horse industry or have your own place, be prepared because most likely during your career with horses, you will come across one or two extremely aggressive horses. They can be very difficult to place in a herd and you will need to be prepared with a plan if the horse never settles down. This was a very challenging part of herd management that I never had to deal with before we started our horse boarding business.

Different opinions on grouping horses

There are so many opinions on how to put horses together in herds. Different boarding facilities in our area all do it different. I believe some ways are better than others to transition or introduce a horse to a herd. I think it depends on a few different elements. How big are the paddocks that the horses are going to be in? Is there plenty of room for the horses to get away from each other and not get cornered? Some places put all their geldings in one herd and all mares in another. Some places mix them. One of the biggest complaints I hear from potential boarders is that the boarding facility they are at does not have enough paddocks to be able to move horses if a big problem arises. I have also had people share with me that their horse is at the bottom of the herd and can't get enough hay to eat and is losing weight. I hear often from potential clients that their horse is getting picked on and they can't get away from the other horses in the paddock and the facility does not have any other options.

Having more paddocks never guarantees that horses will always get along. You can have two horses together and they can have all kinds of problems. I think the biggest way to make the job of herd management a little easier and cut down on problems is to have enough paddocks to be flexible if you have to move a horse. You will always have scuffles with horses but if you can cut down on them by having more flexibility to move a horse when it needs to be moved it will make a huge difference.

Someone I know used a very unique comparison of horses to our children. They said to me, "We would never make our kids hang out in their bedroom with other children that they don't get along with or with kids that are always mean to your child. This is exactly what we do to our horses. We force them to eat, drink and live with other horses in a very small area of land and sometimes they are not going to get along. They can't get away from each other and they end up fighting with each other at times." I know horses are not children and the way they communicate is completely different than people but it does give us something to think about when designing paddocks and expecting horses to get along. It was a very unique way to look at it.

Sometimes horses are not going to get along at first and you just need to give it a few days for them to work it out. And sometimes I believe they need to be moved. I have heard of barns where they have to work it out at any cost. I believe you need to find balance in herd management because to me it's not worth a horse getting beat up day after day for weeks on end or possibly getting seriously injured when the problem might have been easily fixed by a herd change.

The best thing you can do for your horse facility if you have the chance to design it yourself or make changes to an existing one, is to make more paddocks so you can have great flexibility. Because I can promise you that you will have horses that don't get along and when they cross the line and horses get hurt then bigger problems happen with the owner of the horse. It is not fun at all and I can say that from experience.

I have learned a tremendous amount through these years about herd management and I have had my share of mistakes when it comes to reading a horse's personality. I am always learning and new situations are always on the horizon. That is what makes these beautiful animals so amazing. They each have their own personality and if you watch them long enough you will be amazed at how easy they are to read. To this day I still love to go out and watch them in the paddocks. They always amaze me and I am always learning from them.

~40~
THE BOARDER AND HERD MANAGEMENT

As I had said in the previous chapter there are many different opinions on herd management. What makes it even more complicated are the owners of the horses. No school could ever have prepared David and me for what we were going to learn about herd management and how to handle an angry boarder when their horse got a bite mark, kick or even worse becomes lame due to another horse in the same paddock. I never dreamed how personal people would take this.

This is truly going to be one of the most sensitive issues I will be addressing in this book and my goal is in no way to offend anyone at all (even though I have learned through the years, that is not always possible) but to share the experiences we have gone through dealing with herd behavior and especially when horses bite or kick each other and dealing with the owners of the horses involved. I am writing this through my eyes and experiences of running our business and being the barn owner and manager.

Vinland Stables has been open for many years now and I can still say that once in a while when a horse gets a mark on them or a cut, the owner of the horse right away wants to put the blame on a horse they feel did the damage even if they don't know who the culprit was. When this happens it must be addressed right away before it gets out of hand. I have seen boarders take it personally and get upset at the owner of the horse that they were blaming and feelings get hurt by both parties. I have learned so much over the years about people and trying to keep everyone calm under these circumstances. Trying to get them to trust me is extremely hard when emotions are involved. I have made many mistakes in this area throughout the years as I was learning to deal with clients. There have been times that I can make everyone feel better by explaining and educating what is going on in the herd and they understand and trust me but once in a while I lose a boarder over the issue of the horses. No matter what I say they are not going to agree.

I have had to stand my ground and not move a horse because I didn't see a problem that a boarder insisted was happening and in certain situations

I have lost a boarder over that. The thing you have to understand as a barn owner is **you cannot keep moving horses every time someone gets upset or a horse has a new bite mark.** If you don't stand strong in your belief that you know what is best for the herd then you will be moving horses every week and then your job will become twice as hard dealing with herd management. This truly is one of the most important parts of the job and you really need to know how to read the horses and be strong in your decisions. You also need to know when enough is enough and it's time to move a horse to a different herd

The Reactions of Your Clients

When we opened our business I never realized the reaction I would get by the boarders when two horses were not getting along. I was used to my own horses getting a bite mark or kick mark every now and then. I never worried about it because I know that is how they communicate and some horses catch on faster than others and learn to stay out of trouble. Yes, it is not pretty when you have to clean up a bite mark and it always seems to happen right before a horse show but I also knew if I was going to keep my horses together outside then these things would happen once in a while. I was willing to take the chance because I know they are happier when they are with other horses. My personal belief is it is better for their well-being. I am not saying one way is right or wrong, it is just my personal choice.

When we designed our boarding facility I wanted the horses that were going to be boarded here to be in small herds. I also knew because we were going to offer daily turnout in herds it might not be the right place for people that wanted their horse to always be on private turnout or in a stall. I believe there is the right barn for every person and horse and you need to find the right one that fits your needs and desires. We did decide to offer private turnout but it is used mostly for the horse in rehab. We have had horses during show season pay for private turnout and I completely understand that.

As the horses came to our barn and we were in full operation, learning to deal with people under all circumstances became a daily thing especially when it came to the horse herds and their behavior. We were having horses that were getting into scuffs and at times worse and I was trying to figure out where to draw the line and when to move a horse. What made it more difficult was that even though we had great boarders, when they would come out to see their horse and there was a bite mark a few boarders would get extremely upset. I never wanted to make anyone feel like it was not a big deal but on the other hand I was not going to make it into something bigger than it was. All of a sudden I found myself on a tight rope trying to balance both sides and I think this is something that takes years to learn and in some cases it doesn't have a happy ending. I had to learn how to comfort and educate all at the same time. Above all else I really needed to make sure I knew what was going on out in the herds and if there was a problem I wanted to be the first to see it.

EDUCATING WILL BE A PART OF IT

Another part of the equation was educating and making sure the boarders understood the difference between aggressive behavior and playing. This was very challenging at times. What was hard for people to understand was the fact that horses will bite and kick out when they are playing and in that case if you are worried that your horse is going to get marked up or hurt then it is best to pay for private turnout. I was very surprised back then and still am today at how many horse owners do not know the difference between two horses playing or fighting. The other side of the coin is that sometimes with private turnout you have new behaviors that develop because the horse is bored or suffers some kind of anxiety from being alone. It is a balancing act to the highest degree.

Frequently over the years I have had a person drive into the drive way and catch the tail end of two horses that were playing and immediately they call me to tell me the horses are being aggressive and beating each other up. This is frustrating and I believe that if you have the time and can watch horse behavior out in the paddocks, quite often you will be amazed at how much you will learn and be able to tell the difference between fighting and playing. The problem is most people that board horses don't have the time to come out before work or after work just to watch the horses in the herds. When they come to see their horse they want to ride not to watch them out in the paddock. I know as long as we have our barn this will be an area of the job that will have to be addressed every now and then. I just hope over the years I get better at making the boarder understand what I am trying to tell them and they learn to trust my judgment. I want them to know above all else that I do not want their horse to get hurt either.

It has been frustrating over the years when a boarder had decided to move their horse because they were upset that their horse was getting bite or kick marks. What I have tried to explain in the past and still do is there is absolutely no guarantee even if your horse is just with one other horse that something won't happen. My own horses come in at night and I still once in a while find a mark on one of them. You either choose to keep them together or keep them by themselves. We even had one horse get hurt on private turnout. We still don't know to this day how it happened. It is interesting to me if you watch any herd of horses for many days you will find out that some horses are into everything. They are constantly bugging other horses and wanting to play and really are never quiet. They are the ones that usually end up with marks of some sort. Then you have other horses that are quieter (or smarter) whatever you think and stay out of the mix and never have a mark on them. It really tells me a lot about their personality.

To this day I still love to watch the herds outside and the geldings are always especially fun to watch. People forget that they are thousand pound animals and when they play it is not always going to be gentle. If I watch the horses long enough I will still once in a while see something that amazes me and it makes me even laugh out loud at times. I wish more people would take the time to watch their horse in a herd setting. They would learn so much more about their horse and his personality.

If you are going to have a horse business I am sure this will be one of the most difficult parts of your job. It was for me. The early years of our business were extremely stressful for me when dealing with an upset boarder. No one likes conflict but if you are going to be in the horse industry then you will have conflict once in a while and you need to learn how to deal with it in a professional way and help make that boarder feel better about the situation. I never knew this would be part of the job when we opened our boarding stable.

As I said in an earlier chapter, I boarded my horses when I was younger and all I had to worry about was my one horse. When I became the barn owner I saw the situation from a completely different perspective. I wasn't just thinking about my one horse anymore. ***I was now thinking***

about forty horses all the time. I have found it has gotten much easier over the years because I believe I have earned the trust from our boarders and I am confident in my decisions on horse herd management. Our boarders know I try my hardest to make sure their horse is in a compatible herd. It is not always perfect but we continue to try.

~41~
HORSES ON PASTURE GRASS

Having horses in Southern California is unbelievably different than Wisconsin. The idea of having acres and acres of lush green grass to let your horse graze on all day long was something I had never dreamed of living out west. You just don't have it. The summer days were extremely hot in Southern California and if there was any grass it turned brown fairly quickly in the dry hot temperatures. The only green I ever really saw were the golf courses and yards of people's homes and that was because they were watered every day with automatic sprinklers.

Turning horses out on grass in Southern California was never a topic of conversation because it didn't happen. Fast forward many years to Wisconsin and it was an equine culture shock. I had never seen so much open land and it was all green. Horses enjoying the country side with their heads buried in green grass. It was like the pictures of Kentucky I had looked at in magazines when I was younger.

When we designed our pastures it was so much fun for me. It was an easy thing to do because we had the land and it rains so much here. We seeded most of our pastures a couple of years earlier even though we didn't have our loan at the time and if we didn't get the loan, we could cut and bale the pasture and sell the hay. Either way would work for us. If we waited until the loan was approved we wouldn't have any grass pastures for our new boarders the next year. We decided to take a chance. We let it grow and then later began our fencing.

When our barn opened for business and people would come for a tour I was amazed at how important large pastures were to everyone so their horses could graze freely. We don't have very large pastures but they are big enough to give the horses some enjoyment.

How long to graze?

What really caught me off guard were all the different opinions of how long horses should stay on grass and how slowly we should introduce them to grass. I knew how I wanted to run the daily routine of putting horses on grass and for the most part everyone agreed with how we did it here at our farm. I did have a few boarders over the years that never wanted their horse on grass or wanted us to put grazing muzzles on their horses. This was also something new for me that I had not experienced before.

Our horses don't stay on the grass for a very long time. At the height of summer they are on grass about seven hours a day. We still feed them hay in the morning and evening. I really thought at the time we opened that having horses on grass would be wonderful and it is for the most part but once in a while I will get someone that can make it very difficult and it doesn't have to be. What's more natural than a horse eating in a pasture full of grass?

If you take precautions when introducing horses to grass in the spring and do it slowly you shouldn't have any problems. We are extremely conservative and turn horses out on grass very slowly in the spring and we increase by small increments the first week and then gradually increase time by longer periods. We also take great care in making sure the horses are not getting diarrhea from too much rich grass all at once.

Remember with many different horses at your barn, weight will also be something to keep an eye on. Some horses will never gain a pound and then you might have one that blows up like a balloon as soon as he is on grass for long periods of time. Some horses don't need all that extra food and they do better with a little less. A heavy horse doesn't need to be on grass all day and it is not good for their health

Special Dietary Needs

You might have to modify some of the routine for some horses especially if you have a horse with special dietary needs. Your boarders will also appreciate it if you are willing to make adjustments for their horse in special situations. I have had people come to our barn for boarding because the barn their horse was at would not make changes for their overweight horse and they were worried about laminitis. They would watch as their horse became heavier and heavier and the barn owner would not put their horse in a paddock without grass or agree to putting a grazing muzzle on. If you are going to run a boarding business make sure you can be flexible because if you are in it long enough, you will eventually have a horse or two that has special needs when it comes to food.

Some horses are chow hounds and will never bring their head up for air and tend to be on the heavy side and some horses stay thin no matter how much they eat. Be prepared for clients with both types of horses. This was something we had to learn after we were already open and we have modified our program over the years to accommodate the horse with special dietary needs. When designing your pastures keep all these things in mind. We never gave it a thought before we opened and just assumed all the horses would go out on grass. It was another learning curve for us in the beginning.

~42~
CHALLENGES OF OUTDOOR BOARD

Rough Board was a term I had never heard before I moved to Wisconsin years ago. Everywhere I boarded in California was all outdoor board due to the hot weather. Each outside stall had a metal roof to keep the horse out of the hot sun. There were a few of the bigger places that had box stalls but the barns are not enclosed at all due to the warmer weather.

To this day I have never really liked the term "Rough board." It sounds so harsh. But I guess here in Wisconsin if your horse is outside all winter and has no shelter to face the elements, it truly can be harsh. I knew that when we opened our place for boarding we were going to have two paddocks where the horses would be outside all the time in all kinds of weather. We built large shelters to house three horses in each paddock and I wanted to use the stalls in our old dairy barn to bring everyone in if the weather became extremely bad during the wintertime.

I decided back then I wasn't going to use the term "Rough board." We were just going to call it "Outside board." When we were filling spots for boarding back in early spring of 2006 it was pretty easy to fill the outdoor spots. I figured the labor involved with outdoor board would be so much easier than the stall board because we would not have to clean stalls every day and we had automatic waters in each paddock. We would not have to fill water buckets twice a day and we would only have to grain horses in the morning. It seemed like a lot less work for David and me. I was in for a huge education on outdoor board, weather and clients and I didn't see it coming.

THE NEW HORSES CAME FOR OUTDOOR BOARD

Our six new horses came and we had to decide which of the two paddocks they were going to live in. Because they were going to be together 24/7 I wanted to make sure it was a good fit. With six new horses (that I knew nothing about previously) it was going to be a little challenging. We had mostly geldings at first with a couple of mares. I put the mares together with one gelding and the other geldings together. We were lucky it worked out pretty good to start. The summer went by without too much drama between the outdoor horses. The horses seemed content and they would be on grass during the day and fed twice a day also. The weather was good and our outdoor boarders seemed very happy. Everything was so easy with outdoor board and we added two more boarding horses to live with my horses in a different paddock. It seemed at the time like easy money.

Summer Was Over

Then fall came and the weather was changing fast and it became cold and wet. Our beautiful paddocks became total mud because the ground had been used for generations as farm land so it was very soft and it was terrible. Here we had six new horses in two new paddocks with brand new shelters and the horses were in knee deep mud! The boarders were upset and we were upset and because it was so cold the paddocks were not drying. Outdoor board was supposed to be easier for us but became so much harder overnight.

We decided that until it dried up a little we would bring all the outdoor horses in at night and let their legs and feet dry out overnight and they could go back outside during the day. We were hoping the ground would freeze soon but it turned out it would be a long time before the temperatures were cold enough to freeze anything.

I was so worried about the word getting out about our outdoor board and the mud that I really tried hard to go over and above to let the boarders know we were putting their horses first. Some of them were very understanding but a couple of them were so upset and they ended up leaving. There wasn't anything we could do that fall to fix the paddocks and so we waited for a hard freeze. With all these extra horses in at night this would be eight extra stalls to clean every day plus the twenty-stalls in the new barn and then there were my own horses! Back then David and I did all the work cleaning the stalls and it was exhausting to say the least. Our life became even crazier and we were trying to please our boarders the best we could under the terrible conditions we were dealing with. We got through that fall and the ground froze and new boarders came in. I was so glad to see frozen ground! Spring seemed very far away so I wasn't going to worry about the mud until the temperatures started to warm up in March. I thought things were going to be easier for a while.

Winter came in that first year and I can remember it was very cold with little snow accumulation. A new problem developed as we got into winter. My idea of when horses should be brought in at night due to a storm or extreme cold was a different than the boarders. I was not sure how other barns handled outdoor board and weather so I gave in to pressure from our clients. Basically I knew the weather was not bad enough to bring them in but we were a brand new business and they didn't know David or me and I didn't want to lose more boarders again. It was a vicious circle and very stressful.

When I was a boarder I never realized all the extra work the owners or employees taking care of the stable had to do when horses are moved or put in stalls. I am sure it was the same for the boarders at our barn. They didn't realize how much more work it was when the outdoor horses came in and I never asked for help and we didn't charge extra for shavings or labor back then. I really was going into it blind and it took many years before I really figured out how we wanted to run outdoor board on our farm.

As the years have gone by we are much more confident on how we care for our outdoor boarded horses and we have also earned the trust of the people boarding here. I also now ask for help from the owners of the horses that are kept outside and if the horses are brought in for a few days due to bad weather, they come out and clean their own horses stall.

Weather is always going to be the biggest challenge with outdoor horses and we can only take it one day at a time especially during winter. We still have mud in our paddocks in fall and spring but not as bad as we used to and no two years have ever been the same. As a business owner of a boarding stable, outdoor board can be just as challenging as stall board but with different problems. These were things I never thought about when we opened. I hope I can help others by sharing some of the problems we went through so you can learn from our mistakes and experiences and make your job easier right from the beginning.

THE OLDER HORSE AND THIN SKINNED HORSE

Another problem I have run into over the years has to do with horses that do not do well on outdoor board either due to their old age, breed or surroundings. So many things play into the whole equation and once in a while a horse doesn't thrive well, being out 24/7 in all types of weather. I have had a couple of horses that really struggled due to the extreme cold and needed to be blanketed or in one case the horse was extremely old and the weather was wearing him down. Like I said earlier, winter in Wisconsin is harsh and it can be even harder on the senior horse or the horse that doesn't grow a good winter coat. There have been a few times over the years when David or I have checked on a horse in the morning or evening and they are shivering and I have needed to get a blanket on them right away. I have had to bring horses into the barn to warm them up and borrow a blanket to keep the horse warm. With these horses I have told the owner that they need to get a blanket right away and the blanket needs to stay on.

What I found out early on is that many people that own horses don't realize that different breeds handle the cold better than others and age can make a huge difference on how a horse handles the cold. I believe when horses get up in their senior years some of them need special attention during the extreme cold weather. I own a thoroughbred and she gets absolutely no coat in the winter. Believe me when I tell you that she wears blankets all fall through spring because of the cold temperatures. On the other hand I have a miniature horse that gets such a heavy coat that he sweats if the temperatures get above forty degrees in January.

YOU WILL BE DOING MORE EDUCATING

One of your jobs as the barn owner will be to educate as much as you can so the horse does not suffer. I have found that some horse owners have the *"Living out on the range"* mentality where they believe all horses should be able to handle the elements because the wild horses can do it out on the range. What they forget is that most of those wild horses don't live as long as the horses that are owned and fed hay twice a day and have shelter. Wild horses are very hardy horses. They had to be tough to survive all these hundreds of years in extreme weather. They are bred for that. Many of the breeds we have today are not hardy enough to withstand a hard winter out on the range. The more you can do to educate your clients the better off the horses in your care will be

One last thought - Your idea of when horses should be brought in due to bad weather and the boarder's ideas might be different. You have to feel secure in your decisions and it might not please everyone. We did have people leave over the years because they wanted their horse brought in at night for every little thing that popped up on the radar and I would keep explaining to them that this was outdoor board not inside stall board. I would always tell them that if they were going to worry that much they should just get a stall in the big barn and they would feel better. You see, almost all the time the horses are just fine. It's the owners that are having the hard time. I have tried my best to educate new horse owners over the years and it is something that will always come up once in a while during the winter especially here in the Frozen Tundra! Patience and education mixed in with a little laughter is always good.

THE HORSE THAT CAN'T KEEP WEIGHT ON

Another challenge I have had over the years with outdoor board has to do with having a horse that can't keep weight on. When we feed our horses we always feed a separate pile of hay for each horse. They will switch piles continually but they always have a pile to go to. Once in a while I will have a horse that comes to outdoor board that is a hard keeper. Either they are light eaters or have a hard time keeping weight on and need special attention. This can be upsetting for the owner of the horse when they notice their horse is losing weight. During those situations I have had many talks with the owner to find out what we can do to put weight back on the horse. What many horse owners don't understand is that sometimes hay alone is not enough. Sometimes a horse whether it is a very young horse, a senior horse or even a hard keeper like a thoroughbred will need some extra help nutritionally. I have had clients that didn't understand that in the past. It can be a very sensitive subject but needs to be addressed and when I have a horse that can't keep weight on, I encourage the boarder to have the veterinarian come and do a physical exam on the horse and then have a game plan from there. Sometimes it can be as simple as having the boarder come out to give their horse extra grain in the evening. There have been a couple of situations where the horse had a tooth problem and was losing weight. Some horses just can't keep their body warm in the winter and they end up burning more calories than they eat. Those horses benefit from blankets to help keep them warm and keep their weight on.

Each situation will be completely different so be prepared. The last thing you want is for the boarder to worry that you are not feeding enough hay each day. Make sure you have good hay and they have plenty of it during the winter months. If all your horses are a very healthy weight and you have one that is losing weight then it is time to talk with the boarder and create a plan for the horse. They may not know what to do and they will look to you for guidance.

~43~
VETERINARIANS AND FARRIERS

Whether you have your own place for your horses or board them, choosing a veterinarian and farrier will be part of owning a horse. When you decide to cross over to the other side and own a horse business, especially a boarding business with many horses and different people, you will need to decide if you are going to allow your clients to choose veterinarians and farriers of their choice or if you will only allow the ones you recommend. I have seen it done both ways at different barns.

When I was deciding how I wanted our boarding facility to run I knew I wanted the boarder to have complete control of who they wanted for their veterinarian and farrier. I believed that it was their horse and their choice. As long as they were pro-active on making sure their horse's feet were taken care of and up to date on shots, I was good with that. When our doors opened and all the horses came I was very surprised at all the different farriers and veterinarians that came to our barn. That was fine with me and I really enjoyed seeing how different farriers and veterinarians did things. What came as a surprise to me were the different beliefs and practices behind each of the professionals that came to our barn.

FARRIERS
We have had a lot of great farriers that have come through our barn over the years and did a great job and off they would go with no problems. They are professional and very knowledgeable about horse's hooves and shoeing. We have also had some farriers that have worked on horses out of our barn and by the time they left, they had the owner of the horse changing feed and putting on a grazing muzzle and in a couple cases had the owner of the horse in tears! Now changing dietary needs of a horse in itself is not a bad thing and in some cases it is needed. But there needs to be a balance and I have seen the extreme other end where changes were made that caused more problems in the long run. In the worst case scenario we have had a couple of farriers over the years who did not know what they were doing and caused severe damage to the horse's feet and the horse would end up becoming lame for a very long time.

I never realized all the different ideas out there and as the barn owner you will be asked to participate in these ideas for the boarder's horse. Be ready to have an answer. I didn't many years ago and I did a lot of things that I didn't want to do or that I questioned. It took me a couple of years to figure this out.

I have learned as I have gotten older that people are gimmick followers and I will admit that I am at fault once in a while also. When you have a barn with a lot of boarders you will see things you have never seen before, I sure did. Sometimes the boarder will look to you to see what your thoughts are on any particular subject. I have seen many tears through the years due to people trying new things that ended up hurting the horse. I am not trying to sound harsh at all but some of the things I have observed were not positive ones for the boarder or the horse. As the barn owner I felt I needed to be there to help them fix what was done and move forward. Even if the boarder may not do what you suggest, they might want you there to listen to their thoughts on the situation. As the barn owner you will be the one picking up the pieces most of the time.

If you are going to allow different farriers at your barn and you have a client that is asking what farrier you recommend, make sure it is one that has good references. Like any good service oriented business, check with other clients and see what kind of history the farrier has with people and other horses.

VETERINARIANS

I have tried over the years to have a good working relationship with all the veterinarians that come to our barn. Get to know your veterinarians and talk to them when you have some concerns in your barn with medications or a possible sickness or anything else out of the ordinary that may come up. They are there to help and I have found that the more I talk to them and we keep an open line of communication between the barn and the doctors, the better it is for everyone especially the horses. Remember, they are there to help and make your job easier when questions come up in the barn about sickness, viruses or the many other things that can affect the health of the horse.

People will panic if they think their horse's health might be compromised. It can start by something they read about online or all of a sudden they hear a horse start to cough in the barn or a number of other things they might hear about through the grapevine. I have had this happen several times over the years and when it does and your clients start to call you with lots of questions you will want to have answers. Talk to your veterinarian and tell them what is going on and they will help you to give an appropriate answer to your boarders. Your veterinarians will be your biggest supporter but they need to know what is going on ahead of time so they are not caught off guard either. The relationship with your veterinarian is invaluable. Creating a good partnership can really help your barn run smoothly and will make your job easier when something does come up where you need a doctor.

It's Okay Not To Have All The Answers

In the beginning of having our business one of the biggest fears I had was I didn't want any of the boarders to think I didn't know what I was talking about when it came to their horse's health. I put so much pressure on myself that I should know all the latest in medical problems and what can happen in different parts of a horse's body. I was worried that if I was not knowledgeable on everything that soon the boarders would wonder how I could be running a barn and properly taking care of their horses. I know now that was foolish thinking. I did not go to equine veterinarian school and neither do most barn owners or barn managers.

Years later I feel very comfortable telling a boarder that I don't have the answer but we can call the vet and ask them. If you are going to run a horse business, don't put that kind of pressure on yourself. You don't need to have all the answers. That is why you have doctors that went to school for many years to learn all the things they need to know to help a horse get better.

Work as a team with them. They need your input because you will know the horse's personality better than most anyone (even sometimes the owner) and you need them for their medical expertise. Together you will make a fantastic team and make the job much easier and safer for all when something does happen to a horse in your care.

WHEN YOU ARE ASKED TO GIVE MEDICATIONS

At my barn I decided as part of a service given to our clients I would give medications during the morning and afternoon feedings without any extra charge. With this many horses you are bound to have a horse or two on something. During the early years of business I was asked by a couple of boarders to give an extreme amount of a medicine for a very long period of time. It was way beyond the normal time you would give the medicine. I knew what the medicine was but I didn't feel comfortable giving it for the extended time period without the veterinarian's written direction. In one particular case the person could not come up with the doctor's written directions for the medicine and I told them that I would not give it any more without the proper paperwork. This person became very upset with me and because I was a new barn owner I really didn't know how to handle it. I had not ever dealt with a situation like this before and so I called my veterinarian and asked them what I should do under the circumstances. They gave me sound advice on what could go wrong and told me that I would be the one at risk of losing everything if something bad happened to the horse because of the medicine I was giving. That was all I needed to hear. I stuck to my decision not to give the medicine and this person left our barn eventually.

You will be asked to give many different things to the horses in your care through the years. Be prepared and know what you are giving. It is not worth the risk if something goes wrong. Some people are chance takers but I am not and I was not willing to take a chance with the horses under my care at my barn. Just remember if you give a medication without the proper paperwork from the veterinarian and the horse gets sick or worse dies, you will be at fault.

Before we started our boarding business, I had really only hung out with horse people that were like minded. Isn't that what we all do? When we opened for business I was all of a sudden thrown to a whole new world of different personalities and beliefs and I was not prepared for it and I now had to deal with it on a daily basis. My goal in this book to make you aware of the entire world of barn management which includes farriers and veterinarians and how they are an extremely important part running your horse business. I want to give you a realistic look at barn management so you are prepared for the unexpected.

~44~
BOUNDARIES

When I decided to write a book about our horse boarding business I really didn't know at the time what each of my chapters would be about. As I started thinking about what it takes to run a large boarding operation and all the people that are involved, I quickly realized there would be some sensitive subjects to talk about. Creating healthy boundaries between the barn owner, barn manager and clients was something I wanted to talk about in this book because it will become a big part of your day to day life when running your business. You might be wondering why I am even writing a chapter on the subject of boundaries and what could it possibly have to do with starting and running a horse business. Let me tell you right now that it has a lot to do with it!

Owning and running a horse business is unique in itself but then add into the equation that most horse boarding facilities are on the same property that the owners live on. That means that you never get away from it! Did I catch your attention now?

Think about most businesses. Many people have a business on their property and that in itself is not uncommon. It can be a store, trucking outfit, car repair etc. Most of the businesses people have on their property can close their store on a Sunday and not think about it at all until Monday morning. The exception to this of course would be farmers, ranchers and any other business that has animals on the property. Now you look at the horse world and of course because they are living breathing animals they need to be taken care of seven days a week, twenty-four hours a day. Your business will never close. I am not telling you this to freak you out, I just want you to get a clear picture of what you are about to embark on.

Now you add in the customer. As a boarding facility or training barn, your boarders or clients will most likely be able to come to your barn seven days a week. Our barn is open every day of the year. What makes the job of running and owning your own business a little tough (at least it was for me) was figuring out the boundaries so my family had family time. Most of us know what it is like to go to a job five days a week and see the same people every day. You might be best friends with some of your colleagues and enjoy being around them and even go out with them on a Saturday night. You can choose not to go out if you don't want to. You can take the entire weekend and stay at home and not see anyone or talk to anyone all weekend and then catch up with them on Monday. Having alone time without thinking about work is a very good thing. This was an area we had never thought about before and was an extremely hard adjustment for David and me.

There were many times through the years when I would be outside on a weekend to do chores and maybe I didn't feel the greatest or David and I had a huge disagreement and then I would still run into boarders in the barn and feel like I needed to be polite and nice. Don't get me wrong, I have wonderful people that board at our barn. But sometimes putting on a smile can be hard if you don't feel good or your dealing with a personal crisis and don't want anyone to see how you're feeling. The last thing I wanted was for our boarders to think something was wrong at the barn and then they would panic.

TRYING TO FIND A BALANCE IN HEALTHY BOUNDARIES

Boundaries between the boarders and my family became a difficult area for me to find the right balance in. When we first opened I would go out in the barn and talk for hours to people and share too many things that I should not have shared. I would talk about my personal problems and barn problems. **I know now that was not the right thing to do.** A lot of people come to see their horse and are private people and don't want to be bothered. I am sure I made people uncomfortable at times. The other side of the coin was that I got too involved in our clients problems and I really should have kept it more professional.

Over the years I have developed some very close friendships with some of our boarders and sharing personal things has been fine. I just had to learn not to share with everyone. Not everyone in the barn wants to hear about my private life and they also don't want to share theirs. They come out for enjoyment and peace in a hectic world. They might have just had a horrible day and just want to ride quietly by themselves.

When talking about boundaries and running a business on your property, it can come in different forms. Over the years we have had boarders that walk right into our home and never knock first. This might be someone that I barely know. I have had a boarder ride their horse right up to my living room window while my family was eating dinner. Privacy was gone at that point. I have had a boarder use our farm equipment without asking. I am just mentioning a couple of examples but you will see many as you go through the years with your business. Set your boundaries early on and make them very clear and it will cause much less stress in the future. Remember it is a business and it took me a long time to embrace that concept and own it.

Sundays became a day that I had a hard time with boundaries. Our barn doesn't close and I still do chores on Sunday but we try to make it somewhat of a day off (if that is possible). I am finally after all these years finally telling our boarders that if they call me, I might not get back to them until Monday unless it is an emergency. Even though we don't get a day off, my phone will ring seven days a week and it has rung as late at 11pm at night. To some of you reading this you might be thinking, what is the big deal? It is never a big deal to start with most brand new businesses but it will become one as you realize your time is really never your own when you own the business. Your personal and private time will become extremely valuable.

After running your business and realizing the extremely hard work it takes every day, you will see how important it is to set boundaries and time for you and your family. You have to or it will wear you down and burn you out. We live in a day where people want a response right away. Before cell phones and texting, if you called a business after hours on a Friday night you knew you would have to wait until Monday to get a call back. Not anymore. People want answers immediately and if they don't get it within a few hours, often they will call or text until you finally respond. Setting clear boundaries of hours in the barn and letting your boarders know you might not get back to them until Monday needs to be understood. You will have less stress if you do this right from the start. This took me many years to figure out.

Boundaries are a very good thing that help keep a business healthy. Not everyone that boards at your barn will want to share their life. Be careful not to make them feel uncomfortable and pressure them that they have to talk. It can lead to unhappy boarders and eventually they will leave and they might have been one of the nicest boarders you will ever have.

Trust me when I tell you that these things will come up and you will need to be prepared on how you want to handle them. If I could give any advice, let your clients have their space and enjoy time alone with their horse if that's what they want and enjoy. If you feel you have a client that has crossed over the line into your space and personal life and it makes you feel uncomfortable then you will need to be honest with them. It is not easy to do but once you start running your business like a business many of these problems will disappear on their own.

~45~
HANDLING THE BOARDER'S HORSE

Every one of us that owns a horse most likely spent countless days, months or even years looking for the perfect horse. When we found him we knew it. Our heart raced and we were the most excited we had been in a long time. Do you remember that feeling? I sure do. After we bought the horse and brought him home we did everything to make his life perfect. We thought he was perfect. As time went on we slowly started to realize that this beautiful horse we bought had a mind of his own and at times was not perfect and in fact could be naughty. Some of us chose to fix the naughtiness and a lot of us chose to ignore it.

In steps the barn owner and/or manager. As we opened our facility I was very comfortable with my horses and how to handle them. My world of experience was small dealing with the *horse/owner* combination. In fact it was zero. I had worked on horse farms and handled many different horses as the employee but now I was on the other end of the business.

After our barn was in full operation and I was handling almost forty horses every day, my eyes were truly opened up to all the different personalities, habits and behaviors both good and bad. Because our new barn housed twenty-seven horses we would hand walk out all those horses each morning and bring them in each evening. We had twenty-seven horses with twenty-seven personalities and lots of behaviors.

It was amazing to me that out of all horses that we would walk outside each morning, many of them could not walk quietly to the paddocks. Many of them pulled on me and tried to drag me around or worse, rush the gate as you open it and knock you over as they go through. I would have the ones that would continually try to bite at me while I was walking them out. I was finding out fast that I really needed to learn about each of these horses like they were my own and in some cases if the behavior was terrible I would need to bring it up to the owner. It was a new situation because if my horse would have been doing some of these behaviors I would have done something immediately to correct it but since all these horses belonged to other people, now I was trying to find a balance between correcting the horse and knowing when I needed to talk to the owner of the horse. I found myself in new territory again with owning a business. I knew that there would be some clients that would get upset if I talked to them about their horse's bad behavior.

I learned very early on in our business that many of the owners that had horses with bad behaviors really didn't mind the behavior or didn't see a problem with it and many times didn't want to do anything to fix it. We have had boarders that under no circumstances wanted to discipline their horse for any aggressive behavior because they thought it was cruel. I have seen both ends of the spectrum at our barn. This is where my job became very hard when dealing with the boarder that had a horse that is hard to handle. I am not a trainer and it is not my job to train a horse and correct these behaviors while walking them out to their paddock and bringing them back inside in the evening. Believe it or not you might be asked to help fix these problems. I don't think it is in the description of "barn owner or manager."

What the owner of the horse doesn't realize is how dangerous it is at times and when they are only dealing with their own horse they can't see beyond that. I have had owners upset at me a few times over the years because I have had to tell them about a behavior that needed to be worked on and corrected because it would only get worse. They would take offense to it the same way some parents do when they hear from their child's teacher that their son or daughter has been in trouble at school.

It was amazing to me the view of what different owners have as far as appropriate discipline. It is very hard dealing with a horse that is constantly trying to bite you but what makes the situation worse is when you see the owner constantly giving them treats and letting them chew on their winter coat and think it is cute. These are the horses that the behaviors continually get worse because of what the owner is doing. I have had a time or two over the years when I had a horse with a dangerous behavior and when I brought it up to the owner they told me they had never seen it before. It is human nature to want your horse to be perfect but they are a very large living breathing animal and it is very hard dealing with an owner that is in denial. I was again finding myself having to learn how to deal with people as much as the horses. In many cases dealing with the horse was easier.

Throughout the years David and I have been run over, bitten, head butted, kicked, body slammed and dragged (when we should of let go of the lead rope). I used to be nervous to discipline a horse in front of anyone at the barn because I was worried about what the owner would say. Now I realize I can't put my life in danger and I will very quickly tell the owner the problems we are having with their horse if I need to and then I will let them know there will be correction if it happens while I am leading their horse. As the barn owner you can't always worry about how the owner of the horse is going to respond. They might not like what you are saying but they need to know the truth and if said in a calm and professional manner it could make a difference in how the owner takes it. When I need to talk to a boarder about a bad behavior I now try my best to find something positive to tell them about their horse. It truly can make them feel better in a very tough situation.

COMMUNICATION IS SO IMPORTANT

Because I am better now at communicating with the owner right away and telling them my concerns, it is easier and it works out better in the long run. I haven't had any problem with the owners of a horse at our barn in a long time. I still once in a while have a difficult horse but good communication is *key* with the owner. If you are going to be running a larger size barn, there is a good chance you will have one or two horses with unruly behaviors and then you will have to deal with the owner. You might be surprised at their response. They will need to understand and work with you or you might need to tell them this is not the right barn for them. The bottom line is you don't need to get hurt on the job and it can happen in a second. Horses with bad behaviors make the job much tougher and you will get to a point where you realize it is not worth it. At the end of the day you have to do what is best for yourself and your business.

We have wonderful people at our barn and they have great intentions. We all do. If you get into this business you will eventually come across a horse that is dangerous or has extreme bad habits and when you do, you will need to be prepared on how to address it and handle the situation with the client. It was something I had to learn on the job. I had never dreamed I would be dealing with these situations when we opened.

As a barn owner I now believe it is so important to network with other barn owners so that you have a sounding board to talk about some of these issues and how other professionals in the business handle them. Talking to others in the business lets you know you are not alone and it is a great way to get ideas on how to make a tough situation better.

If I can give some advice in this area - If you are going to spend time discussing problems you have on your farm with other barn owners, make sure you find someone that can help you in a positive way and give good advice or even mentor you in the business. I wish I would have had someone to mentor me when we first opened years ago. Make sure that they can give you healthy positive solutions because believe me, you will hear many negative ways to fix a problem and that doesn't help anyone and it is not good for your business or your reputation.

~46~
ASKING A BOARDER TO LEAVE

Asking a boarder to leave our barn and giving them a thirty-day notice was an area that I never once gave a thought to when we we're talking about starting a horse boarding business. I had never known anyone that was asked to leave a barn and I didn't think we would ever have a problem where I had to make that decision. I was in for another big surprise with this part of the business.

Why on earth would we ever ask anyone to leave? What could go wrong? This was an area that no one ever talks about unless you are the owner of a business. Since I was new to the horse boarding business world I didn't know who to talk to about their experiences. I just went on thinking it would all be fine and we would have wonderful boarders and I wouldn't ever have to deal with this. This is another time when you can laugh!

Our boarding contract had a paragraph in it detailing the events that could lead up to an eviction of a horse and that was the most thought I gave it. In my mind the only possible reason that I would ever have to ask anyone to leave would be because they didn't pay their board or maybe if someone was caught stealing. I never dreamed I would have to ask someone to leave for other reasons.

DRAMA ON THE HORIZON

As you have read in earlier chapters, the first couple of years were pretty rough with getting accustomed to owning and running a boarding barn. I was learning very fast how drama can run a barn down very quickly and can make everyone very unhappy. It was starting to happen in our barn early in the first couple of years with very strong personalities and people that were into everyone's business.

I really tried hard to stay out of my boarders business and their personal life was to be private but we experienced situations where trainers and boarders were causing a lot of negativity in the barn and were not following barn rules and even making up their own rules. In our barn we had people that were gossiping and talking about others, tearing others down and trying to dominate the barn. People were accusing each other of selling drugs in the barn and pretty much anything else you could think of. The atmosphere in the barn became very bad very fast. The worst part about the entire thing was everybody was calling me and I had people crying and people that were telling me they were going to leave if something wasn't done about the small group of people that were controlling the barn. Yes I was in shock and my husband was even more. We couldn't believe this was happening.

This was when I was going to experience my first time asking someone to leave our barn. It was extremely hard but I knew where the problems were coming from and they needed to be addressed and stopped immediately and that would not happen unless these people left our barn. I wrote my first letter and explained all the problems surrounding the people involved and I suggested a different barn might be a better fit. I told them that they would have thirty days to find a new home for their horses. I tried to keep my letter as professional as possible. I was sick to my stomach. I gave it to the people involved and asked if they wanted to talk. I got no reply from them. The boarders left our barn the next day and I lost money. We had five boarders and horses leave over this situation but at that point the money didn't matter. What mattered most was that we had to get our barn back to a positive environment for everyone else.

Over the next few years I have had to ask a boarder to leave a couple more times and it is one of the hardest parts of the job that I have ever had to do. It has always been because the boarder has a different idea of what the barn should be and run like. When another boarder or trainer starts trying to change your barn and doing things differently than how you have set them up and then gets others to join in, that is when you have big problems. These are problems that can be far more damaging than not paying the board.

I have always tried to treat each boarder with respect even when I have had to ask them to leave. What they say after they leave is beyond your control but as long as you know that you tried your best to handle the situation as professional as possible, that is all anyone can ask for. I have made mistakes in this area through the years and have lost my temper a couple of times. To this day I still regret losing my temper and all I can do is learn from each situation.

Asking someone to leave is never easy and every barn owner might do it a little differently. You will need to find what works best for your business and what you feel is appropriate for your barn. The few times I have asked a boarder to leave I have always given them a thirty-day notice with the plan that I would treat them as best as I could while they were at our barn. They have always left a day or two after the notice was given which was less stressful for everyone. I hope you never have to ask someone to leave but if you find yourself in that situation, always be as professional as possible. I know it is hard because there is so much emotion involved in it. I have found that the times that I was professional to the boarder the smoother everything went.

I believe now that many of the problems we had in the early years stemmed from the new boarders not knowing us and trusting us. David and I were not being the leaders we should have been. We let people walk all over us and run the barn and that was our mistake. We had some very strong personalities that questioned everything we did at our farm and then they would talk and put the seed of doubt in other people's heads about the care of their horse. Be prepared and be open to explain how you do things at your barn and why you do them the way you do. All it takes is one person to start talking and it can get everyone worked up.

I know when I boarded my horses I wanted to make sure my horse had the best care. I am positive that goes through every clients mind because they have not yet learned to trust the barn owner. It takes time and it could take a very long time if you are starting a brand new facility. Once your barn gets a good reputation for being a safe and caring place for horses, I believe your job will be much easier even under the most difficult of situations.

It is okay for a client to have a difference of opinion but your clients need to understand this is how you are going to do things at your barn. If they don't agree how you do some things that is fine as long as they don't cross the line and start trying to change things. If they start to cross the line and create drama because of things they don't like then they need to find a barn that is better suited for them. There is a fine line between a difference of opinion and trying to change the entire barn.

What is even worse is when one person starts spreading the seeds of doubt to everyone else in the barn. It happens and it can start to make things into a real mess. Balance is something that is so vital for a healthy barn. Once you learn to be a leader many of these problems will disappear on their own. They did for us.

The few times we have had to give a thirty-day notice were all for emotional problems and difference of opinions all entwined together to make a volatile relationship between us and the boarder. You always hope you can reconcile the problem but sometimes you can't and that is when it is better for everyone involved to say goodbye and have them go their separate ways.

~47~
SAYING GOOD-BYE TO A HORSE

Euthanizing a horse is by far the hardest thing any of us will have to do if we are put in the situation where our horse has to be put down. There is nothing more heartbreaking than to say goodbye to our equine companion. As I am writing this chapter it brings tears to my eyes thinking about the last few years and the wonderful horses that have crossed my path and the ones that took their last breath here on our farm.

I knew when we opened our doors it would eventually happen where we would have an injured horse, very sick horse or a horse that had lived a very full life beyond his years and now it was time to say goodbye. I wasn't sure how I was going to handle it and as the barn owner I felt a very heavy responsibility to make sure I was there for the owner through the entire process. The problem was I didn't know what that process looked like on my end as the barn owner. I didn't know how other barn owners handled it when a horse dies or what their responsibility was to the owner. I never asked anyone but I knew in my heart that out of all the things that happen at our stable, this was by far one of the most important times when I needed to be there for the owner as much as they need me to.

A VERY PRIVATE DECISION

The one thing I was not prepared for when the time came was how involved and at times opinionated other boarders would be when someone in the barn was going to put down their horse. For something that was so private and heartbreaking I was not ready for the slew of questions I would be asked about the reasons behind the decision to put the horse down. This is an extremely sensitive area and I was learning real fast to keep it professional at all times and not give out any information without the owner's consent. It was amazing to me all the different views of when a horse should be put down. What should be a very private decision will be everyone's business very quickly and with that comes many different opinions. I realized early on I needed to make sure others in the barn knew that the euthanizing of a horse is a private matter and I didn't want to hear gossip running through our barn.

We have had several boarders put their horse down over the years and each one was for a completely different reason. One of the biggest worries that the boarder will have during this time is what others think and feel about their decision. They don't want others to think they made the decision too fast or without thinking it through. It can be very stressful on them and I realized after the first time that it was my job to make sure people didn't cross the line and say things that would hurt the person losing the horse.

I had to learn quickly that as the barn owner, the boarder is going to look to you for support and answers and many times your opinion on what you would do. Sometimes they just need you to be there to listen and be the shield so they don't have to deal with others while they are saying goodbye. You will have boarders that want to be there when the horse is euthanized and you will have boarders that don't want to be there at all. I have truly learned so much about people during this process and realize now that we all handle death differently and there is no right or wrong way to say goodbye. It really opened my eyes to how others handle the death of their horse.

As the barn owner or manager you will be asked about the best way to dispose of the body. We have had boarders that chose to cremate their horse but most often they are taken away by a rendering company that takes the body and uses it for meat and other byproducts. Be prepared by having some answers for the owner because they will not know what to do with the body or who to call afterwards and they will be too upset to deal with it. They are going to look to you for guidance with the entire process.

Could We Have Done More?

As I was writing this chapter I am saddened by the unexpected loss of a beautiful and very sweet senior Arabian gelding that was boarded at our farm. The night of his passing my husband did not sleep well at all and when we got up early the next day for chores he told me he kept wondering if there was anything more he could have done to prevent the passing of this horse. We talked about it for quite a while and I tried to reassure him that we did everything the veterinarian's had told us to do and there was nothing more we could have done. I realize more and more now as a barn owner that these thoughts will go through your head each and every time this happens. Prepare yourself because even though it may not be your own personal horse it will still be a horse that was in your care for possibly a very long time and it will be hard and very emotional for you as the barn owner. It has been for David and me every time. This was again another area that we were not prepared for when we opened our business.

What an Honor

Every time that a horse has been euthanized on our farm I felt it was an honor to be there with the owner even under the saddest of circumstances. I always wondered how I would handle it when it happened and each time has been completely different. It is never easy but it truly is one of the most important jobs you will ever have as a barn owner or manager.

~48~
It's a Working Farm

We live in a world that does not like to be inconvenienced. Not everyone is like this but the mentality for many people in our beautiful country has become- ***We want things done now, done to our liking and done after I am in bed so it doesn't inconvenience me.*** Are you wondering where I am going with this chapter? Keep reading because this is important!

Growing up in Los Angeles California I knew absolutely nothing about farm life except for what I had read or saw in pictures in school. I knew I always wanted to live in the country and always had the dream of living on a horse farm but I had no idea of what it took to keep a farm operating. The day to day chores and hard work that happens on a farm every day of the year never entered my head. The only chores I was familiar with were cleaning stalls and feeding horses and I only helped with that on the weekends. Not a true picture at all of a working farm. When I dreamed of working on a horse farm I thought about giving horses baths and hand-grazing them out in the warm sun while they eat the tall green grass. Brushing them for hours and watching the farrier put shiny new shoes on my horse and then proudly riding off. Can any of you relate to this? I wanted so bad to be part of the life I saw in pictures. Did you ever think about the fact that most of the pictures they show in children's school books are beautiful summer pictures? Where are the winter pictures?

I was such a city slicker that I didn't even know that farmers worked seven days a week milking cows and they had to be milked every day of the year or they would get sick. I was about to learn a lot about living and working on a horse farm and the daily jobs that need to get done no matter what the weather is.

YOU HAVE TWO CHOICES

When our business opened many years ago I wanted it to be perfect for our boarders. I wanted them to have a slice of heaven at our farm and never be bothered with the day to day grind of a working farm. David and I didn't want to be in the way of our clients as they got their horses out and groomed them in the crossties and we didn't want to do anything to make their horse nervous or possibly spook. I was quickly learning that things still need to get done on a farm and you have two choices. You can do everything after hours when the barn is closed and give up sleep all together or you can do the things that need to get done during the day and the boarders will have to deal with it.

At first when we opened for business, David spent a lot of time after hours doing projects that he couldn't do in the barn because he didn't want to bother a boarder with noise or being in the way. Some of the things he would need to fix involved tools that were noisy. He wouldn't cut the grass or trim next to the building or arenas until after people and horses were done which was often late in the evening. He was working himself ragged because he didn't want to be in anyone's way. Then winter came and he would get up extremely early, sometimes at 2am in the morning to plow snow so he wouldn't be in the way when they came to ride. This was his business and he was trying so hard to make it the best boarding facility around and bending over backwards not to bother the boarders. He was putting in hours that were killing him. We couldn't afford to hire someone to plow snow or cut grass and he was doing it all himself beside the other ten hours of work on our farm. He tried so hard to not bother the boarders but it was going to come with a cost to us. We had to make a change and the boarders were going to have to realize that this was a working farm and things have to get done and we were going to do them during the day.

As the first couple years rolled on our stable was very busy all the time. David was always using the skid loader to move hay or snow or fix something. Trucks were always coming in with hay or shavings and our small utility vehicle is used every day to feed horses outside and drag the arenas. Then of course the grass needs to get cut. Whenever he was using any of the machines to take care of a job of course it was noisy. He is an extremely careful man and always very aware of what is going on around him but it was still noisy.

I can remember one time after a heavy snowfall David went into the arena to let the people riding know that he was going to be moving snow that was outside the arena wall. There was a lot of snow and it needed to be moved before it got hard packed and he didn't want to be doing it late at night when everyone was gone. He went in the arena and let everyone know he would be moving snow outside and it would be noisy. Everyone was okay with it. It was their decision to ride even after he told them what he was doing. We did have a boarder fall off his horse during the time that David was working outside and there were different opinions of why he fell off. Some say the horse spooked from the noise and others said that was not the case. The boarder was upset and ended up leaving our barn.

We have had boarders early on in our business ask us if we could do some of the jobs in the evening or before we open. Back then we would have always said yes. We were trying too hard to please our clients. Now we have learned to politely tell our clients no and that we will be doing these jobs during the day. We would always be nice but now our boarders understand that the job needs to get done and it will get done during the day. So many different types of personalities will fill your barn and most of them will love the idea of desensitizing their horse to new sounds. You most likely will get a boarder now and then that will be extremely nervous of everything and it might make your job a little tougher.

What the general public doesn't realize (and I didn't either at first) is that most farms are run by the owner and it is not realistic to do all the maintenance before or after hours. Who wants to cut grass or fix things at 5am in the morning? We sure don't. Running a horse farm and keeping up on all the jobs that need to be done is never ending. You will feel like you are walking on egg shells sometimes with a boarder and trying not to be in their way and other times you will just have to let them know you have no other choice but to get the job done now.

It is a balancing act and something that we never gave any thought to when we were starting our business. I do believe most of the time your boarders will understand that the jobs need to get done. We have great boarders now that understand and like the fact that David takes care of things around the farm and they don't mind if it is done in the middle of the day. I sure wish we would have started out that way but it was a learning process and it taught us a lot about dealing with people and running a business on a daily basis.

~49~
Let Them Know You Care

As I sat down to write this chapter I started to think about the special things people have done for me over the years that made me feel important or that I mattered. When I thought about some of the things people have done for me that really touched me, it had nothing to do with money. Most of those kind gestures were very inexpensive or didn't cost anything at all but they made me smile and even made me feel that what we were doing for the horses in our care was important.

The same goes for your clients. They want to feel like they are important and that their horse is important to you. It is so easy to get caught up in a world where everything is about money but just as my grandmother told me years ago, her favorite gifts from her grandkids were always the homemade ones. Many years later I feel the same thing with my daughters.

If you are going to start a boarding business, the truth is unless you are financially well off to begin with you are going to be strapped for money. Most businesses start off in the red and it takes years to show a profit. That was so true about our business so I needed to find little ways to let our boarders know they were special and I truly cared about their horse without it costing us a lot of money.

Here are a few ways I have tried to let our boarders know I care about their horse and them

Communication is one of the most important elements of running a business and without it your business can fall apart overnight. Because I am on the computer so much I found it very easy to communicate through email often.

If the horses are left in their stalls for the day due to bad weather or extreme cold temperatures, I send out an email early in the morning so the boarders know we left the horses in and then they can make arrangements if they want someone to come and get their horse out to stretch his legs or pick his stall. I have found that the boarders greatly appreciate that I take the time to let them know this through email and they can plan accordingly.

I also will let the boarder know if their horse has lost a shoe or a blanket strap has broken or if their supplements are gone. Because quite a few of our boarders work, they may not make it out until the weekend so this way if they know their horse has lost a shoe they can call their farrier and get the shoe put back on. It makes life a lot easier for them.

I found texting is a great tool. It is extremely easy to use and almost everyone uses it. It is a great way to communicate and keeps you in touch with your clients. I also found it much faster when I don't have time to talk but I need to send a short note.

Another thing I try to do for our boarders is to get back to them in a timely manner. If they call, text me or email I try to get back to them the same day. The only day I don't get back to them quickly (unless it is an emergency) is on Sunday. They know this and understand that I try to make Sunday somewhat of a day off. It may sound simple but they will appreciate it.

When a new horse comes to our facility the owner is usually very nervous about the first introduction in the herd. I will call the owner and let them know how the first couple of days are going so they can rest a little easier. They usually can't be out at the barn all day long to watch so if I let them know how everything is going, they can relax and not worry.

We have forty horses at our facility, so when spring and fall comes it can be crazy when scheduling for shots, teeth and anything else that needs to be done. I let our boarders choose who they want for veterinarians but I do schedule an all-day appointment with our local clinic to take care of all the spring and fall needs for the horses. The only thing our boarders need to do is sign up and put down what they want done for their horse. If they can't be there I will take care of their horse for them no matter what is being done. These are the only two times during the year when I don't charge the boarder to hold their horse. Many of them work and can't be out so they really like the fact that I will be holding their horse and taking care of them afterwards.

It's all the little things you do that make a difference. If a horse has all of a sudden stopped eating all his grain or doesn't like a supplement the owner just purchased, I let them know. I keep a close eye on each horse and if they look like they are starting to lose weight I let them know. Then we can discuss it and have a plan. All these things will set your facility apart from the others and your boarders will greatly appreciate it.

It is the highest compliment when a boarder tells me that our barn is the first barn they have boarded at where they don't have to worry about their horse at all. They can go on vacation and enjoy it and never worry. When you have a client tell you that they completely trust your judgment then you know you have succeeded in your business and making it the best that it can be. All anyone ever wants is a kind word or a smile and taking a quick moment to tell them about something special you might have seen their horse do will make your clients day. I know it would for me.

All these things I have shared with you don't cost a penny but they are worth a million to the owner of the horse in your care.

~50~
ENCOURAGEMENT GOES A LONG WAY

I was sitting in church this morning as it was about to begin and I have to admit that my mind was in another place. As I have been writing this book it has been self-consuming and church should be the one place that I should not be thinking about it. But here I was thinking about what I was going to write about in the next chapter and starting to realize I am almost done with this book. It is winding down but I still felt like something was missing in the pages that I hadn't talked about yet but I could not pin-point what it was. That was until this morning at church.

Church and horse barns have always been a place of comfort for me. I always try to listen to what the pastor is saying and then my mind starts thinking about how God wants me to use it in my daily life on our horse farm and running our business. As I was listening this morning something he said hit me upside the head and I realized I wanted to write about it and how it goes hand in hand with my business and really any business. **Our pastor told us we should encourage and challenge each other**. He was sharing about our faith and our daily walk but also about the daily life that we live after we leave the church building.

It hit me that I need to be more encouraging to my boarders at our barn and gently challenge them to step out of there comfort zone and try new things with their horse. I realized as the barn owner that when I walk in to the barn and see a boarder with their horse, at that moment I need to be encouraging to them if I see them struggling and help them if they need help. They may not tell me with words but they might be very nervous inside and not sure what to do with their horse but they don't feel comfortable asking for help. They might be having a behavior issue and feel stupid in front of the others so they keep to themselves. Instead of asking for help they let the behavior continue because deep down inside they hope it will go away and no one will notice. I have been in that same spot with horses I have owned and feeling like I had no one to go to for help. I can remember places that I boarded years ago and when I was younger and the last person I would ask for help from was the barn owner. I decided I didn't want that to be the same with my barn.

I started to think about the wonderful people at our barn and how some of them have always wanted a horse but have never been able to afford one until later in life and now that they have this thousand pound animal, they are not quite sure what to do when a problem arises. A behavior creeps up or they have new tack and don't know how it goes on correctly and they feel uncomfortable asking for help. I believe this happens more often than we know. I need to remember that not every person was able to have or afford a horse as a child and getting your first horse in your fifties is a lot different than getting one as a teenager. It made me realize I need to be more encouraging and to let them know I am always here to help them if they need help. I needed to make myself more available to them if they have a question. They need to feel it is a safe place to ask questions and if I don't know the answer then I will find out the correct answer for them.

WE ALL GET NERVOUS AT TIMES

Almost thirty years ago I had a chance to work at this horse farm and I had not been around horses for a few years. I was newly married and I was busy with my new life in Wisconsin. I went to the farm for an interview and the owner asked me to put a halter on one of the horses. This was something I had done thousands of times throughout my life but all of a sudden I froze and I couldn't remember how the halter went on! I was so nervous and wanted to look like I knew what I was doing but in the process I blanked out and I am sure I looked stupid. I am sure the owner could see that I was nervous and helped me and all of a sudden the fear left and it was just like I had been working at this farm for years.

All it took was a gentle and encouraging word. I now try to remember that, all anyone is looking for is a smile and encouraging words. When running your own business, remember that when you walk in to the barn you will set the tone of the moment just by what you say to your boarders or clients. They just want to make sure they are doing everything right and if something is not right then gently help or correct the issue and try to remember when you first started handling horses and how nervous you were. We all have been there at one time or another and we all have made mistakes. I have made some really stupid ones over the years. It will truly make your barn a safe place for your boarders to learn and it will create a positive atmosphere in your barn and separate your business from the others.

~51~
THINGS I'VE LEARNED OVER THE YEARS TO MAKE THE JOB EASIER

As I was writing this book it really was amazing to me how different we do things at our barn now compared to how we did them in the beginning.. I have learned many different things to make the job easier and to save money. I thought I would share a few with you.

Leaf Blower-Our barn is two hundred feet long and has a cement aisle way. When we first opened we would take a push broom and sweep the entire aisle way each morning after all the stalls were cleaned. It was exhausting to say the least and very time consuming. My arms would feel like they were going to fall off. I have to admit, it was too much work for me but David would do it every morning and evening.

After we were in business for about a year one of our boarders told us that a barn they were at previously would use a leaf blower to blow the aisle way and it was extremely fast and did a much better job than any broom could do. We decided to give it a try and we have been using a leaf blower ever since and it blows everything from dirt and hair to cob webs off of the stalls. I would highly recommend it for your barn.

Ivory Soap-One of the hardest things to watch is a horse chewing on the wood in a stall. It was even harder when our stalls were brand new. I would watch a horse start to chew and down to the store I would go to buy an expensive product to paint on the wood so the horses wouldn't chew. There are many types of products out there and if you have to use them enough it can become very expensive.

I had a trainer who worked out of our barn tell me to use Ivory Soap or any strong smelling soap and rub it all over the area that the horse is chewing. It works fantastic and the horses do not like the taste of soap. We even had a couple of horses last year start chewing on the lid of our automatic waterers and after I put the soap all over the lid they stopped. I haven't gone out and bought any horse products for chewing wood in years. I always use soap and it is much cheaper.

Baling twine for crossties-If you have crossties, you are going to have horses at one time or another spook and try to break loose out of the crosstie area. It can be dangerous to the point where they can get hung up or they can pull so hard that they bring down part of the wood the crosstie is attached to. The last thing I want is a horse getting hurt and if I am going to be honest, I don't want my barn destroyed also. Another great tip that was given to us from a previous boarder was to take a little baling twine and tie it to the ring (that the crosstie hooks to) and then attach the crosstie to the twine. If the horse pulls hard enough they will break the twine and that is better than breaking anything else or hurting themselves in the process. This was a great tip and we have used twine on all our crossties for years now.

Composting Horse Manure-If you have horses than you will have manure! We have many horses and we have lots of manure. During the first three years of our business we would spread the manure out in the fields in the fall and we always kept horse manure on hand (which wasn't a problem) for the winter when we would get ice everywhere. During our fourth year of business we had a wonderful family move to Wisconsin from the U.K. and they started boarding at our barn. Karen would help with cleaning stalls and asked me one day what we do with our manure. I told her how we got rid of it and she told me how they compost it and sell it in the U.K. She went on to explain how composted horse manure is a fantastic source of nutrients for flowers and vegetables and we should give it a try.

I had never heard of composting it before but I started reading up on it and decided I was going to compost most of our manure for a year and then sell it. I now sell our composted manure in our fifty pound grain bags (great way to recycle all those grain bags) and in bulk. I have been doing this for years now and I sell completely out of it each spring. People come back year after year for our compost and it also gives me a little spending money on top of it.

I am always looking for ways to save time and money and make the job easier. The longer you are running your barn the more you will find yourself looking for ways to make your job easier. Be open to suggestions that a boarder might give you. I have had many great suggestions over the years and many of them we still use to this day.

~52~
CLINICS ARE ALWAYS GOOD

People love clinics and when you own a horse, there is always something new to learn. I love having clinics at our barn and it always brings new people to our barn and it gets our name out there at the same time. I enjoy having many different types of clinicians here at our barn because I believe you can learn something from all of them. From a financial stand point, it is also a good way to make a little extra money on the side and people will remember your place when they are looking for a possible boarding facility.

I have had clinics of almost every discipline at our barn and they all have been fun and bring a fresh perspective. If having a huge riding clinic might seem a little overwhelming at first, try something smaller. Have a trailer loading clinic or a clinic on nutrition which doesn't involve as much preparation. We have had our local veterinarians come and give a clinic on "health and well-being of your horse" and anything medical that people would like to discuss. Clinics on health and nutrition are always great and it can be done in the winter when it might be too cold to have a riding clinic. One of our most attended winter clinics was a clinic on nutrition. We had a person come in and talk about different grains and supplements and all the pros and cons of each. This is another great clinic to host in the winter.

When deciding on what kind of clinic you want to have, sometimes variety can be fun. We put on a clinic one summer and the clinician came and taught the clients how to do horse tricks. He taught them how to make their horse bow and count and many other fun things. I was surprised that this clinic had more adults in it than kids with all types of horses. It was one of the best clinics we have ever had at our barn.

Learning at a "Mock horse show" clinic with Dan Grunewald of Jefferson, Wisconsin

When setting your fee for the clients that are going to participate in it, you want to make sure that you include the cost of insurance for the day. You will want to talk to your insurance agent to find out what kind of extra insurance you will need. It is usually not very expensive. Your auditing fee might change a little depending on who you have for your clinician also. It is better to charge a little less and have it well attended than to make your price too high and have very poor attendance. Make it affordable and they will come.

Here is a list of different clinics to give you some ideas:

Trailer loading

Nutrition

Health and Well–Being

First Aid clinic

Saddle fitting and correct tack

Clipping

Braiding

Farrier and learning about the hoof

Blanketing and different types of blankets (There are so many types of blankets out there and it can be very confusing)

Trail riding clinic

Horse show clinic

Jumping clinic

Problem solving clinic

Having a foal clinic

Breeding clinic (There are many people that have thought about breeding their mare but don't know where to start.)

Showmanship clinic

Western or English riding clinic

Dressage clinic

Driving clinic

Natural Horsemanship clinic

Teaching tricks to your horse clinic

Learning to ride all over again - for riders fifty and over

Facing your fears clinic (This is a great clinic for the older person that has fears which many of us do!)

Reining clinic

People always want to learn new things about their horse and themselves. Clinics can be a huge positive experience for everyone. The trailer loading clinic we had at our barn was one of my favorites because it is such a problem area for so many people. If you think about it most people that show or trail ride work hard all winter riding as much as they can. Then the day comes to go to a show or trail ride and their horse will not get into the trailer. A lot can happen over the winter and some horses develop a fear all over again. I have seen boarders all ready to go to a horseshow and never get there because they could not get the horse loaded even three hours later! It is heartbreaking for the person and very stressful on the horse. Trailer loading and nutrition are two clinics you could probably have each spring and people would never get tired of it. They are topics that always need refreshing and are very easy to put on.

I hope this gives you some good ideas and remember most of all, if you have never hosted a clinic at your farm then start small and keep it simple. We made the mistake of hosting a very large clinic for our first clinic and it was very stressful. We had ten horses coming in from all over the state for this big dressage clinic we were hosting and it turned out to be an unbelievable amount of work. A dressage trainer that was working in the area had connections to a clinician who also happened to be an "O" Dressage Judge. What that meant was that she was one of the judges for the Olympics dressage competition. This trainer approached us and asked us if we would be willing to host the clinic at our barn. The clinician would fly in from Florida for the clinic and it would be a two day clinic. I was so excited and right away I said yes! It was going to be so exciting to have an Olympic judge here at our barn giving a clinic and the caliber of horses that were going to attend would be amazing.

The trainer that was taking care of all the details would let me know what was going on and she told me what we should charge for the stalls for two days and David and I would not need to do any work at all. The owners of the horses would be responsible for making sure the stalls were completely cleaned out before they left on Sunday. This trainer also set the auditing fee and I would be splitting it with her. I would make a little money from the auditors and at the time I thought I would make some extra money renting out the stalls.

Well the day came and the ten horses arrived from all over the state of Wisconsin and I got them all situated in their stalls. The owners of the horses all seemed very nice and the clinician flew in and the clinic started.

This clinic was geared for higher level dressage riders and it all seemed to go well but very poorly attended by auditors. The trainer had also contacted a couple local tack vendors to set up their trailers at our barn for the weekend. After both vendors had been here for a couple of hours one of them approached me and was very upset because she told me that normally only one vendor comes to a clinic so there is not competition between the two vendors. She felt this was a waste of her time. I had to explain to her that I did not set this clinic up or make any arrangements. She stayed but due to the low attendance she sold very little and neither did the other vendor.

Sunday afternoon came and the clinic was over. The clinician had left to catch a flight back to Florida and all the riders and horses loaded up and left also. Do you know that out of ten stalls that were rented only one person cleaned out their stall! I am not sure if the trainer forgot to tell them since she took care of all the details but David and I were stuck cleaning nine stalls completely out and we made very little money. It definitely was not worth our time for what we were paid. I charged way to low of a stall fee and ended up doing a ton of clean up all through the barn for all the people that attended the clinic. The trainer never checked on one stall and she left in a hurry also.

I said never again would I let someone else make all the arrangements for a clinic here at our barn without everything going through me first. It was poorly run and I believe would have had better attendance if the auditing fee was not so expensive. I have to say that David and I felt taken advantage of that weekend and did not make enough money for all the work we had to do afterwards.

If you are going to put on a clinic be in charge of it yourself. If someone else wants to run it through your barn then make sure every detail goes through you first for your approval. Things can get out of hand fast and it is not worth the little money you might make. Since that first clinic here at our barn we have had many clinics throughout the years and they all have been wonderful and fun now that I know what to expect.

~53~
THINGS WE WOULD DO DIFFERENTLY

Over the years I have had many people come look at our barn to see how it is built and what the design is like. People that are interested in building their own barn will ask us what we like and don't like about our barn. One of the most often asked questions we get about our facility is, "What would we do differently in the building design now that we have been in operation for a few years?"

It is funny how you can have an idea in your head about how you want something to look and after you build it and start using it, you find out that some changes would have made much more sense. I think this is so common with people who build houses and I know now it is common with people who build barns.

I talked to David about this chapter and asked him about things he wished he would have done differently in the design of the barn and he also gave me his list. Here are some of the things we would do differently.

BUILDING TOO BIG TO START AND GOING INTO HUGE DEBT

This is a huge one for us. This is the most important one for me to share because when we were trying to decide what size our barn should be we didn't have any idea how the debt would affect our lives. Looking back, David and I built too large to begin with. We should have started out smaller and took our time adding on as money came in.

Most businesses have some kind of debt when they first start out. We didn't have any of our own money to put into the project and we borrowed one hundred percent of the loan. I would not do it that way if I could do it over again. I never realized until we were into it for about five years how much you are a slave to the business and bank if your debt ratio is too high compared to what you are bringing in. With too much debt it doesn't leave you room to hire help and you will end up working seven days a week for many years. I would never wish that on anyone because we have done it now for several years with very few vacations and a few days off here and there. Because of the huge building mess we got ourselves into and all the lawsuits, our debt load has not let us live life like we thought we would be able to. You can get burned out over time and your dream business can become a very hard life.

Don't get me wrong, I love our business but I had envisioned having employees by now for the weekends and that is not the case. If we would have had less debt we would have been able to hire after a few years. These are all things to think about when applying for a loan and the long term of your business.

GROOMING STALL

We have a large barn with twenty-seven horses housed in it and we only put in one grooming stall. With all the traffic of horses back and forth down the aisle, I know now if I could build again I would put three grooming stalls up and down the barn so that people can get their horses out of the aisle way. We have many crosstie areas but this means you have to walk your horse by each one and it can sometimes be congested and not safe. When the farrier or vet come to our barn they usually use the grooming stall but I have had two farriers here at the same time which means one of them are out doing feet in the main aisle. Our barn is a very busy barn and now that we have been open for a while I would definitely add more grooming stalls.

AUTOMATIC WATERERS

This is a big one for David and me. It is a ton of work filling water buckets two (sometimes three) times a day and it is even harder in the winter. It takes up a lot of time morning and night and that is *time* that we could be using to do something else.

Time vs. Money-When thinking about building your barn, there is a lot of things that go into it and many of them you will not figure out until it is done and your business is up and running. Putting in automatic waterers can be expensive initially. We have twenty-seven stalls so automatic waterers would have been very expensive when you add in all the cost of the water lines and hooking all of them up.

Now that we have been in business for many years, I am sure the automatic waterers would have paid for themselves a few times over. If you live in a cold climate state then you need heated water buckets in the winter if your barn gets below freezing temperatures. Our barn gets very cold in the winter so we have our heated water buckets running for about six months out of the year every night and if the days are extremely cold then they are running during the day also. It cost a lot less to heat a little bit of water in an automatic waterer than a six gallon heated water bucket. I was in shock at how much our electric bill shot through the roof when we starting running the heater buckets. I believe now it would have saved us time (which is so important) and money which is even more important.

WASH STALL

I am very happy with our wash stall but if I was to do it all over again, I would have put the wash stall on the back end of our barn. When we designed our barn we put the wash stall right in front as you enter our barn. It causes a lot of congestion as you enter our barn and the wind blows right in the front and it can be cool and drafty at times. We also were not looking at our cement as it was being poured and if I had to do it over I would make sure the cement in the wash stall was slanted more into the drain area then what it is now. We always have problems with water running down the aisle. These were things I never gave any thought to when we were building.

HAY, GRAIN & SHAVINGS ROOM

When we designed our back room that would house our hay, grain and shavings, we underestimated how much hay we would go through in a year's time. Our back room is big but not big enough to hold all the hay we need for a year. We are very lucky that the farmer we buy our large bales from will save fifty to seventy-five large bales for us that we always have delivered around late March or April. I know it is a pain for him and it takes up storage room in his barn but he always has been so kind to do this for us. When he delivers the rest of our hay in the early spring it gets us through to the first cutting in early summer. If we were to build over again, we would have made our hay room much larger. Better to have it too big than not big enough.

Barn Design

When David and I were talking about things we would do differently, one of the first things he mentioned that was high on his list was the overall barn design. Our barn has basically three different buildings that are all connected. We are happy with how it looks on the outside but the problem comes in the winter time. Any kind of snow accumulation makes it much harder for snow removal. Because we have a lot of ins and outs with the building itself, it means that snow gets piled up in lots of corners and David has to remove it by hand because it is too small of an area for the skid loader. The problem occurs when we don't remove the snow right away and water seeps into the barn in all the corners. If you live in a state where you have a lot of snow, think about snow removal because it can truly be a headache. David always tells me he wishes our barn was a complete square! It would be boring for me but then he could take his truck and just plow all the way around the barn and be done.

If you can afford to hire someone to plow all your snow then the design will not matter but if you have to do all the work yourself then the design will become very important.

Storage for Arena Stuff

We have a very diverse group of horses at our barn and with that come all kinds of equipment. We have carts for horses and minis and jump standards, trail equipment and lots of poles. If I could do it all over again I would design a small room attached to our indoor arena that would store all this stuff and make it easy to bring in and out of the arena. Because we don't have that, all the equipment is stored in two corners of the arena. We are very lucky because everyone is very good at keeping everything nice and neat but it would look so much nicer if it wasn't all stored in the corners. Because our arena is so large it works out fine but if you have a smaller arena it can really take up a lot of riding space.

Location of Paddock Automatic Waterers

We have five large paddocks on the east side of our barn and this is where most of the horses enjoy their day outside. When we decided to put automatic waterers in each paddock we thought it was a pretty easy decision on where to locate them. We had the water line dug and the electric put down in the ground and placed each automatic waterer in the front of each paddock about six feet from the gate where we bring the horses in and out. Big mistake!

After it was all done and the automatic waterers were working great then the horses arrived. During the day the water system worked great and the horses were drinking out of them with no problem. What we never anticipated was the huge problem we would have in the afternoon when it was time to bring the horses in for the night. We found out very fast that many of the horses would pace right next to the gate and the automatic waterers. If the ground is hard and dry then it is no problem. But in springtime when the ground is thawing out and we have water and mud everywhere, it becomes a soupy mess very fast. Each spring this happens and our automatic waterers start to tip forward or tilt to one side because the ground is so soft and the horses have pounded it down so low.

Almost every summer David has to go out and unhook all of it and re-due the base and re-hook up each automatic waterer. It is all due to the fact that the horses are constantly walking by the gate in the afternoon. The ground becomes too soft to hold the automatic waterers firmly in place. We have since the first year put heavy cement slabs down under each unit and it has helped a little but it cannot hold up to the weight of horses pounding the ground continually when the ground is so soft.

If I was to give any advice on location of putting your waterers in your paddocks, I would advise not to put them anywhere near your gate where you bring horses in and out. Many years later David and I still talk about having our water line dug up and relocated and then move our waterers. It is an expensive job to have your water lines moved so if you can, do it right the first time. I wish someone would have told us this when we were putting ours in.

INSULATING OUR BARN

When we built our barn we only put insulation on the ceiling of the entire barn. Now after many very long winters we are talking about insulating the entire barn. If you live in a state that gets cold in the wintertime, the winter will be much harder and longer if you are working all day in a barn that is colder than a freezer at times. It is worth it to spend the money and insulate if you can.

It is also good for business. I have lost boarders over the years because our barn is extremely cold in the winter. It becomes very hard for people to ride under these circumstances and sometimes they will go elsewhere even if the barn is not as nice just to have a warmer barn. Weigh out the options. I wish we would have in the beginning. This was something we never really gave much thought to.

~54~
LIFE LESSONS IN RUNNING A BUSINESS

As I was finishing this book I realized how many things I have learned over the years about myself and running a horse business. When I put all the chapters together I really wanted one about growing and learning from the mistakes I have made and I really wanted to share some of the deeper life lessons I've learned from running my own business.

When you walk into any business and you meet the owner of the establishment, we usually assume, they must know what they are doing because they own and run a business. In most cases they had to learn just like everyone else from trial and error. There is a good chance they did not know very much about running their business in the beginning. Most successful business people learn from their mistakes and change what they are doing wrong. This is something that will be so different for each and every person.

Now understand you still need to have experience in the type of business you want to start and you need to be familiar with how your business is going to operate on a day to day basis but don't let a mistake ruin your day. You will have plenty of mistakes especially at first and if you let it control your day you will have many bad days ahead. Stand up and shake off the dust and learn from them. In the arena of horse professionals and clients you are going to be bombarded with many opinions and you will learn to stand your ground and also be open to new ideas. Listen to those around you that have done it longer and then take the ideas you like and use them and put the rest away.

Listening to others that have been in the business longer does not mean you have to do it their way but there is a very good chance they will be able to help you. I wish to this day I had taken the time to talk to more people when we started our business. Remember, if someone doesn't want to take the time to talk with you about the business you are starting then keep looking. We have such great tools for communication now and social media is wonderful for hooking up with others in the same field as you. I have met some very nice people on Facebook and there are wonderful groups you can join for the horse professional.

GOING INTO DEBT

This is a big one for David and me. Many people believe the lie that if they go into debt for their business that it is a good debt because they can write it off on their taxes. The whole idea of writing purchases off on your taxes doesn't change the fact that you still need to make the monthly payments. Buying a new truck or tractor for the farm is a huge write off but if you have a monthly payment of four or five hundred dollars a month for the purchase you still need to come up with that money. What if your business is not bringing in an extra four or five hundred to cover the payment? This is how businesses ***go out of business!*** It was too much too soon and they were not prepared for the rainy days their business will have. You need to remember that at the beginning of almost every new business you are going to have a lot of debt. Don't keep increasing it to buy more stuff for the business. I had that mentality in the beginning. I realize now that my life would be much easier and I would be freer to enjoy life if we didn't go into so much debt. Don't be a slave to the lender and take control of your business destination.

I absolutely love the saying ***"Slow and steady wins the race."*** Nothing is truer and if you go slow it will eventually pay off. Before you sign your life away really make sure you know what you are getting into and remember that with horses, it is seven days a week, twelve months a year and you will burn out real fast if you can't afford to hire anyone to give you a day off.

IT'S NOT PERSONAL, IT'S BUSINESS

This was probably one of the hardest lessons for me to learn over the years of running our business. It can be exhausting trying to please everyone and eventually you will hit the bottom and be heartbroken because you did everything and it wasn't enough.

Every decision you make every day regarding your business will have positive feedback and at times negative feedback from your clients. Above all else, you need to do what is best for the business because it does absolutely no one any good if you go out of business. As the years have gone by I have learned not to make such quick decisions regarding our business and that was hard for me at first. I was always the person that would run with an idea before thinking it through. I have finally learned to slow down and really think about the changes I want to make in the business. I have also learned that not everyone will like the changes or ideas I want to make but you have to do what is best for the business and it usually works out. Some of the poorest decisions I have ever made were decided on the emotions I was feeling at the time. Anytime you take the business part out of the business, emotion will take over and that is when problems can start.

Take time to think about some of the most successful and best run businesses in the world or even in your city and I would venture to believe most of them are very professional all the time. You may not like some of the changes they have made in the business but I would have to believe you respect them well enough to stick it out. If you can get that from your clients then you are on your way to a successful barn and business life.

THE BUCK STOPS WITH THE BUSINESS OWNER

Remember that everything that happens on your farm will come back to you. I was amazed that even when I wasn't in the barn for a few days that eventually I would get calls or notes about something that happened. Take your time to hear the whole story and **both** sides of the story. Be fair.

Whether it was gossip or disagreements in the barn or maybe something more along the lines of theft or non-payment for something purchased, it will always stop with the owner of the business. Be ready to set the tone for how you want your barn to run and what you will and will not tolerate. This took me many years to figure out and I believe you cannot learn this until you are in the owner's chair. No amount of school can truly prepare you for the decisions you will need to make in each circumstance that comes up.

Running your business will become much easier when you understand and accept that it will all fall back on you. And I want you to be glad that it does. To me there would be nothing worse than running a business and not knowing what is going on in the business. That is how I was in the beginning and I was caught off guard many times and had no idea how to fix the problems that were coming in all directions.

Accept your new position as business owner and eventually your job will be much easier and you might find out like me that you really love owning and running a horse barn. Remember there is no perfect job and even though you can decide your hours of operation and what hours you want to work, the job never really leaves you so be prepared to set the boundaries of how it is going to run.

BE PATIENT AND FORGIVING

I have to be honest and tell you that years ago I was much quicker to jump on someone that was doing something wrong at our barn. Many times after I had gotten upset at the person I realized that they didn't understand that they were doing something wrong. I have lost boarders over the years because I didn't take the time to find out why they were doing the things they were doing. Are you ready for real honesty? One of my biggest regrets was the time I made someone cry at our barn. That was life changing for me and after that incident I have tried very hard to not speak until I have calmed down. I still to this day feel bad about that situation. Sometimes it is something as simple as giving them another copy of the barn rules and going over it with them.

Now I know at times as the barn owner you will run into someone that doesn't care about your barn rules and does whatever they want. Then you need to be firm and take action if need be but for the most part, people really do try to follow the rules and most of the time they just need a reminder. **Sometimes I have to make a conscience choice to cool down before I talk to the boarder so that I don't say things I will regret in the future.**

One more thing-If you have crossed the line, then say "I'm sorry." Those two little words can make all the difference in the world to your clients. We all make mistakes and I have had my share of them. Treat you clients the way you would like to be treated and they will respect you for that.

IT IS A SERVICE ORIENTATED BUSINESS

When we first built our barn in 2006 I was so proud of our facility. I am still as proud as ever about our farm but I look at it much differently now.

When we opened our doors I have to admit that I believed people would come board at our barn because we had a beautiful brand new facility. I never expected that any of them would leave. I actually told myself that no one would leave because after all why would they? They were keeping their horse in a brand new barn with many great amenities. I was looking at our business completely the wrong way. Back then I thought the barn itself was enough for our clients. I believed we gave great care but I didn't think that was the reason people came to our barn. I learned a very hard lesson with this. Many people left in our early years and we had a very high turnover. It took me a few years to realize that the barn itself is not what makes a great boarding facility. It is so much more than that.

What makes a great boarding facility is the service that you offer and the atmosphere you create. A safe place for their horse with shelter, good quality hay and fresh water are the most important things a client is looking for. Yes, they might come at first because of the great amenities you offer but the atmosphere and care will soon outweigh any other things.

As the barn owner you are offering a service of care. Do the best you can. Give good quality hay to the horses and make sure their water buckets are clean and filled. Make sure they feel safe in the barn as well as out in the paddock. If you do those things right then people will stay.

In the beginning I thought it was impressive to have a large barn with a big arena. I don't think that anymore at all. I am so much more proud of the wonderful boarders who stay year after year and know and trust that we will do the best in our power to make sure their horse is safe, healthy and happy.

A barn is nothing without the people and horses that are inside. Create an atmosphere where people will want to stay and remember good service is what your clients deserve.

DON'T ACT LIKE YOU KNOW IT ALL

This is something that I see often with many people in all walks of life. We live in a society where people are scared to admit they might not have the answer. For some reason many people feel like they need to be an expert on everything. As you know that is impossible.

As the barn owner you are going to be asked many questions all the time about every topic under the sun when it comes to horses. In the beginning I was very insecure and I didn't want the boarders to think I didn't know what I was talking about. There were times in our early years that I bluffed my way through an answer. NOT anymore. It is so much easier and less stressful to tell your client that you don't know the answer to what they are asking and you would be glad to help them find out what the correct answer is. It is amazing how much weight is lifted off your shoulders when you can be honest with your clients. Remember that they already know you didn't go to veterinarian school so don't act like you are a doctor. It is so much easier to call the veterinarian's office and ask to talk to a doctor and ask them the question.

Only through life experiences and years of dealing with many different types of horses and problems will you become more knowledgeable about all the different areas that involve horses. You will sound much smarter if you call the vet and get the correct answer instead of giving them the wrong answer and end up with a bigger problem down the road. I have seen that happen between boarders and it can end up being a real mess and you will be the one having to clean up and help fix the damage that was done.

If you *do* know the answer to the question then feel confident in your answer and move on because there will be many more as the years go on.

I have always loved another old saying ***"Try to learn something new every day"*** I think this is so profound for the horse industry because horses cannot tell us what is wrong so we have to try to guess through observation and process of elimination. As a barn owner be open and ready to learn something new every day. It still amazes me when I see something new I have never seen before either in the herds or with one horse in particular. It keeps me on my toes and the job is never boring.

THINGS NEVER STAY THE SAME IN BUSINESS

This is another big one. When we opened our doors I just assumed how we did things back then would be how we were always going to do them. That is just a crazy way to think! We do many things the same but we have changed in so many ways. We do many things much differently now than we did when we opened. I have to say our business runs much more efficiently and smoother as the years have gone by and that was due to the fact that we were open minded to change things that needed changing and staying current with the times.

Change is not always easy for the barn owner but you need to remember, it will most likely be even harder on your clients. When you are going to make a major change and we have made a few big ones, give your clients time to take it all in and be ready to give them answers to why you are making the changes. They will take it better if you give them time to talk if they have concerns and they will greatly appreciate it. It will also make them feel important and it shows them the same respect you want from them.

OWNING A HORSE BUSINESS IS HARDER THAN I THOUGHT

Before we started our business I would always watch (and still do) shows on television that had to do with starting and running your own business. They make is sound so glamorous and easy. I love owning a horse boarding business and after all these years, it is finally becoming a little easier. But the truth of the matter is, it is not glamorous at all and it is the hardest I have ever worked in my entire life! When I look in the mirror at my reflection I realize it has aged me a little. There are many days where I end up working all day before I realize I didn't even put make-up on.

Very few people make it big owning a boarding operation. My idea of success is not making it big at all. I have learned to be content with making an honest living and hopefully as the years go by we hope to have a little extra money to enjoy life a little more. What I believe keeps people in the horse business is not the money. It is a hard living to make money at. I believe the passion for horses is what keeps people in the business. At the end of the day they make it all worth it.

It is not a glamorous job working on a horse farm and there will be times when you wonder if you could possibly get any dirtier or more tired than you are. I have worked in every type of weather and have come in completely soaked from a down pour and have had frozen toes and fingers from doing chores in sub-zero temperatures in the winter. I have been knocked into the mud and been so hot in the summer that I thought I was going to pass out. Remember that this career will never be a 9 to 5 job with four weeks paid vacation. It will be job of hard work and endless wonder. Horses are tremendous amount of work but the endless wonder of them never stops for me. Being a barn owner has been a great experience and I believe it has made me much stronger as a person inside and out.

There is a need for good quality horse boarding stables and I truly believe you can be a success at running your own horse business if you take it slow and do it the right way. If you have the drive to start your own business and are not afraid of hard work then do it. Just remember, when the days get long and the pay checks are next to nothing and you wonder why you ever wanted to start the business in the first place, you might need to take a walk down your barn aisle after the barn is closed and the horses are quietly munching on hay to find the reason again. It will be there.

~55~
BUSINESS OWNERSHIP IS A LOVE/HATE RELATIONSHIP

I have the most awesome job in the world. I get the privilege of taking care of so many beautiful horses. Having your own business whether it is boarding horses or being a trainer, breeder or other professional in the equine world comes with many ups and downs. It can be the most exciting job in the world and the loneliest job on earth at times.

There are going to be days that you truly love your job and you can't believe you get paid to be around horses all day. Then you will have days when the weather is bad and it is below zero outside and you are putting four layers of clothing on and you don't like your job at all and you begin to feel you are not paid enough to do this job. You will have days when the horses all walk in calmly from the paddocks and it doesn't take much time at all to get chores done. Then you will have days where the horses all seemed to have lost their brain out in the paddocks and trying to walk them into the barn is a hazard in itself and you are glad that you renewed your life insurance policy. They will make you smile and laugh and once in a while scream!

When I think of the business that David and I started many years ago, I can see after writing this book how it has truly evolved over the years and also how much we have changed as people and business owners over the years. I never realized until I started to write this book that it really does take years to become the business person you need to be to run a business properly. Very few people are true business people right at the start unless they have run successful businesses before. Most of us have not and David and I had zero business experience. Be open to change over the years in your business and yourself because it will happen and it can be a very good thing.

Is our boarding stable a successful business? I would say in a heartbeat yes it is. It is successful in the fact that I believe we have truly content boarders here at our barn and I believe all the horses in our care are happy and healthy. It is successful in the fact that through all the hardships and changes we have gone through over the years, our business has persevered under every situation that was thrown at us.

Have we had our hearts broken when someone leaves? Yes. Have we been so tired that I cried at times? Yes. Have I met the most wonderful and diverse group of people and horses throughout the years? Yes. I have learned so much about myself and how to work with others and how to lead. I have made mistakes throughout the years but instead of quitting I was driven to make it better and not make the same mistake twice.

If you are willing to work harder than you have ever worked in your entire life and be on call 24 hours a day, 7 days a week, 365 days a year and you love horses as much as I do, then go for your dream of having a business in the horse industry. It is an amazing career and if you do it right from the start, it will be much easier on you and everyone that is involved in it with you.

All the stories I have shared in this book are put in this book solely to help you. Our way of running our boarding stable is not the only way to run a barn. There are many successful boarding facilities out there. I am just truly hoping that by sharing everything that we have learned it will help you with your business endeavors and help you avoid some of the pitfalls we went through.

I wanted to be as transparent as I could into our world of starting a business from absolutely nothing because when we were starting our business I could not find one book out there that really talked about how to start and run a horse boarding stable on a daily basis. I wanted to share everything as honestly as I could and hold nothing back.

It truly is an amazing job and life and I feel blessed that I am able to go to work each morning and hear nickers when I step into my office.

I hope and pray that your horse business will be successful and is everything you hoped it would be.

Wishing you many blessings in all that you do with horses,
Sheri Grunska

Sheri's Books and Website

You can catch Sheri's blog articles every week at
www.probarnmanagement.com

Sheri has written several books on horse barn management and inspirational books about horses and running a business. You can find all her books on her website at www.probarnmanagement.com and Amazon.com

A Step By Step Guide To Starting And Running A Successful Horse Boarding Business
(The comprehensive book of horse boarding and effective barn management)

The Total Horse Barn Management Makeover
(Practical business wisdom for running your horse business)

One Horsewoman To Another
(Trading in your high heels for muddy work boots and finding Courage, Confidence and Joy in all of it!)

Caring For Horses with a Servant's Heart
(A daily Devotional for the horse professional and the horse lover in all of us)

Printed in Great Britain
by Amazon